HACKING
THE BOMB

HACKING THE BOMB

Cyber Threats and Nuclear Weapons

ANDREW FUTTER

Foreword by Lord Des Browne,
Former Secretary of State for Defence and
Former Secretary of State for Scotland,
United Kingdom

Georgetown University Press
WASHINGTON, DC

Library of Congress Cataloging-in-Publication Data
Names: Futter, Andrew, 1983– author.
  Title: Hacking the bomb : cyber threats and nuclear weapons / Andrew Futter.
Description: Washington, DC : Georgetown University Press, 2018. | Includes
  bibliographical references and index.
Identifiers: LCCN 2017035576| ISBN 9781626165649 (hardcover : alk. paper) |
  ISBN 9781626165656 (pbk. : alk. paper) | ISBN 9781626165663 (ebook)
Subjects: LCSH: Nuclear weapons. | Nuclear weapons--Security measures. |
  Hacking. | Command and control systems. | Cyberspace operations (Military
  science) | Information warfare.
Classification: LCC U264 .F877 2018 | DDC 355.8/25119—dc23
LC record available at https://lccn.loc.gov/2017035576

19 18   9 8 7 6 5 4 3 2   First printing

Printed in the United States of America

Cover design by N. Putens.

For Rehana

⫶ CONTENTS

⫶ FOREWORD

A DECADE AGO, as the United Kingdom's secretary of state for defence, I was responsible for overseeing the beginning of the replacement of the Trident nuclear-armed submarines. This was a complex and difficult process, with many on both sides of the debate advancing passionate and important views about the necessity or desirability of retaining a nuclear weapons capability, well into the second half of this century. Absent from this discussion, however, was any mention that our submarines or nuclear weapons systems could be vulnerable to nonstate hackers or sophisticated state-based cyber warriors. Stuxnet was yet to be revealed, and though cyber operations and attacks had been ongoing for some time, news of them rarely reached public consciousness, and few, if any, had considered, far less written about, the vulnerability of nuclear weapons to the cyber threat.

It was not until 2013, when I read the US Defense Science Board's *Task Force Report: Resilient Military Systems and the Advanced Cyber Threat*, that I appreciated the seriousness of the situation and the scale of the challenge needed to "address this broad and pervasive threat." The report explained in no uncertain terms that the most sensitive US military networked nuclear systems were vulnerable to a high-level cyberattack by a "sophisticated and well-resourced opponent" because, among other reasons, the networks themselves were built on inherently insecure architecture. Reading also that the authors of the report assessed that the equivalent systems of US allies were equally vulnerable, I raised my concerns with those now responsible for the United Kingdom's strategic deterrent, only to have them brushed aside by bland but unspecific assurances that all was well. After further research, it seemed to me that those in charge of nuclear weapons complexes in all the other leading nuclear-armed states were demonstrating a great deal of complacency about the cyber challenge. Many experts and military spokespeople assert that, because their weapons systems are not connected to the internet, there is no need for concern and, of course, submarines are deployed at sea. To me, this approach avoids many of the major aspects of the challenge. For example, increasingly, nuclear command and control structures rely on complex computer systems, and so too do the weapons themselves, and nuclear-armed submarines actually spend most of their time in port, linked up and essentially online. Admittedly, attacking these weapons systems would not be easy—but no system is invulnerable, no matter how much we may wish this to be the case. This is why I have sought to push the issue in various international forums over the past few years, and have attempted, unsuccessfully I have to admit, to make cyber risks a major issue in the 2016 Trident renewal debate in the United Kingdom (see Watt, "Trident Could Be Vulnerable," in the bibliography).

In almost all aspects of our lives, we are becoming more and more reliant on complex computer systems that fewer and fewer people really understand. We are living in a world where cyberattacks are likely to be more frequent, more sophisticated, and more pervasive. Purported ongoing US attacks against North Korea's missile program; alleged Russian interference in the US election in 2016; and the recent WannaCry attack on, among others, the UK National Health Service—not to mention the extensive leaks from whistleblowers, such as Edward Snowden—are indicative of a fast-changing global security context. At the same time, global nuclear weapons complexes are becoming increasingly sophisticated, digitized, and reliant on ever more lines of computer coding and high-technology hardware. It is not impossible to foresee an accidental, miscalculated, or even unauthorized use of a nuclear weapon as a result of computer errors or cyberattacks. Certainly, the cyber threat will only grow, constantly and increasingly challenging established notions of mutually assured destruction, deterrence, crisis management, and proliferation. Thus, before it is too late, it is imperative that we take this threat seriously, include it in public nuclear discussions and debates, and, above all, secure our systems against hackers.

With all this in mind, Andrew Futter's excellent book could hardly be more timely. In this very readable and accessible overview, he outlines the key elements of the cyber challenge to nuclear weapons, helps the reader unpack its various aspects, and sets it all in its proper context. As he explains, the cyber challenge is far more than a teenage hacker crouched over a computer in his bedroom, accidentally starting World War III—although this is a possibility. Rather, the threats vary considerably across a spectrum, ranging from nuisance and espionage attacks right up to the possibility of national offensive cyber operations waging cyberwar. Each of these various versions of the threat have differing implications for how we think about and manage our nuclear weapons policy.

I have had the pleasure of knowing and, occasionally, working with Andrew during the last four years. During that time, he has written extensively, accessibly, and wisely about the impact of emerging technology on nuclear strategy, stability, and arms control. I have watched his reputation grow as his expertise has been sought further and wider. To my knowledge, his research, analysis, and advice have been deployed to the advantage of the deliberations of think tanks, academic institutions, and legislative committees here in the United Kingdom, in the United States, and across Europe. His research, analysis, and recommendations merit attention and should give policymakers food for thought as they set about building a cyber capability or deploying it in the nuclear realm and begin establishing a norm of "hacking the bomb." I sincerely hope his groundbreaking work marks the beginning of concerted global engagement with this topic in both the academic and policy worlds.

The Rt. Hon. Lord Browne of Ladyton,
Former Secretary of State for Defence and
Former Secretary of State for Scotland, United Kingdom
June 2017

⋰ ACKNOWLEDGMENTS

THIS BOOK would not have been possible without the support provided by the UK Economic and Social Research Council, and specifically the Future Research Leader's Grant, which I was fortunate to be awarded in 2013. This three-year award allowed me not only time to think and develop my ideas, but also to test them out in different international forums, and to learn from a wide variety of global experts on this subject. If it had not been for this grant, I would not have been able to spend time in the fall of 2015 as a visiting fellow at the James Martin Center for Nonproliferation Studies in Monterey, California, where many of these ideas were developed and honed. I also benefited greatly from being part of the Cyber-Nuclear Threats Task Force run by the Nuclear Threat Initiative in Washington, where I have been able to discuss and develop my ideas with some exceptional people. Thanks must also go to the many others who commented and made helpful suggestions on the presentations I have given on this topic in Australia, Belgium, India, Pakistan, Russia, the United States, and of course, the United Kingdom.

I also owe a great debt to James Acton, Greg Austin, Dave Blagden, Des Browne, Steve Cimbala, Erik Gartzke, David Jarvis, Peter Hayes, James Johnson, Martin Libicki, Herb Lin, Jim Miller, Jon Moran, Sir David Omand, Mark Phythian, Bill Potter, Thomas Rid, Nick Ritchie, Elke Schwarz, Nikolai Sokov, Page Stoutland, Kris Stoddart, Michael Sulmeyer, Ian Wallace, Heather Williams, Ben Zala, Kim Zetter, and the many others that gave their time to speak with me, either on or off the record. Don Jacobs and the team at Georgetown University Press also deserve special mention for all their hard work, enthusiasm, and help. Any errors in the book are of course entirely my own.

Finally, I am grateful to my friends and family for their encouragement in so many ways; to my mother, Alison, and my late father, John, for motivating me to follow my interests; and most of all for the love, inspiration, and support of my partner, Rehana.

Introduction: *WarGames* Redux?

IN 1983, a teenager sat in front of an IMSAI 8080 microcomputer in his bedroom in Seattle, hacked into a Pentagon supercomputer that controlled nuclear war planning, and almost started World War III between the United States and the Soviet Union.[1] This was, of course, the plot of the Hollywood blockbuster film *WarGames.* To many at the time, this film seemed a rather farfetched and unlikely piece of science fiction—most people did not have a personal computer in the 1980s, let alone a connection to what would become the all-pervading World Wide Web. Moreover, the first *Hackers' Handbook*—the how-to guide for breaching networked computers and systems—was not published until 1986, some three years later.[2]

But when US president Ronald Reagan had finished watching a private screening of *WarGames* as part of his regular Sunday movie night, he was sufficiently worried to instruct the chairman of the Joint Chiefs of Staff, Gen. John Vessey, to find out whether hackers could ever gain access to the most sensitive US computer systems.[3] A week later, Vessey told the president that the problem was much worse than they had realized.[4] In fact, part of the plot of the film had been based on information supplied by the computer pioneer and RAND Corporation employee Willis Ware—the man who had helped design the most sensitive computer systems at the North American Aerospace Defense Command (NORAD)—where any information on a nuclear attack would be collated and analyzed. The screenwriters Lawrence Lasker and Walter Parkes had apparently been told by Ware that NORAD's computers were vulnerable to outside hackers and that "anyone could get in if the right number was dialed."[5] The result was NSDD-145—the National Policy on Telecommunications and Automated Information Systems Security, which was released by the US government on September 17, 1984, and marked the beginning of an awareness of what would later be termed "cyber threats."[6] In the words of the Pulitzer Prize–winning journalist Fred Kaplan, "It's fitting that the scenario of *WarGames*—which aroused Ronald Reagan's curiosity and led to the first national policy on reducing the vulnerability of computers—owed a crucial debt to the man who'd first warned that they were vulnerable."[7]

Some three decades later—with the exponential spread of computing technologies, access to the internet, and the rapid expansion of complex networks and systems reliant on millions of lines of software code—the risk that hackers might somehow breach or interfere with nuclear weapons and related systems has grown considerably.[8] Although computers have always been central to the nuclear weapons business (as David Blagden has phrased it, "nuclear has always been cyber"[9]), the need for a fundamental reassessment of what this new digital context means for the safe and secure management of nuclear forces—and the state strategies, global relations, and strategic balances underpinned by these weapons—could hardly be more pressing. What is often rather loosely termed as "cyber" is transforming how states experience and understand threats, and how nuclear weapons systems operate, communicate, and are thought about. As a result, many of the central tenets of nuclear orthodoxy that were developed for a different era need reassessing. This is not to say that these are wrong, but rather to highlight the fact that there is an inherent risk in making policy and strategic assumptions about nuclear weapons today, based on frameworks from a very different global technological context of yesterday.[10] In fact, thanks to the cyber phenomenon, we may well be standing at the edge of a major technological challenge to—or even revolution in—the global nuclear order.

Most nation-states now devote considerable resources to the "cyber challenge"—even though the term remains contested and continues to escape an accepted definition. Some nations have even established cyber warfare units in their militaries and are seeking or have developed offensive cyber capabilities and cyber weapons. Perhaps as many as sixty countries now have, or are developing, cyber capabilities that might be used against the sensitive computer systems of other states, and this only seems likely to grow in the years ahead.[11] Various nonstate actors are also thought to be interested in using cyber capabilities for their nefarious purposes. The result has been a certain degree of cyber hyperbole. Two former high-ranking US politicians have even gone as far as to warn of the possibility of a future "cyber Pearl Harbor" or "cyber 9/11," and the hysteria surrounding the possible implications of cyber threats has grown exponentially in the past two decades.[12] Although information is sparse and the literature is very much in its infancy, the cyber challenge is also thought to extend into nuclear weapons systems. In 2012, for example, Thomas D'Agostino, former director of the US National Nuclear Security Administration, cautioned that US nuclear weapons and associated systems were under constant attack from a full spectrum of hackers, and face millions of attacks every day.[13] Others have warned that cyberattacks that might have placed nuclear weapons and related systems at risk may have already taken place.[14] The result is that it appears to be increasingly likely, as Gen. James Cartwright, the former head of the US Strategic Command and former vice chair of the Joint Chiefs of Staff, has warned, that the cyber threat has extended into nuclear command and control systems.[15]

Notwithstanding a very few notable exceptions, the potentially catastrophic scenario played out in *WarGames* a generation ago—not to mention the relationship between the incipient digital age, cyber threats, and nuclear weapons more broadly—remains understudied, little understood, and largely unaddressed.[16] Given the considerable number of nuclear weapons that remain in the world today—many of them held on high alert and increasingly reliant on unfathomable lines of digital code and complex, often commingled computer control systems—and the growing spread of both cyber and nuclear weapons technology and know-how to a range of new actors (often referred to as the transition to a "second nuclear age"[17]), we are fast entering a period where the central dynamics, beliefs, and thinking that underpin the ultimate weapon need to be reassessed while considering the new cyber context.

However, the implications of this new cyber context for nuclear weapons' security, management, and utility remain far from clear. Could hackers—whether state-based or terrorists—break in to nuclear command and control networks, breach defenses, and launch missiles and warheads, as the former US nuclear launch officer Bruce Blair has warned?[18] Could attackers steal nuclear authorization codes and transmit them to weapons? Could they cause a nuclear explosion through other cyber means, or acquire various types of sensitive design or operational information that might be used either to compromise systems or aid proliferation? Might an adversary spoof early warning systems—as Israel is believed to have done during Operation Orchard in 2007[19]—or disrupt vital communications or interfere with signaling during a crisis and precipitate overreaction, as the Global Zero Commission has cautioned?[20] Are nuclear weapons and related nuclear infrastructure vulnerable to sabotage—perhaps through a Stuxnet-like attack, meaning that they will not work, or at least will not work as intended, when required? Could these attacks be carried out in advance, from afar, and without an adversary knowing about them?

Questions also abound at the strategic level. How, for example, might cyber operations and a new computerized global security environment affect the confidence in maintaining a secure second nuclear strike force, the credibility of deterrence, or the pressure to act first during a crisis? Does the possible use of cyber weapons against nuclear systems transform our existing thinking about counterforce strategy, the offense/defense balance, and preemption in the nuclear realm? Does this mean that there is a role for nuclear forces in deterring cyberattacks or cross-domain attacks that involve the use of cyber weapons—or are the two fundamentally different? Are some nuclear-armed states, weapons systems, doctrines or postures, and different nuclear weapons facilities more vulnerable or susceptible than others? What impact will the threat of cyberattacks on nuclear forces have on strategic stability, future crisis management, and an embryonic

international cyber-nuclear security dilemma? And how might these new challenges affect the perception of risk and vulnerability associated with retaining
nuclear weapons—particularly for states that keep weapons on high alert, tightly
coupled to warning systems, or that exist in a heightened threat environment,
and therefore conceive their perceived utility and role more broadly? Taken
together, the need for a fundamental reassessment of what this new digital global
security environment means for the safe, secure, and reliable management of
nuclear forces, and the state strategies, global relations, and power balances
underpinned by these weapons, could hardly be more pressing.

Although some of these questions, possibilities, and scenarios might seem
somewhat alarmist, the central aim of this book is to assess, examine, and explore
what this new global context means for the way that nuclear weapons are thought
about, how nuclear forces are managed, how nuclear strategy is conceived, and
how global nuclear order is maintained. To do this, the approach taken here is
deliberately designed to be as inclusive, wide-ranging, and holistic as possible,
both in terms of the nature of the cyber challenge and what this includes, and in
its analysis of the various facets of the nuclear weapons enterprise across different
nuclear-armed actors. In this way, the cyber challenge involves two distinct but
also intrinsically linked dynamics: The first is the importance of a new digitized
global *context* dominated by the use of information technology and the digital
information flows that are changing the way that national security is thought
about and performed, and where all nuclear-armed states are coming to rely
increasingly on complex computer systems for all aspects of nuclear weapons
management. And the second is a new and novel suite of cyber *capabilities*—
which includes, but is not limited to, cyber weapons—that could be used against
nuclear systems and associated infrastructure, and which have been spawned by
this new context. We can think of these key variables as cyber *context* and cyber
operations.

Thus the cyber challenge is viewed here as being more than simply hacking and
the internet. Instead, it includes the security implications of a more extensively
digitized global nuclear order and a greater reliance on information technology
throughout the nuclear weapons enterprise—*and also* measures designed to attack,
compromise, destroy, disrupt, or exploit activities involving computers, networks,
software, and hardware/infrastructure, and the people that engage with them.[21]
Moreover, it also seeks to differentiate between the different types, goals, and
potential severity of cyber operations, because these are far from being homogeneous and have very different implications for nuclear thinking. Likewise, the
book seeks to address cyber-induced challenges across the entire nuclear weapons
enterprise, and not simply focus on whether a cyberattack could directly cause a
nuclear detonation (the so-called *WarGames* scenario mentioned above).

Consequently, the conceptual emphasis is broadened to include all associated
nuclear weapons infrastructure—such as research laboratories, contractors, and
command facilities—as well as the weapons, warheads, and systems, and the

people who operate them. It also seeks to look across three levels of the nuclear weapons enterprise—from single-unit variables and the nuclear command and control apparatus (e.g., missiles, warheads, specific computers, sensitive data, early warning systems, and people); through state-level structures and national security thinking (e.g., about nuclear deterrence, strategy, and posture); right up to international strategic relations, crisis stability, and a possible future cyber-nuclear security dilemma. Accordingly, the book seeks to develop and provide a framework for understanding the nature, nuances, and implications of the cyber-nuclear nexus rather than a set of country-specific, threat, or scenario-based case studies.

The Emerging Cyber-Nuclear Nexus

The main argument of the book is twofold: First, the burgeoning cyber age is transforming the way that we should think about, manage, and control nuclear weapons; and second, establishing a norm of hacking the bomb is a bad idea fraught with danger, uncertainties, and risks. Specifically, the book argues that the emergence and spread of an ever more pervasive cyber context is changing, recasting, and exacerbating existing tensions right across the nuclear weapons enterprise and, in some cases, providing new dynamics and threat vectors that need to be understood and addressed. These challenges are diverse in their scope, and range from the safe, secure, and reliable command and control of nuclear forces and trustworthy and robust early warning and communications; to an increased threat of nuclear accidents and mistakes (especially as systems become more complex and pressurized, and are modernized); to new problems for information systems security and the protection of sensitive secrets that could lead to nuclear proliferation or the compromising of weapons; up to an incipient set of complications for strategic and cross-domain deterrence, and the emergence of a cyber-nuclear security dilemma that must be factored into future crisis management and strategic stability. To unpack these challenges, it is worthwhile to outline eight key themes and important dynamics that flow throughout the book and that help give its overarching arguments both depth and context.

First, *cyber capabilities and nuclear weapons are fundamentally different*. Thus, though cyber threats and the digitized global environment are unquestionably becoming a central component of both national and international security thinking and strategy, these new technologies and dynamics are not—at least not yet—undermining or superseding the role of nuclear weapons in global politics. Cyber threats are profoundly different from nuclear weapons, not least in the degree and nature of the destruction they might cause, and this has significant implications for how the cyber-nuclear nexus should be viewed and understood. As Martin Libicki puts it, "Nuclear war creates firestorms, destroying people and things for miles around. By contrast, even a successful widespread information attack has more the character of a snowstorm."[22] Essentially, this makes it both complicated and problematic to attempt to transfer the lessons, models, and frameworks from the nuclear realm—such as deterrence, mutually assured destruction, and arms control—to cyberspace. Moreover, it is a central argument of this book that "cyber" refers to both the emergence of an incipient digital global context within which we think about nuclear weapons *as well as* a new set of tools, dynamics, and weapons that might be used against them.

Second, *nuclear weapons systems have always been vulnerable to interference and attack*, and nuclear weapons management has always been difficult. The challenges of the digital age are therefore principally exacerbating and reshaping, rather than fundamentally transforming, the intrinsic difficulties and pressures associated with nuclear forces. This is particularly the case with the ever-present need for nuclear-armed states to balance the twin requirements of keeping nuclear weapons safe and secure but at the same time ready to be used—the so-called always/never dilemma. But it also applies to the challenges of ensuring the credibility of deterrence, maintaining strategic stability, and safely managing nuclear crises, as well as protecting sensitive nuclear secrets and designs, and providing information about the nuclear personnel who operate these systems. Although nuclear systems are of course likely to be among the best-protected against cyber operations, and are where possible air-gapped from the wider internet and unsecured networks, this is not a panacea. It is therefore, principally, the *methods* and *threat vectors* rather than the overarching *problems* of nuclear weapons management that are changing in the digitized world.

Third, some *cyber challenges may not involve attacks or attackers at all*. Although the cyber threat has become synonymous with hacking, attacks, and weapons, the increasingly digitized global context is itself creating new problems and pressures both within and for nuclear weapons systems and their operators. The nuclear past is littered with accidents, mistakes, and near misses—many of which, at least the ones we know about, occurred because of computer errors or problems. Unfortunately, complex nuclear systems, particularly nuclear command and control systems, represent a perfect test case for the theory of normal accidents, that is, the notion that complex systems are bound to fail and go wrong, and often in ways that no one could foresee. Though the likelihood may be small, it is at least possible that a computer-induced error or malfunction could lead to a normal *nuclear* accident or unintended use—it is important to remember that computer systems do what they are programmed to do, not necessarily what is intended or expected.[23] More broadly, the digital age is creating innumerable technological-deterministic pressures that complicate nuclear weapons management, and this is expanding the range of possibilities for things to go wrong.

Fourth, *the threats posed by cyber technologies are fundamentally diverse and different*. In fact, the wide variety of activities that fall under the rubric of cyber operations, or that are characterized as cyber threats, is far from being homogeneous. Cyber operations range across several different spectrums, and vary considerably in terms of severity, sophistication, frequency, and intended target. The challenge therefore includes everyday hacking, exploitation, crime, and espionage, and also range up to sophisticated attacks designed to disrupt, damage, and even destroy computers and associated systems. Thus, only the most severe of these might be considered as involving weapons or thought of as strategic or as constituting warfare. Moreover, to date, the clear majority of "cyberattacks"—itself a contested and often misused label—do not fall within the weapons category but rather are designed to steal information, gain access to secrets, or prevent computer systems or networks from working as intended. Likewise, cyber threats not only involve operations carried out over the internet but also include actions that target physical infrastructure, operational software, information, and people. Thus, it is not just cyber operations (e.g., attacks or exploitation) but also nefarious activities *in cyberspace* undergird the challenge. Such operations might be conducted either remotely or by a person in situ, and could be done with or without that person knowing. Humans, therefore, remain a key part of the cyber challenge. As such, it is essential to be clear what is meant by the word "cyber," and about how the concept is being used.

Fifth, *actors in the cyber-nuclear realm have varied intentions and capabilities.* In addition to cyber espionage, which is likely to be employed (albeit possibly for different purposes) by both states and nonstate actors, we can think of two distinct goals of cyberattacks in the nuclear realm: (1) *disabling*—those who seek to disable, undermine, and prevent nuclear weapons from being used and working as planned; and (2) *enabling*—those who seek either directly or indirectly to cause these weapons to be used, launched, or detonated. In general, state actors are more likely to opt for cyber operations designed to disable an opponent's forces, whereas nonstate actors and cyberterrorists would likely seek to precipitate nuclear use (either deliberate or inadvertent). States are more likely to be able to develop sophisticated cyber capabilities that could be used directly against nuclear systems (and over a longer period of time), whereas nonstate actors are perhaps more likely to pursue indirect measures to achieve their aims, such as attempting to cause confusion and miscalculation by manipulating information, early warning systems, and the broader information space. The problem for managing both risks lays in perception, and particularly in the inability to know for sure if key systems have been penetrated and if the information on which a state and its systems are relying can be trusted. Unfortunately, protecting against one set of risks might necessarily involve weakening protections against the other set.

Sixth, *cyber threats should not be viewed in isolation,* and it is often unhelpful to view cyber operations as a separate domain of military operations. This is because though cyberattacks may well be used independently for low-level operations—such as general hacking, testing system defenses, and espionage—at the military or strategic level, cyberattacks will almost certainly be used in conjunction with (either before or at the same time as) other means of force. This has two implications. First, it must be assumed that any future conventional conflict will include cyber operations and that this will have implications for escalation management, signaling, and resolving crises between nuclear-armed actors. And second, if things escalate to the strategic level, cyber capabilities are likely to be used alongside other advanced conventional military technologies, such as precision strike missiles, missile defenses, and other weapons with counterforce potential. When these are taken together, and placed in context, the cyber challenge at the nuclear level is in fact magnified and augmented considerably, and states must now consider a much broader suite of challenges to nuclear surety and strategy. The combined impact of these advanced conventional technologies—all of which are being facilitated by considerable advances in information technology—and their consequent challenges to nuclear thinking, utility, strategy, balances, and escalation control are only likely to increase in the years ahead.[24]

Seventh, the impact and implications of *cyber threats will become magnified and exacerbated during a nuclear crisis*. This is true on three levels: First, state actors would naturally try to limit or disable an opponent's forces through cyber means (and have already been open about doing this); second, terrorists or other third-party actors might seek to interfere in various ways (e.g., false flag attacks) and cause a crisis to escalate, potentially leading to nuclear use; and third, the reliance of modern militaries on increasingly vulnerable computerized systems is likely to create significant problems for communicating and seeking to understand what is happening. To borrow from Clausewitz, this could be thought of as a digitized or cyber-enabled fog of war. Ultimately, even the perception that weapons, communications, or early warning systems *could* be compromised or that weapons *might not* work as expected will place more pressure on decision makers, and could potentially make unintended nuclear escalation far more difficult to prevent or manage. The challenge is particularly acute in crises where nuclear forces are kept on high alert or where warning times are limited, such as the United States–Russia or India–Pakistan relationship. It also becomes highly problematic when states share command and control apparatus and other capabilities across nuclear and conventional forces—and particularly for so-called dual-use systems. Indeed, and irrespective of whether such cyberattacks have taken place or whether systems have been compromised, the effects are likely to be increased perceptions of risk, a more clouded nuclear information space, and reduced time for decision making. Thus, though the most serious aspects of the cyber challenge are likely to become particularly pronounced and influential during periods of instability and crisis, they may well be at least manageable during times of relative peace and stability.

Eighth, and finally, *nuclear modernization is a double-edged sword*. This is because as nuclear-armed states set about modernizing their nuclear systems, and especially command and control apparatus, various tensions and problems are likely to become aggravated and possibly worsened, and new potential vulnerabilities are expected to emerge. As such, it may be that the less sophisticated nuclear systems are, the less tightly they are coupled (both to warning sensors and other weapons systems), and the less they rely on complex software and high-technology computers, the safer and more secure they will prove to be. Nuclear modernization, which all nuclear-armed states are currently undertaking—and particularly the digitization of nuclear infrastructure, weapons, and support systems—is therefore inherently problematic. This is because though more powerful, networked, real-time systems may offer greater functionality, options, speed, and processing power (and guard against the subversion of static technology), they also increase the chances of errors and unintended consequences, and the potential for attackers to interfere with or compromise nuclear weapons systems. To be sure, the extent of the challenge will vary depending on the types of weapons system being deployed, and particularly the doctrine and requirements placed on these forces; but all nuclear-armed states will likely be affected in some way.

The challenges of the cyber age for nuclear weapons are therefore far subtler and nuanced than perhaps they first appear, which complicates and obfuscates the inherent difficulties associated with the management of nuclear forces rather than fundamentally transforming them. That said, cyber challenges do, when taken together, and particularly when combined with other advanced military-technological developments (particularly advanced conventional weapons), represent an important shift in the environment within which nuclear weapons are thought about, managed, and used as a component of security strategy by states. Increased uncertainty about the integrity and security of nuclear systems, their component parts, and the sensitive nuclear information on which they and their operators rely necessarily raises questions with implications right across the board for all nuclear-armed states. These include the methods and procedures used for nuclear force management and procurement, and for updating key nuclear systems; the shape and implications of future nuclear proliferation; and how to maintain the credible force postures and structures that underpin nuclear strategy. The cyber challenge will therefore have different implications and be interpreted and responded to in different ways by different nuclear-armed actors, depending on their nuclear doctrine, force structure, and immediate threat environment. A possible growing predilection for preemptive cyber operations against enemy military systems will also present another barrier to trust and confidence building between nuclear-armed adversaries. This, in turn, will have both direct and indirect implications for global and regional strategic balances, for the maintenance of current nuclear arms control agreements and regimes, and for any foreseeable future moves toward nuclear disarmament.

Ultimately, the evolution and deepening of a digitized and computerized global nuclear order is changing how nation-states think about and manage nuclear weapons. But it is also forming a context where many of the challenges, or at least the key dynamics, are not necessarily new. In many ways, rather than creating an entirely new strategic landscape, the cyber challenge primarily is exacerbating existing tensions and problems within the nuclear weapons enterprise, is drawing more attention to many aspects not previously at the forefront of the debate, and is providing new means and tools that need to be incorporated into global nuclear management and thinking. That said, these challenges are of fundamental importance, and thus they must be understood and addressed as nations go about securing their nuclear futures. Although it may be unlikely, it is certainly not impossible that nuclear weapons might be used either as a direct or indirect result of a cyberattack, mistakes caused by a reliance on complex digitized systems, or some future scenario involving cyber operations and complex computers. It also seems probable that cyber threats will negatively influence arms control, strategic stability, and long-term notions of disarmament, unless we start addressing this challenge now. Above all, we should think long and hard before establishing a norm of hacking the bomb.

Outline of the Book

To assess, address, and examine the numerous and diverse challenges to nuclear weapons in the burgeoning cyber age, this book adopts a four-part framework that focuses on the different facets and dynamics of the cyber-nuclear nexus. In doing so, the chapters seek to place these new cyber dynamics in a historical and broader context; to evaluate what is changing, how, and why; to consider what is new and what is not; and therefore to provide both a rounded and grounded basis for understanding, analysis, and policy recommendations.

Part I of the book focuses on the nature of the cyber challenge and begins in chapter 1 with an examination of what exactly we mean by the term "cyber." The chapter explains how the complicated evolution of the concept has led to considerable problems with its definition and use, and why it is fundamentally unhelpful to view the cyber challenge as homogeneous, before going on to introduce the new types of mechanisms and methods that might be used to attack nuclear systems and their operators. Chapter 2 looks at how nuclear weapons systems might be vulnerable in the emerging cyber context, and explains why many of the new cyber challenges stem from the foundational nature and inherent tensions within nuclear weapons management. It then goes on to describe the two main challenges for nuclear systems: those deriving from the risk of accidents and mistakes caused by complexity, and those driven by the new vulnerabilities that might be exploited by an adversary's cyber operations.

The main objective of part II is to consider the different types of threats and challenges to nuclear systems that fall under the rubric of cyber operations, and to begin unpacking what might be vulnerable, how, to what extent, and to whom. Specifically, it distinguishes between the challenges posed by cyber *exploitation* and those posed by cyber*attacks*. To this end, chapter 3 looks at the new risks posed to the safe and secure management of sensitive nuclear information and secrets, details the growing number of cases that have and are taking place, and then explains the various, diverse implications of the challenge posed by cyber-nuclear espionage. Chapter 4 examines the serious concerns of whether hackers could cause a nuclear launch, create the conditions that might precipitate or deepen a nuclear crisis through cyber means, or prevent nuclear systems from working. It also looks at what different hackers might want and can do, the important differences between direct and indirect attacks, and the distinctive challenges posed by states and nonstate actors.

In part III, the analysis moves on to consider the impact and implications of cyber threats and the new digital context for nuclear weapons management at both the strategic and international levels. To this end, chapter 5 outlines the key differences between nuclear weapons and cyber threats, and explains why any strategy to manage cyber risks must include the full panoply of state capabilities—including both deterrence by denial and deterrence by punishment. Finally, it considers the question of whether nuclear weapons could ever be used to deter either counterforce or countervalue cyberattacks against critical national infrastructure. Chapter 6 looks at how new cyber dynamics (both contextual and in terms of operations and threats), and particularly the possibility of using cyber capabilities to attack nuclear systems, are making an impact on global and regional strategic stability and on arms control, and are increasing the prospects for future arms racing. The chapter analyzes the likely consequences of this cyber context for crisis management and escalation between nuclear-armed states, and explains why we may be moving closer to a cyber-nuclear security dilemma, where we will need to rethink previous notions of signaling and risk management, and perhaps the central tenets of nuclear orthodoxy.

Part IV examines several key dynamics that together seem set to fundamentally shape the future global cyber-nuclear operating environment and strategic context. Chapter 7 explains why nuclear modernization—and particularly the digitization of key nuclear weapons and support systems—is likely to create numerous new problems and vulnerabilities that could be exploited by attackers, and at the same time exacerbate the current challenges involved with nuclear weapons management. It then seeks to place the cyber challenge in a broader technomilitary context, alongside other potential destabilizing emerging technologies, which, when taken together, may have the potential to fundamentally challenge the central axioms and thinking of nuclear orthodoxy in the medium to long terms. Finally, it considers how these new dynamics might play out in various contexts and what this might mean for the thinking and strategy of different types of nuclear actors.

The conclusion brings together the key arguments and insights from the book, and begins to consider ways forward and possible recommendations for those both directly and indirectly involved in managing the global nuclear order. Specifically, it elucidates and outlines the key dynamics that need to be considered if we are to mitigate and perhaps prevent the worst effects, dangers, and risks of our cyber-nuclear future as we move further into an ever more complex cyber-nuclear age.

Notes

1. This machine was first released in 1975 and came with a choice of 32 kilobytes or 64 kilobytes of memory. In contrast, a modern Apple iMac computer has 8 gigabytes of memory (i.e., 8,000,000 kilobytes). In the film, the computer was paired with an acoustic coupler modem.

2. Cornwall, *Hackers' Handbook*.

3. Kaplan, *Dark Territory*, 1–2.

4. Ibid.

5. Ibid., 9–10.

6. Reagan, "National Policy on Telecommunications."

7. Kaplan, "'War Games' and Cybersecurity's Debt to a Hollywood Hack."

8. On this development, see, e.g., Cross, "After Moore's Law"; and Burkeman, "Forty Years of the Internet."

9. Private conversation with the author.

10. Interview with Ian Wallace, Washington, March 30, 2015.

11. See Devries and Yadron, "Cataloguing the World's Cyberforces."

12. On "cyber Pearl Harbor," see Panetta, "Remarks by Secretary Panetta on Cybersecurity." In fact, the same phrase had been used nearly two decades before by US deputy attorney general Jamie Gorelick at a hearing of the US Senate's Government Affairs Committee. See Kaplan, *Dark Territory*, 48. The phrase "cyber 9/11" was used by US homeland security secretary Janet Napolitano in January 2013. See Charles, "US Homeland Chief: Cyber 9–11 Could Happen 'Imminently.'"

13. Quoted by Koebler, "US Nukes Face up to 10 Million Cyber Attacks Daily."

14. Boulanin and Ogilvie-White, *Cyber Threats*, 3–4.

15. Quoted by Burns, "Former US Commander: Take Nuclear Missiles Off High Alert."

16. The main works looking at the cyber-nuclear nexus include US Department of Defense, Defense Science Board, *Task Force Report: Resilient Military Systems*; Fritz, "Hacking Nuclear Command and Control"; Gady, "Could Cyber Attacks Lead to Nuclear War?"; Reed, "Keeping Nukes Safe from Cyber Attack"; Futter, "Cyber Threats and the Challenge of De-Alerting US and Russian Nuclear Forces"; Futter, "*War Games* Redux?"; Futter, "Cyber Threats and Nuclear Weapons"; Cimbala, *Nuclear Weapons in the Information Age*; and Global Zero Commission on Nuclear Risk Reduction, "De-Alerting and Stabilizing the World's Nuclear Force Postures." Similar themes have also been covered in the popular television series *Battlestar Galactica* and more recently in the novel *Ghost Fleet* by August Cole and P. W. Singer.

17. See Bracken, *Second Nuclear Age*.

18. See Blair, "Could Terrorists Launch America's Nuclear Missiles?"

19. See Fulghum, "Why Syria's Air Defenses Failed to Detect Israeli's."

20. Global Zero Commission on Nuclear Risk Reduction, "De-Alerting and Stabilizing the World's Nuclear Force Postures," 29.

21. This builds on a definition by provided by Andres and Winterfeld, *Cyber Warfare*, 167.

22. Libicki, *Conquest in Cyberspace*, 39.

23. Libicki, *Cyberdeterrence and Cyberwar*, xiv.

24. Such "advanced conventional weapons" include increases in precision strike, conventional counterforce and C4ISR (command, control, communications, computers, intelligence, surveillance, and reconnaissance) capabilities, new antisubmarine and anti-space technologies, and the spread of ballistic missile defenses. Many of these systems have reached maturity due to the rapid increases in information technology and engineering that characterize the cyber age.

PART I

> The Nature
> of the Challenge

1

> What Exactly Do We Mean
> by the Cyber Challenge?

"CYBER" IS A NEBULOUS and contested concept that means different things to different people. This is a central reason why the cyber debate lacks coherence, and why there is such disagreement about the nature and extent of the cyber challenge and cyber threat. Indeed, it has become commonplace to use the prefix or adjective "cyber" as a one-size-fits-all descriptor for the challenges posed by the numerous new tools and dynamics associated with computer systems, complex technologies, and the latest information revolution. As a result, it often is not clear what is and is not new, what is at risk, in what ways and to whom when we talk about cyber. At least part of this is because the cyber revolution is "still incipient," and because we cannot yet be fully sure with any confidence what it means for theory and practice.[1] But a failure to be clear what is meant by the term has often led to overhyping and a general misunderstanding of the cyber challenge, which in turn has made it far harder to devise and agree to a set of responses, frameworks, and protections. This has also left the concept dangerously devoid of strategic meaning, which has meant that "cyber" is too often used as a catchall that means whatever the user wants (consciously or not).

Despite a tendency for conflation in both the academic literature and policy debates, there are many different types of cyber challenges—some that are intrinsic and are the product of the emergent digital context, some that involve cyber operations, and some that might even include strategic attacks or cyber weapons. But perhaps the most important distinction when seeking to conceptualize "cyber" is between the challenges derived from the pervasively computerized global *context* in which we all live, where complex technology forms an ever-increasing part of everyday life, and those challenges emanating specifically from cyber operations and new methods of exploitation and attack. Cyber threats vary considerably across a cyber spectrum—which ranges from the use of capabilities for nuisance, crime, and hacktivism; through espionage; to denial-of-service attacks and the infiltration of systems; to activities that cause damage, involve weapons, or might even be considered warfare. Depending on the use of the term "cyberattack," it could therefore be argued that nations and critical infrastructure are constantly under attack or that such attacks are a minor concern and are very unlikely to materialize. For example, when Adam Segal warned in 2012 that US nuclear weapons face "up to 10 million significant cyberattacks every day," this did not necessarily mean defending against millions of versions of Stuxnet, cyber-terrorists trying to cause a nuclear explosion, or some other highly sophisticated piece of malware that could destroy these systems, but rather "automated bots, constantly scanning for vulnerabilities," or even just curious, would-be hackers.[2] The difference is distinct, and the lack of clarity often drives hyperbole, leads to confusion, and complicates issues of cyber security, cyber defense, and cyberdeterrence. Such semantics also often obfuscate what is new and what is not when we talk about the cyber challenge, and particularly how this emerging suite of new and inchoate dynamics interacts, builds on, or transforms the current nuclear threat landscape. As a result, there is a strong case for treating the cyber challenge as both context *as well as* a set of new tools, operations, and weapons, and therefore for viewing it as both a societal development and a technological transformation in military operations and international security.

Accordingly, this chapter proceeds in three sections. The first explains the complex and complicated cultural heritage and the etymological development of the "cyber" concept, and the problems of agreeing on a single definition that this has caused; the second introduces the notion of a cyber threat spectrum and outlines the very different and differentiated nature of the challenge; and the third section looks at the new range of tools, mechanisms, and dynamics that have emerged as part of the transition from an analogue to a digital nuclear world. The conclusion makes the case for treating the cyber challenge as both a context *and* a set of specific threats, operations, and tools when we assess the challenge posed to the nuclear weapons enterprise and the nuclear order more broadly.

A Complicated Heritage: Genesis and Definition

The complicated and diverse background of "cyber" is a fundamental reason why its nature and definition—and, therefore, its implications for security thinking and practice—remain such a contested subject. This is because cyber challenges are both new and novel—and, broadly viewed as a phenomenon that is synonymous with the digital computer, the internet, and the latest information revolution or age—and at the same time are the most recent iteration in how information is used, communicated, and stored that can be traced back through history.[3] Consequently, it is often difficult to outline exactly what the cyber challenge includes and what is and is not new, issues made even more complicated by the relationship with the Revolution in Military Affairs, electronic warfare (EW), and the broader field of information warfare (IW) or information operations. Thus, there are three often-competing and co-constitutive aspects of how we understand the cyber challenge: (1) the evolution, use, and etymology of the term itself in popular culture; (2) its status as the latest iteration in the role of information in warfare; and (3) its relationship with the broader notions and established traditions of IW and EW. It is this mixed heritage between recognized military traditions, cultural movement, and new societal dynamics that have made "cyber" such a difficult concept to define, and why the debate on the nature and seriousness of the cyber threat is still opaque, diverse, and divided.

The word "cyber" began life with nothing to do with computers, hackers, or the internet—or, for that matter, anything to do with warfare. Its etymology can probably be traced back to Ancient Greece and the phrase *kybernetes*—which translates roughly as "helmsman" or "the art of steering."[4] But the word as we know it did not emerge until the 1940s and the publication of *Cybernetics* by Norbert Weiner; *Cybernetics* was the study of the importance of systems in both living beings and artificial machines.[5] The term then became popularized in the 1980s as part of the "cyberpunk" movement (a subgenre of science fiction), and most notably with the novel *Neuromancer* by the science fiction writer William Gibson.[6] Neither of these developments had much to do with security or politics. In fact, "cyber" did not really become part of the national security lexicon until the 1990s, with the development of SIMNET (the first virtual battlefield) by the US military,[7] and the publication of the seminal article "Cyberwar Is Coming!" by John Arquilla and David Ronfeldt in 1993.[8]

"Cyber" and particularly the notion of "cyberwar" did not start being used within US policymaking circles until about 1995, when an interagency task force investigating the weaknesses of the United States' critical national infrastructure needed a phrase to capture the challenges posed by the new computer vulnerabilities within these systems. According to Fred Kaplan, "cyber" was the name advocated by Michael Vatis, a Justice Department lawyer in the task force who had just read *Neuromancer*.[9] Since then, "cyber" has become one of the most utilized words in existence and has emerged as something of a catchall prefix or adjective referring to almost every aspect of modern life. Some estimates suggest that as many as 150 words now contain the prefix or adjective "cyber."[10] It is primarily due to this unusual evolution that the term "cyber" is often seen as referring to broader societal and even cultural development and the technological transformation of society, as well as a discrete set of new and novel capabilities, vulnerabilities, and threats.

At the same time, the cyber phenomenon is also the latest iteration in the centrality of information and the nature of the so-called infosphere (where information is created, stored, shared, and used) in warfare and strategy.[11] The security, safe storage, secure communication, and reliability of information have been intrinsic to national security and warfare throughout history. Equally, stealing, altering, and destroying key information; attacking, sabotaging, and compromising the means of storing and sharing this information; and seeking to alter perceptions and policies through deception and psychological operations have also always been a central part of warfare too. But though the methods, skills, and technologies used to achieve this have undoubtedly changed over time—from messengers, semaphore, and telegraphs to wireless networks, satellite communications, and network-centric warfare—the central principles and importance of information to and within warfare and strategy have remained relatively constant. If anything, they have become more important. This is particularly the case in the last two hundred years, as states have come to rely more on electronics and telecommunications for military operations.[12] Thus, many cyber challenges can actually be traced to "classical military and intelligence fields."[13]

In this way, we can think of the cyber challenge as not fundamentally altering the nature or the importance of information but rather as creating new ways of managing and targeting this information and therefore new problems for defense, assurance, and security. Or, as David Lonsdale puts it: "The information age has raised our awareness of information."[14] Therefore, the cyber phenomenon, the proliferation of complex software and networked computers, ever-increasing real-time interconnectivity, and particularly the wholesale transition from an analogue to a digital world, constitute the latest iteration of this technological evolution. This suggests that the cyber phenomenon has principally transformed the infosphere within which politics and strategy play out, and therefore how international security is understood and managed.

A final complicating factor is that the cyber challenge has become intertwined with the broader field of information warfare—itself a product of the recent information age and the associated Revolution in Military Affairs. The concept of IW probably began back in the 1970s, with the development of "command and control warfare,"[15] and specifically to a staff scientist at the Boeing Company called Thomas Rona—who speculated in a paper written in 1976 that in the emerging computer age, the most effective means to attack an adversary would be to focus on its information systems.[16] But it would only become formalized in the 1990s, with the introduction of IW (also often referred to as information operations) as a specific field of (primarily US) military activity and strategy.

IW is a multifaceted concept covering many different activities, including sabotage, espionage and intelligence operations, telecommunications eavesdropping and fraud, psychological operations, perception management, and electronic warfare.[17] But it also includes computer network operations (CNO), or what we would come to think of as cyber operations. Although cyber operations or CNO have often been conceived as just another component of IW, the new technologies and dynamics associated with the cyber challenge are also changing each of the other components, and thus the entire concept of IW as well. Thus, the cyber phenomenon should be treated both as a new niche component of and within IW and at the same time as a broader transformation in the way in which IW is carried out. Cyber capabilities (and context) therefore provide new methods and vectors for the established tactics of deception, destruction, degradation, denial, and disruption.[18]

This is particularly the case for the subfield of EW, an established component of strategy, but also another concept often combined under the general heading of IW.[19] EW can be thought of as operations using or taking place within the electromagnetic spectrum to attack an adversary's electronic systems—including computers. Thus, methods such as the ability to jam communications, eavesdrop, obtain secrets, and to deceive, exploit, or interrupt activities taking place across the electromagnetic spectrum have been around for decades. But EW is being transformed by the incipient cyber age as well—in fact, EW may be becoming more rather than less important in the cyber context.[20] Cyber operations essentially represent a shift in IW and EW from targeting analogue rather than digital systems, and from primarily seeking to intercept or disrupt information flows to being able to alter, corrupt, or delete this information. As Fred Kaplan explains,

> Information warfare took on a whole new dimension in the cyber age. Until the new era, the crews gathering SIGINT—signals intelligence—tapped phone lines and swept the skies for stray electrons, but that's all they could do: *Listen* to conversations, *retrieve* the signals. In the cyber age, once they hacked a computer, they could prowl the entire network connected to it; and, once inside the network, they could not only read or download scads of information; they could change its content—disrupt, corrupt, or erase it—and mislead or disorient the officials who relied on it.[21]

As such, though EW and computer security have often been treated as separate entities in the past, even though they use many of the same technologies, the spread of cyber capabilities, and a concurrent greater reliance on the electromagnetic spectrum for both military operations and for society in general, creates multiple new pressures to be understood and vulnerabilities to be exploited.[22] The cyber challenge can therefore be thought of as comprising both a new and growing subset of IW and EW—specifically the new "battlefields" of computers, networks, and digitized data—and at the same time as a phenomenon that transforms each of the other aspects and subsets of IW, such as psychological operations, intelligence warfare, perception management, and particularly electronic forms of exploitation and attack.[23]

A direct result of this unusual heritage is that when one looks at the nature of the current cyber debate, it quickly becomes clear that many analysts, analyses, and even states are talking past each other when they address the challenges posed by the cyber phenomenon. In some cases, this may be a conscious and instrumental choice, designed with a particular purpose in mind, but often it is the result of a lack of understanding and agreement about what the term "cyber" means and includes, and how it is being used. As the computer scientist Dan Craigen and colleagues have pointed out, "The term is used broadly and its definitions are highly variable, context-bound, often subjective, and, at times, uninformative. There is a paucity of literature on what the term actually means and how it is situated within various contexts."[24] The result is that when the term "cyber" is used, some very basic questions and clarity of assumptions are often lacking. Although most people accept that it involves computers and broader developments in information technology, what constitutes "cyber" therefore remains an esoteric product of individual views. In this way, it often also fuels hyperbole and misunderstanding—and makes for excellent sensationalist tabloid headlines (and sometimes policy sound bites). In fact, some have even suggested that we might be best served by getting rid of the term altogether, because it has become so dangerously devoid of meaning and complicates rather than elucidates such an important issue.[25]

There is no single accepted definition or conception to which all adhere to when using the term "cyber," or that denotes cyber operations or attacks on computer systems and networks.[26] In fact, use of the term spans a wide variety of different areas and scenarios, and incorporates a plethora of different referents and phenomena. These understandings range between very narrow and discrete uses of the term, which essentially refer to an expansion of electronic warfare operations against specific military targets during conflict, and much broader, inclusive conceptions that include a wide variety of operations involving all types of civilian and military systems, which are ongoing all the time.[27] This holds true at both the individual, analytical level and the strategic level. For example, Russia and China tend to prefer the label "information"[28] and a far broader conception of information-based attacks that include political or psychological actions designed to destabilize governments and influence policy, as well as more specific CNOs, as opposed to the perhaps more discrete US and Western preference for the term "cyber" as primarily involving attacks on computer networks.[29] That said, as the cyber security journalist Aliya Sternstein has pointed out, even the US military has had trouble defining what "cyber" actually means and includes for its budgetary purposes.[30]

First, there is an important difference between what is meant by "cyber" and "cyberspace"—two words that are often used interchangeably. Although it is often considered problematic to use the word "cyber" as a noun rather than as an adjective or a prefix (e.g., as was done repeatedly by then–US presidential candidate Donald Trump in television debates with Hillary Clinton in 2016[31]), most people would agree with the glossary of the *Tallinn Manual*, produced at the behest of the NATO Cooperative Cyber Defence Centre of Excellence, that cyber "connotes a relationship with information technology."[32] A better definition might be the one provided by Martin Libicki, who conceives of "cyber" as simply "the command and control of computers,"[33] or, as *The Oxford English Dictionary* describes it, as "relating to or characteristic of the culture of computers, information technology, and virtual reality."[34] "Cyberspace," conversely, more directly refers to the broader information environment within which data are stored and shared, and to the larger realm of computer networks. Cyberspace can therefore also include physical and nonphysical aspects of the electromagnetic spectrum,[35] as well as machines and people.[36] Thus, it involves all the interconnected, computerized components around the globe as well as the commands that pass through them and the information that they store.[37] Both cyber and cyberspace can therefore involve humans, and particularly the human–computer interface; they can also involve *both* contextual and operational dynamics. Although work is ongoing to produce an accepted *international* glossary for these terms, there is a real need for clarity if analysts and states are to ensure that they do not simply talk past each other.

Second, we can also think of the "cyber" definition problem as generally vacillating between narrow and broad conceptions of the term. For some, cyber challenges are best conceived of as involving computers and attacks over the internet—essentially, computer and network security. But for others, adopting a more comprehensive framework that incorporates hardware, software, and even people, and that utilizes a more inclusive understanding of cyberspace, is far more useful.[38] This broader framework also operates across several different levels, which therefore raise further questions about what "cyber" should include.[39] This variance has significant implications for the perception, nature, and scope of the challenge posed by so-called cyberattacks, the notion of cyber weapons, or, more broadly, the challenges for national security driven by the advent of the cyber age or context. The cyber challenge is perhaps best thought of as involving *four* different domains of analysis: physical/mechanical, logical, informational, and human/cognitive.[40] The first, the *mechanical* domain, involves physical infrastructure and hardware—such as wires, computers, communications nodes, and mainframes—that permit the creation, circulation, and storage of information. The second, the *logical* domain, includes the commands that tell the hardware what to do and the software that allows the transmission, interpretation, and sharing of key information. Third is the *information* and data domain, which includes all the data that the system collects, stores, generates, and relies on to function. And fourth is the cognitive domain, specifically, *human* beings and their interaction with the hardware, software, and information.[41] As a result, we must consider the nature of the cyber challenge vis-à-vis machines, software, data, and humans. That said, any particular cyber challenge, cyber operation, or cyberattack may span more than one of these domains.[42]

The conception favored here is the broad model and an amalgam of the definitions noted above. The cyber challenge is therefore conceived as the command and control of all information technology involved in nuclear weapons management and operating across the four domains of the information environment. It is important to note that this means the challenge should be understood as stemming from both a ubiquitous contextual dynamic and a specific set of operations and threats.

The Cyber Threat Spectrum: Exploitation and Attacks

According to Peter Singer and Allan Friedman, the internet security firm McAfee discovers a new piece of malware every second.[43] But these bits of malware vary significantly in their sophistication, seriousness, and especially in what they are intended to achieve. Indeed, while each of these challenges are likely to raise different questions and represent very different types of threats, they are too often grouped together as one. A closer examination shows that though there have been no "cyberwars" and only a handful of strategically significant cyberattacks during the past couple of decades, thousands of other cyber activities have been going on at a lower level.[44] Most of these cyber operations have been designed to test systems, steal information, and perhaps discover new vulnerabilities rather than to implant highly sophisticated malware into sensitive machines and systems or to cause damage, although there is an increasing "gray area" in between. As such, it is important to be clear about the different and differentiated nature of cyber threats, and therefore to be accurate about the exact nature and shape of the challenge. This also has implications for how we might conceive of a cyber weapon and whether certain activities might fall under the rubric of warfare or be classified as "strategic."

The first thing to note is that the cyber challenge varies considerably, depending on the types of actors involved. More sophisticated attacks are likely to be the preserve of the handful of nation-states with very advanced cyberattack capabilities (usually thought to include the United States, the United Kingdom, Russia, China, and Israel, but could also include a handful of others). Less sophisticated attacks, operations, and nuisances are more likely to be perpetrated by criminals, hacktivists, or small substate groups. Despite the often-held view to the contrary, cyber weapons and sophisticated cyberattacks are therefore not automatically the best weapons of the weak (particularly terrorists), due to the considerable barriers in development and use, and the threat of retaliation by a stronger adversary in the case of states.[45] Instead, they seem most likely to exacerbate the relative power of the strong.[46] As a former director of US national intelligence, Vice Adm. Mike McConnell explains, "There is a hierarchy. You go from nation-states which can destroy things, to criminals, who can steal things, to aggravating but skillful hackers."[47] Indeed, the destructive potential of a cyberattack is likely to be inversely proportional to the number of actors that are capable of carrying out such attacks and to the types of targets that can be struck. Sophisticated strategic attacks on sensitive systems (e.g., nuclear weapons systems) are therefore likely the preserve of only a handful of nation-states, given the considerable resources, time, and intelligence required for such operations.[48] That, said, espionage and penetration testing are often a state-based activity, and it is at least possible that individuals, small groups, or terrorists could carry out a sophisticated cyberattack in certain circumstances.

Second, the cyber challenge varies enormously in terms of the type of activity being undertaken. These can range from (1) simple hacking, hacktivism (the use of computers and networks to promote political ends), nuisance, vandalism (e.g., that believed to have been conducted by North Korea against Sony Pictures in 2014),[49] and crime—which might be carried out by any type of actor—such as the "WannaCry" ransomware that targeted the British National Health Service and other institutions in 2017;[50] (2) denial-of-service attacks and espionage through compromising systems and networks (the vast majority of cyber operations to date—notably in Estonia in 2008); (3) the use of cyber capabilities to inflict sabotage and destruction by targeting specific processes, software, and hardware; and (4) existential attacks or warfare—much more likely to be the preserve of powerful actors or nation-states—and that may involve sophisticated cyber weaponry, perhaps even able to act autonomously as an intelligent agent.[51] These challenges can be broadly split between activities that are best classified as *exploitation*, those that involve *attacks*, and some that might include the use of cyber weapons.

Cyber *exploitation*, or computer network exploitation (CNE), is best thought of as an intelligence-gathering activity or operations designed to probe and test systems. These operations include enabling actions and intelligence collection via computer networks that exploit data gathered from a target or from enemy information systems or networks, and may involve the use of advanced persistent threats to steal data over a prolonged period. Cyber*attacks*, or computer network attacks, conversely, are cyber operations designed to disrupt, deny, degrade, or destroy information resident in computers and networks, and the hardware that facilitates this.[52] However, the term "cyberattack" is often used to conflate many varied activities with very different intentions and implications, and this misuse also serves to reify the notion that all uses of cyber capabilities are in some way similar to a conventional military attack.[53] The conflation of the two in the cyber discourse is yet another factor that leads to misunderstanding and threat inflation.[54] That said, exploitation might often be a precursor to an attack, particularly as part of an active cyber defense policy.

There are two key ways to differentiate between exploitation and attacks: by intention (whether operations are designed to test systems, steal information, or cause damage and disruption) and by the type of malware or payload involved.[55] For example, we can think of most cyber operations as involving both a delivery vehicle and a payload (much like nuclear weapons). But though the method of delivery of the malware may come in many guises and be contingent on the vulnerability being exploited, its payload will likely be specific to the task required (much like a nuclear or conventional bomb or missile). Thus, espionage primarily requires a way in and perhaps some method of exfiltration of data, whereas an attack is designed to deliver a piece of malware to its target within the system with a specific objective—such as interfering with a particular process in a particular way. The clear majority of cyber activities to date—and, arguably, the most important—are low-intensity, such as crime, economic competition, hacktivism, and intellectual property theft, and therefore are best labeled as CNEs.[56] However, because the delivery vehicles for exploitation or attack can be very similar, or may even be the same, it is often very difficult to distinguish between CNEs and computer network attacks in practice. As a result, a cyberattack might be better understood as a statement about methodology rather than a description of intention, impact, or effect.[57]

A closer examination of use of the term "cyber threat" therefore shows that it is often used to refer to everything from denial of service, vandalism, and simple hacking or hacktivism through exploitation and the stealing of secrets, right up to attacks that might have physical, widespread, and destructive implications. The nature of cyber threats, and particularly the broad spectrum of challenges to which these threats lead, produce markedly different pressures for the global nuclear weapons enterprise. The most prevalent, persistent, and numerous attacks occur at the lower end of this spectrum, and the quantity of attacks diminishes considerably the further along the scale you go. These range from preventing the use of systems, to stealing the information that they contain, and to seeking to interfere with them and cause them—or their operators—to operate or act differently. As noted earlier, it is also important to note that different actors have different possible intentions and of course differing abilities to carry out cyber operations against nuclear systems.

How we conceive of and define cyber operations, cyber threats, cyber security, and cyberspace clearly also have implications for the nature, extent, and severity of the challenge and threat, and what can or might be done about them. The lack of an agreed-on approach and framework for understanding, or at least the lack of clarity about the approach or framework being adopted, has significantly complicated the debate and in many ways has eroded the analytical rigor of the term. It has also, according to some, been done instrumentally by certain parties to increase interest and funding or to exacerbate the threat.[58] Consequently, many opinions and statements about the cyber challenge lack a clear understanding of what the term means and what it involves, and this has meant that the cyber debate has often been clouded and that people with many varied points of view have essentially been talking past each other. It has also led to an ever-increasing "cyber hype," with far-reaching implications for both understanding and policy.[59] The debate and much of the analysis of the cyber challenge are therefore highly polarized, and opinions range considerably about the nature and severity of the threats and dynamics posed by cyber operations.

The truth is that the nature of the cyber threat—and the viability of different ways to respond to, manage, or protect against the cyber challenge—vary considerably, depending on what is at stake; what an attacker's intentions are; and, perhaps most important, what these attackers can actually do. As is explained in the subsequent chapters, the level of threat diverges substantially between actors and cases. It is also true that, to some extent, cyber risks, and especially those associated with nuclear weapons, can only be guessed at, due to the nature and sophistication of the systems being employed. This is particularly the case with systems (e.g., those used to manage nuclear weapons) that have very high consequences of failure; that involve complex interactions between hardware, software, and humans; and that may need to make critical decisions in a very short space of time.[60]

Nevertheless, an important implication of the divergence in opinion about the nature and extent of the threat posed by the cyber challenge is that it is difficult to reach a consensus on what can and should be done to address these new dynamics. Hyperbole and alarmism may be useful in drawing attention to the possible risks and dangers, but too often analysts have failed to be clear as to what exactly they are talking about and referring to. As such, it is useful to break the cyber phenomenon down into more manageable slices and to treat the challenges posed as deriving from both a new, pervasive strategic, political, and technological context and as a set of specific activities, operations, and maybe weapons. Ultimately, how we think about nuclear weapons is being challenged as much by the evolving digitized information environment as it is by specific attacks, operations, or capabilities.

What Is New? From an Analogue to a Digital Security Environment

The tools, dynamics, and methods of attack against nuclear systems have been transformed both by the emergent cyber context and by the development of various offensive cyber capabilities. This has largely been facilitated by a shift from a primarily analogue world—that is, where information is stored and transmitted in its original format through electrical pulses—to a digital world, where information is reformatted as a series of binary codes—0s and 1s. Put simply, digital technology and devices make it much easier to share, store, process, and use all sorts of different information; but at the same time, they make this information theoretically easier to access or attack, and potentially to do so without an adversary realizing this. Although it is possible to attack analogue systems and transmissions, it is far harder to get gain access, steal information from a distance, reprogram them, or interfere with the way that they work.

Cyber operations (both exploitation and attack) therefore provide a new means of stopping systems from working, new methods of instigating and carrying out an attack and finding "ways in" to sensitive systems, and new possibilities for what can be done once a system is breached. Although many of these threats draw on or utilize more established methods of attack, cyber operations are unquestionably revolutionizing how attackers can seek to compromise, interfere with, disrupt, or destroy nuclear systems. This may involve interfering with software and hardware in the manufacturing phase or compromising the supply chain; by attacking human operators directly—such as by inducing them to open or download an infected file;

by attacking over networks; by exploiting a known vulnerability, such as a zero-day exploit; or even by creating a new vulnerability within a system.[61] This is particularly true for the ability to compromise systems remotely and in advance.

The first key aspect of the threat is that cyber capabilities are providing new ways of gaining access to computer systems during their development and manufacturing phases. Sensitive hardware has always been a target for attackers, and nuclear security experts have long warned of the risks posed by an attacker altering hardware components so that they do not work, or at least do not work as expected.[62] But a greater reliance on code and complex systems more generally is making it easier to interfere with the software and data on which the hardware relies. As a result of the digital revolution, it has now arguably become easier and perhaps also less discoverable to attack the coding rather than machinery on which these sensitive systems rely.[63]

With the exponential increase in the sophistication of software and coding, and particularly the use of commercial off-the-shelf software—that is, programs available commercially from different suppliers around the globe—for all types of computing, and worryingly also for nuclear systems, the risks increase markedly. As the computer security expert Ross Anderson notes, "The moral is that vulnerabilities can be inserted at any point in the tool chain, so you can't trust a system you didn't build yourself."[64] But even this is not a panacea. In fact, a 2008 US Defense Science Board report noted that "malicious code could be introduced inexpensively, would be almost impossible to detect, and could be used later to get access to defense systems in order to deny service, steal information, or to modify critical data."[65]

The second set of challenges concerns the role of the humans who operate computer systems—not least, the so-called insider threat. This is true both for unwitting or unknowing exploitation of a human working directly with the target systems, and also for attacks carried out deliberately (perhaps under duress) by those in situ. These "attacks" must also differentiate between remote access attacks—that is, those conducted at a distance and likely over the internet and through networks—and close access attacks, probably carried out by people, which could be logical (i.e., using a Universal Serial Bus drive or other removable device) or physical (e.g., by damaging or corrupting hardware).[66] Although many cyber operations often will utilize new and innovative methods (outsiders are clearly being empowered by new ways to attack systems and people remotely), a considerable part of the cyber challenge will therefore be from insiders and traditional "inside jobs."[67] Indeed, for all the time and money spent improving cyber defenses or air-gapping sensitive systems, such as those used for nuclear weapons, the weakest part of the system remains humans (as it does for most other organizations).[68] As Henry Sokolski explains: "No matter how 'secure' one tries to make nuclear weapons assets procedurally or technically, individuals with enough authority or access can elect to override or find ways around such protections. The political and organizational solutions employed successfully in the past, therefore, may or may not work in the future."[69] That said, it may be that human carelessness or complacency—on the part of either employees or contractors—represents a far bigger threat than malicious insiders.[70] It is most likely that a human with access to the system unwittingly spanned the "air gap" to facilitate the Stuxnet attack against the Iranian nuclear program discovered in 2010 by inserting infected media that had been compromised beforehand.[71] The insider threat may become particularly pernicious when it is combined with the possibility of cyber social engineering (this is discussed later in the book).

The most common method of targeting humans is through phishing attacks via email, which are used to dupe the receiver into supplying sensitive data, such as passwords and other personal details. Email might also be used to induce the recipient into unwittingly downloading an infected file on their computer (or this might somehow be planted physically on their computer by operatives). This file could contain any number of "payloads" (discussed in later chapters) and could be transferred across the network. This might be done through a virus—a program that attaches itself to another program or file, enabling it to spread from one computer to another, leaving infections as it travels, much like a human virus. Almost all viruses can only work if the infected file on the computer is activated, and they vary in severity; some may cause only mildly annoying effects, whereas others can damage hardware, software, files, or processes. A virus cannot spread without human action, although this can of course be done unwittingly. Alternatively, systems may also be infected with a "worm"—malware that is very similar to a virus, except that it can spread to new computers without human involvement. Worms replicate themselves automatically; in many cases, this leads to the computer crashing or the spam that automatically sends itself out to all recipients in an email address book, but it could also be far more sinister.

Finally, systems may be breached though the use of vulnerabilities in the software coding and security programs once systems are up and running. This is perhaps the biggest development created by cyber operations, particularly the ability to exploit systems remotely. Essentially, all computer systems are likely to contain coding errors, or what are known as zero-day exploits—also often referred to as bugs—and these can allow access to particular programs, computers, and networks. In fact, zero days are now being traded on a growing informal international market.[72] Equally, an adversary may employ what are known as advanced persistent threats to carry out a coordinated attack that might be used to search for these vulnerabilities, or once discovered, allow access to them over a sustained period of time. It might also be possible to create vulnerabilities in systems.[73] Although this challenge is likely to be more worrying for widely used programs, even the most carefully designed and highly secure systems are likely to contain vulnerabilities and flaws.[74] In fact, in 2007, a US Defense Science Board report suggested that it was "only a matter of time before an adversary exploits this weakness at a critical moment in history."[75] Because of this, cyber security is as much about managing vulnerabilities and minimizing possible ways into systems as it is about hackers and sophisticated cyber weaponry.[76]

Once an attacker has gained access to the computer system—through the supply chain, through a human in situ, or remotely—they essentially have four options: (1) take control of that computer, and its processes, and issue false commands; (2) steal the information and data that it contains, or data on how the system works; (3) manipulate the coding or inject phony information to mislead the system and its operators; or (4) implant malware that will cause the system to run differently or to make erroneous decisions.[77] In doing this, a successful cyber operation may cause systems to issue the wrong instructions or provide faulty information, run incorrectly, or even not run at all. The effect could be the significant disruption or degradation of critical computer systems used for military operations and possibly even the command and control of nuclear weapons.[78] An attacker may also seek to take control of a computer as the basis for a distributed denial-of-service attack, whereby many compromised computers are used to overwhelm a single system or network, through the establishment of a botnet (a group of compromised computers linked through the internet that, although their owners are unaware of it, have been set up to forward transmissions—including spam or viruses—to other computers on the internet). The use of distributed denial-of-service attacks, as Richard Stiennon points out, "is the strongest weapon available for cyber aggression. Countering them is very expensive and could theoretically be impossible."[79]

In terms of stealing data and manipulating processes, different types of malware might be placed within these systems to allow either exfiltration of data or to interfere with normal operations. Spyware does not harm the target computer but seeks to collect sensitive information—including potentially logging the user's keystrokes (and therefore passwords). A logic bomb is code deliberately inserted into software that will set off a malicious function when certain conditions are met or when ordered to do so by external contacts. Rootkits seek to provide access to all the folders on a certain computer—both private data and operational system files—to a remote user who, through administrative powers, can do whatever they want with that computer (i.e., they seek to control rather than to destroy). A Trojan horse will masquerade as a useful (and legitimate) piece of software and, once installed or run on a computer, will do its damage—this can vary from minor activities that cause annoyance, to more serious operations such as deleting files, stealing information, and even acting to create a backdoor for future illicit entry into the system. Trapdoors and backdoors are a method of bypassing normal authentication to allow ways back in to computers and systems planted by programmers or introduced through malware. A hardware Trojan—for example, a malicious modification of an integrated circuit chip—could also leak information or disable, deny, degrade, derange, or destroy the chip, components, or parts of the system it supports, perhaps at a crucial time. A hardware Trojan might also act as "a backdoor that can sniff out encryption keys or passwords or transmit internal chip data to the outside world."[80]

In general, what each of these types of malware is designed to do is entirely up to the attacker (although what can be achieved will often depend on prior knowledge of the system under attack and the capabilities of the attacker[81]). As Martin Libicki explains: "If hackers get in, they could wreak great damage. At a minimum they might steal information. Worse, they may make systems go haywire. Worst, they could inject phony information into systems to distort what users think they absorb when they deal with systems."[82]

Many of the new challenges posed by cyberattackers draw on established methods and vulnerabilities; in this way, the challenge is bifurcated between old and new, and between weaknesses and offensive capabilities. However, the nature of the cyber challenge, and therefore the methods and mechanisms that might be used to attack nuclear weapons systems, necessarily depend on the types of target. For example, nuclear weapons and delivery vehicles are perhaps most vulnerable during manufacture and development; communication links, early warning systems, targeting plans, and operational security are perhaps most vulnerable during a crisis; and sensitive nuclear information is perhaps most vulnerable at any time, once it has been collated and stored on a computer. The role of humans remains important—if not fundamental—across all these vectors.

Conclusion: The Cyber Challenge as Both Context and Operations

The cyber phenomenon is and remains a nebulous and contested challenge, and this is a central reason why the debate lacks coherence and why there is such disagreement about the nature and extent of the threats and risks it poses. Indeed, it often is not clear what is and is not new, what is now at risk, in what ways, and to whom. This has also left the cyber concept dangerously devoid of strategic meaning, and thus "cyber" is too often used as a catchall that means whatever the user wants, consciously or not. Because of this, there is a strong case for treating the cyber challenge as both a context as well as a set of new tools and weapons, and viewing it as a societal development and a technological transformation in military operations. This in turn allows for a much more holistic and nuanced treatment of the possible problems posed.

Different aspects of the cyber challenge will therefore affect nuclear weapons thinking, security, and strategy in different ways. For example, there are clearly key differences between the impact of an increasingly digitized global context and the tools and capabilities this has bequeathed (although these are of course co-constitutive); the nature of the operation being undertaken (e.g., exploitation vs. attack) and the differences in intention and capabilities of actors in this realm; the target (critical civilian infrastructure or military forces); the mechanisms being employed (low-specification tools vs. sophisticated weapons) either by a human in situ or remotely over networks; and the level at which attackers are operating (crime vs. warfare). This, in turn, will necessitate a diverse and flexible toolkit of responses and mitigation: The specter of strategic cyberattacks, or cyberattacks with possible strategic implications, will require different thinking from those primarily designed for exploitation, espionage, intellectual property theft, or purely nuisance. What this means for the use of the term in the nuclear realm is addressed in the following chapters.

Notes

1. Kello, "Meaning of the Cyber Revolution," 39.
2. Quoted by Koebler, "US Nukes Face up to 10 Million Cyber Attacks Daily."
3. The current epoch is often referred to as the "Information Age" or, perhaps more correctly, as "the Second Information Age." For a discussion of this, see, e.g., Brock, *Second Information Revolution*.
4. See Tabansky, "Basic Concepts," 76.
5. Weiner, *Cybernetics*.
6. Gibson, *Neuromancer*.
7. See Cosby, *Simnet*.
8. Arquilla and Ronfeldt, "Cyberwar Is Coming!"
9. Kaplan, *Dark Territory*, 45–46.
10. Thomas, *Cyber Silhouettes*, 7.
11. Lonsdale, *Nature of War*, 183; and Mitchell, *Network-Centric Warfare*, 32.
12. Healey, *Fierce Domain*, 27.
13. Berkowitz, "Warfare in the Information Age," in *In Athena's Camp*, ed. Arquilla and Ronfeldt, 273.
14. Lonsdale, *Nature of War*, 184.
15. See Price, *War*, 239.
16. Berkowitz and Hahn, "Cybersecurity."
17. Libicki, *Conquest in Cyberspace*, 20.
18. Andres and Winterfeld, *Cyber Warfare*, 175.
19. Anderson, *Security Engineering*, 588.
20. Ibid., 568.
21. Kaplan, *Dark Territory*, 4–5.
22. Anderson, *Security Engineering*, 559.
23. Libicki, *Conquest in Cyberspace*, 16–17.
24. Craigen, Diakun-Thibault, and Purse, "Defining Cybersecurity," 13.
25. See, e.g., Yadron and Valentino-Devries, "This Article Was Written with the Help of a 'Cyber' Machine."
26. Owens, Dam, and Lin, *Technology*, 14–15.
27. Rattray, *Strategic Warfare*, 8–9.
28. Lewis, "Cyber Attacks."
29. See Giles and Hagestad, "Divided by a Common Language," in *Proceedings of the 5th International Conference on Cyber Conflict*, ed. Potins, Stinissen, and Maybaum.

30. Sternstein, "Why Cybersecurity Dollars Do Not Add Up."

31. Wolff, "Cyber Is Not a Noun."

32. Schmitt, *Tallinn Manual*, 258.

33. Interview with the author, March 27, 2015, Washington.

34. See "Definition of *Cyber* in English," https://en.oxforddictionaries.com/definition /cyber.

35. Schmitt, *Tallinn Manual*, 258.

36. Singer and Friedman, *Cybersecurity and Cyberwar*, 13.

37. Tabansky, "Basic Concepts," 77.

38. See, e.g., Libicki, *Conquest in Cyberspace*, 24; Kramer, "Cyberpower and National Security," in *Cyberpower*, ed. Kramer, Starr, and Wentz, 6; and Kuehl, "From Cyberspace to Cyberpower: Defining the Problem," in *Cyberpower*, ed. Kramer, Starr, and Wentz, 28.

39. See, e.g., Libicki, *Conquest in Cyberspace*, 24, Kramer, "Cyberpower," 6, and Kuehl, "From Cyberspace to Cyberpower," 28.

40. This draws on the framework provided by Rattray, *Strategic Warfare*, 17–18.

41. Adopted from Kello, "Meaning of the Cyber Revolution," 18.

42. Andres and Winterfeld, *Cyber Warfare*, 120.

43. Singer and Friedman, *Cybersecurity and Cyberwar*, 63.

44. Lewis, "Cyber Attacks."

45. Lindsay, "Stuxnet," 389.

46. Gartzke, "Myth of Cyberwar," 63.

47. McConnell, "Cyberwar Is the New Atomic Age," 76.

48. Rid and McBurney, "Cyber-Weapons."

49. Perlroth and Sanger, "North Korea Loses Its Link."

50. Newman, "Ransomware Meltdown Experts Warned about Is Here."

51. Rid and McBurney, "Cyber-Weapons," 7–8. See also US Department of Defense, Defense Science Board, *Task Force Report: Resilient Military Systems*, 2.

52. Andres and Winterfeld, *Cyber Warfare*, 167.

53. Valeriano and Maness, "Dynamics of Cyber Conflict," 349.

54. Ibid., 32.

55. Ibid., 150.

56. Healey, *Fierce Domain*, 20; and Lindsay, "Stuxnet," 374.

57. Owens, Dam, and Lin, *Technology*, 11.

58. See, e.g., Lee and Rid, "OMG Cyber," 4.

59. Ibid., 4–12.

60. Stubbs, "Interplay between Cultural and Military Nuclear Risk Assessment," in *Nuclear Enterprise*, ed. Shultz and Drell, 228.

61. Nye, "Deterrence and Dissuasion," 50.

62. Feaver, *Guarding the Guardians*, x.

63. Lynn, "Defending a New Domain," 101.

64. Anderson, *Security Engineering*, 645.

65. US Department of Defense, "Report of the Defense Science Board Task Force," x.

66. Owens, Dam, and Lin, *Technology*, 87–104.

67. Rid, *Cyberwar Will Not Take Place*, 72.

68. Tertrais, "Unexpected Risk," in *Nuclear Weapons Security Crises*, ed. Sokolski and Tertrais.

69. Sokolski, preface to *Nuclear Weapons Security Crises*, ed. Sokolski and Tertrais, viii–ix.

70. Roger R. Johnstone, quoted by Boulanin and Ogilvie-White, *Cyber Threats*.

71. Lindsay, "Stuxnet," 381.

72. Greenberg, "Shopping List."

73. See US Department of Defense, Defense Science Board, *Task Force Report: Resilient Military Systems*, 2.

74. Neumann, *Computer-Related Risks*, 4.

75. US Department of Defense, "Report of the Defense Science Board Task Force," v.

76. Libicki, *Conquest in Cyberspace*, 40.

77. Libicki, *Cyberdeterrence and Cyberwar*, xiii.

78. Gompert and Libicki, "Cyber Warfare," 11.

79. Steinnon, *Surviving Cyberwar*, 62.

80. Mitra, Wong, and Wong, "Stopping Hardware Trojans."

81. Lindsay, "Stuxnet," 378.

82. Libicki, *Conquest in Cyberspace*, 1.

2

> ## How and Why Might Nuclear
> ## Systems Be Vulnerable?

COMPUTERS AND COMPLEX SYSTEMS have always been central to nuclear weapons management, command and control, and global nuclear order. In fact, the need to administer and coordinate increasingly sophisticated and intricate nuclear weapons, early warning sensors, and war plans was a principal driver of early computer technology.[1] However, the numerous and often-competing requirements placed on nuclear weapons systems—principally, the so-called always/never dilemma associated with nuclear command and control—has also meant that these systems have always been prone to accidents and mistakes and have contained certain vulnerabilities that could be either interfered with or exploited by would-be attackers. Despite the availability and use of wide-ranging protective measures, security processes, and systems of control—including various permissive action links on weapons, sophisticated encryption and redundancy for communications, rigorous personnel reliability programs, and the likelihood that most if not all key systems will contain firewalls and will be air-gapped from the wider internet—the emergent cyber context is creating considerable challenges and problems across the entire nuclear weapons enterprise. As the systems security expert Ross Anderson notes, "Despite the huge amounts of money invested in developing high-tech protection mechanisms, nuclear control and safety systems appear to suffer from just the same kind of design bugs, implementation blunders, and careless operations as any others."[2] Consequently, cyber threats are primarily exacerbating and recasting the intrinsic challenges of nuclear command and control, information security, and strategy. But they are doing this by revealing and creating new vulnerabilities and problems within existing systems that hackers might exploit, rather than by fundamentally altering the business of nuclear weapons management itself.

The new cyber context exacerbates and magnifies the challenges associated with nuclear weapons management in two main ways. First, a growing reliance on complex computers, software, and more and more lines of code, in conjunction with sophisticated hardware and sensor technology throughout the nuclear weapons enterprise, is increasing the chances of *normal nuclear accidents*, mistakes, and misunderstandings—that is, computer-induced problems that could cause mix-ups that lead to unwarranted, unplanned, and unintended nuclear outcomes, and even nuclear use. Second, and at the same time, this increased reliance on high-technology hardware and software is creating new ways for would-be attackers to interfere with or compromise the systems on which nuclear forces (and their operators) rely. This might be done either directly or indirectly—and either to enable or disable various weapons, systems, and components. Although the nature and extent of these problems necessarily varies between actors, systems, and types of weapons, all nuclear-armed states will be affected in some way. These challenges are also likely to be aggravated by plans to modernize nuclear command and control infrastructures for all types of nuclear-armed actors.

The main aim of this chapter is to examine and explain the complex nature of nuclear weapons management, outline some of the problems that officials and planners face and have faced in the past, and highlight the inherent weaknesses and vulnerabilities of modern nuclear weapons systems in the budding digital global security environment. The chapter therefore proceeds in three sections. The first looks at the basics of nuclear command and control and the inherent vulnerabilities contained in any nuclear weapons system, before examining the various methods and mechanisms of protection against accidents, mistakes, and attacks. The second section examines how, as part of the emerging digital age, all nuclear-armed states are relying more and more on complex systems, computers, coding, and high-technology components, which have made nuclear weapons increasingly susceptible to normal nuclear accidents, mistakes, and inadvertent and unintended outcomes. And the third section looks at how a reliance on these technologies is creating new vulnerabilities and possible vectors for interference across the nuclear weapons enterprise and increasing the potential for both *enabling* and *disabling* cyberattacks.

The Inherent Difficulties of Nuclear Weapons Management

The systems used to manage nuclear weapons (and the associated infrastructure and information) have always been vulnerable to accidents and mistakes, exploitation, interference, or attacks, although this has varied between states due to the different requirements, specifics, sophistication, and posture of their nuclear forces. The specific risks posed by relying on computers and electronic systems for the command and control of nuclear weapons, and the concurrent dangers of operating these weapons largely outside human control, is not new either. In fact, concerns of this nature can be traced back to the 1960s, when military officials in the United States began to worry that a nuclear-armed missile might inadvertently (or deliberately) be sent the wrong way after launch and detonate on an American city due to computer error or outside interference with its guidance systems.[3] A few years later, in 1972, an official study conducted for the US Air

Force by James Anderson, deputy for command and management systems at the US Air Force Systems Command, highlighted the possibility that "malicious attackers" could potentially penetrate US nuclear weapons systems.[4] These inherent tensions and concerns have remained and are likely to become even more pronounced as we move further into a cyber-enabled global security context where a larger percentage of nuclear functions are controlled by digital computers. In this way, and somewhat ironically, though the modern internet and computer systems were developed in part to help better manage nuclear operations, these same technologies have now become one of the greatest threats to safe and secure nuclear command and control.[5]

Many of the cyber challenges for nuclear weapons addressed throughout this book derive directly from the inherent and central tensions of nuclear weapons management, and particularly from the adversative demands of nuclear command and control. At its most basic, nuclear command and control is about protecting weapons against attack or interference and ensuring that they are never used without proper authorization or by mistake, while at the same time ensuring that they can and will be used if the order to do so is given. We can therefore think of the central paradox of the command and control of nuclear forces as the tension between the *safety* and *security* of nuclear weapons (the threat of unwarranted use) and the *reliability, usability,* and *credibility* of these forces, especially in a crisis (the threat of nonuse and possible decapitation through a disarming first strike). This balance has become known as the always/never dilemma, and is perhaps best summed up by Peter Feaver: "At the heart of nuclear command and control lies the always/never dilemma. Leaders want a high assurance that the weapons will always work when directed and a similar assurance that the weapons will never be used in the absence of authorized direction. Weapons must be reliable: unlikely to fail at the moment when leaders want to use them; safe: unlikely to detonate accidentally; and secure: resistant to efforts by unauthorized people to detonate them."[6]

As such, nuclear command and control comprises two separate but intrinsically linked systems—those designed to provide "positive control" (ensuring that nuclear weapons and systems work and can be used if and when needed) and those designed to ensure "negative control" (ensuring that nuclear weapons will not detonate or launch by accident and are protected against unauthorized use or attack). Both positive and negative control are essential components of nuclear strategy and stable nuclear deterrence; a nation with poor positive control may be seen as vulnerable to a disarming strike (due to a lack of credibility that a nuclear response would be possible), while a nation with poor negative control might be seen as more likely to use these weapons (or at least not be able to prevent them from being launched by an unauthorized actor or by mistake—especially during a crisis).[7] As is explained later in this chapter, both the increasingly digitized nuclear context and a suite of emerging cyber threats are providing considerable new challenges to both these dynamics.

Positive control of nuclear forces means ensuring that weapons will work when required, and that they are protected against attackers intending to undermine or *disable* key systems and weapons so that they do not work or at least do not work as expected. Positive control must therefore ensure (1) sufficient early warning of any attack that might require a nuclear response—especially an attack that might decapitate the nuclear command structure or destroy nuclear forces before they can be used—and (2) that if the decision is made, the correct orders reach the nuclear forces and that these forces operate as planned—that is, that the commander receives the right instructions and knows that the orders being given are genuine, and that the missile/bomb successfully launches and the warhead reaches its intended target. Positive control can be enhanced by hardening facilities against attack, both physically, in terms of bunkers, or with active defenses, such as antimissile systems; through computer network defense, such as intrusion detection systems, air-gapping, and by keeping systems separate from the wider internet; with greater operational and technical secrecy and the enhanced encryption of orders; with redundancy of systems and communications links (although greater redundancy is not necessarily better—it can create more places for things to go wrong[8]); and through robust operational training, personnel reliability programs, and screening. In extremis, positive control could also include predelegation of launch authority to commanders—as is reported to have been the case in the United States in the late 1950s, and may well be true elsewhere, although this in turn raises the risk of unauthorized use.[9] It might even involve partially or fully autonomous nuclear use/response systems—such as the Soviet Dead Hand, or Perimeter, system developed during the Cold War.[10] In fact, some experts and commentators have suggested that this system might even still be active.[11] Given the possibility of accidents, mistakes, or outside interference, both automated/autonomous and predelegated systems would represent a cyber security risk of the first order.

Negative control of nuclear forces, conversely, is focused on protecting against the accidental, mistaken, or unauthorized use of nuclear weapons—or attacks seeking to *enable* nuclear forces and associated systems. Negative control involves (1) making sure that nuclear weapons cannot be used or detonated by accident, mistake, or miscalculation; (2) protection against unauthorized personnel (both insiders and outsiders) gaining access to and using these weapons; and (3) preventing the deliberate use of nuclear weapons (by a rogue commander) or interference that might lead to use by third parties, such as terrorist groups. Many of the mechanisms for positive control described above also apply to negative control. But negative control can be enhanced by procedural measures—such as the two-man rule, where all operations require the agreement and cooperation of at least two authorized personnel; dual phenomenology (utilizing attack or warning information from *at least* two different sensors/sources); a rigid and likely centralized chain of (civilian) command, and rigorous personnel reliability programs.[12] They may also be based on technical means, such as by using permissive action links—either combination locks or coded switches that provide a mechanical barrier to anyone seeking to cause the weapon to detonate without proper authority. These switches maintain the warhead in an electronically disabled condition until the proper code is inserted.[13] However, they are not thought to be used by all nuclear-armed states or on all nuclear devices.[14] Weapons might also be designed to "fail safe" (where warheads will not detonate if a component fails—as opposed to "fail deadly" where they will) or use environmental sensing devices, which are sensors attached to nuclear weapons that permit detonation only when certain parameters are met; for example, strong acceleration and then free fall for a warhead on an intercontinental ballistic missile (ICBM).[15] Other mechanisms— such as using secret codes and encryption for communications, or by detargeting (aiming missiles into the ocean), de-alerting (reducing the time it takes to fire), decoupling or de-mating (separating warheads from delivery vehicles and warning systems)—might also be employed to keep weapons safe and secure. The antagonistic demands on nuclear command and control are explained further in figure 2.1.

The balance between positive and negative control is often a reflection of geostrategic circumstances, but it can also be a direct product of *who* is in control: civilians or the military. Broadly speaking, strong civilian control will tend toward the safe, or "never," side of the nuclear dichotomy, while military commanders will necessarily focus more on the usability, or "always," side.[16] Again, in the words of Peter Feaver, "Civilian leaders feel strong pressure to ensure that things will not go wrong; thus they will be motivated to exert control over nuclear operations. Military officers, responding to the same stimulus, seek as much autonomy over operations as possible in order to keep control in the hands of the most knowledgeable people and the ones least likely to make innovative moves that will have unintended consequences."[17]

Negative control—the threat of unwarranted use		Positive control—the threat of decapitation / first strike
Unauthorized use	**Accidents/mistakes**	
Nuclear forces should be as *secure* and well protected as possible.	Nuclear forces should be as *safe* as possible.	Nuclear forces must not be vulnerable to a surprise first strike.
Delegating authority over nuclear forces increases the risk of an unauthorized use.	Keeping weapons on high alert increases the chance that accidents will happen.	Forces need to be kept on high alert, and control should be potentially (pre)delegated to military commanders.
Nuclear use must always be kept under strict (civilian) control and contain advanced safety measures.	Nuclear weapons should be usable only following a positive command from the relevant authority.	Nuclear use may need to be automated to some degree to be credible.

Figure 2.1 Positive and Negative Command and Control

Historically, many nuclear-armed states have leaned toward the *always* side of nuclear command and control rather than the *never*—particularly the United States and Russia during the Cold War. This essentially means prioritizing the perceived need for credibility in the ability to use nuclear forces over the requirement to keep them safe and secure. The former vice president of Sandia Laboratories, Robert Peurifoy, explains this logic: "For war fighters, (1) more safety means less reliability as a result of the additional operations that are introduced to prevent an accidental detonation; (2) more security means higher costs; and (3) more control means less immediate availability."[18] Essentially, the desire for security and control must always be counterbalanced against the possibility of introducing a new vulnerability or weakness that might be exploited by a potential adversary.[19] The natural result of this tension between the desire of the military for autonomy, readiness, and control, and the requirement of officials to ensure oversight and that commanders cannot overstep their orders,[20] is that nuclear weapons and associated systems will never be as safe and secure as human ingenuity could make them.[21] As is explained below, these tensions are being magnified by the budding cyber context.

Although the challenges associated with using computers for nuclear command and control can be traced back decades, increased reliance on complex software, hardware, and digital code are creating a new range of both inherent challenges and vulnerabilities across nuclear systems that need to be understood and addressed. Thus, both the cyber context and cyber operations build on and exacerbate, rather than fundamentally transform, the complex and delicate nature of nuclear weapons management (both the weapons themselves and the security of associated nuclear weapons infrastructure and personnel). As the next two sections explain, this emerging digitized global security environment (1) increases the risks of normal nuclear accidents, mistakes, and unintended consequences within and by nuclear and associated systems; and (2) transforms how these systems might be attacked, sabotaged, compromised, or spoofed.

Complexity, Mistakes, and Normal Nuclear Accidents

The vulnerabilities and problems that are inherent within nuclear command and control and associated systems are perhaps best highlighted and demonstrated by the number of accidents, mistakes, near misses, and miscalculations that litter our nuclear past. In fact, "normal accidents theory" posits that complex systems—particularly those that rely heavily on computers and high-technology components—will not always work as intended and will naturally go wrong some of the time.[22] This is particularly the case with highly pressurized systems, including systems that can never be fully tested and those that deal with hazardous technologies and for which important decisions need to be made at short notice. Put simply, the more complex a system is, the more likely it is to go wrong;[23] and we should therefore expect that the unexpected will happen due to unforeseen and inadvertent interactions between its component parts.[24]

There is perhaps no better example of a complex—or a tightly coupled and highly pressurized—system than those developed for nuclear command and control, and it should be no surprise that the atomic age is ripe with accidents, mistakes, and nuclear near misses (and these are just the ones that we know about).[25] Scott Sagan has even suggested that "from a normal accidents perspective, the fact that there has never been an accidental nuclear weapons detonation or an accidental nuclear war is surprising." In fact, he indicates that "the nuclear weapons safety problem is like walking on thin ice. The fact that the system has not caved in so far does not mean that it will not in the future."[26]

Although many previous nuclear accidents and mistakes have simply involved human error, a significant number of incidents have involved software glitches or problems with computer technology, and this seems likely to increase as the systems used for nuclear weapons management become more complex, digitized, and intricate, and the broader, burgeoning cyber security context becomes progressively more pervasive. In fact, even as far back as the 1980s, the Soviet physicist Boris Rauschenbach warned that the increasing sophistication of nuclear weapons systems meant that "the very existence of humankind is becoming dependent on hardware and software."[27] But this challenge will become especially problematic as the computer–human interface becomes a more elaborate and multifaceted part of the nuclear mission (as seems likely) and as systems become increasingly complex and largely incomprehensible to all but a few experts. It is also important to note that this change in the global technological context will mean that the problem will apply equally—though perhaps in different ways—to both those with a long history of nuclear weapons management and those whose command and control systems and experience remain nascent.

Normal accidents theory—or, in this case, normal *nuclear* accidents theory— suggests that nuclear systems will almost certainly go wrong at some point and that we must expect unanticipated and unpredictable outcomes. Essentially, this means that the computer systems used across the nuclear weapons enterprise could potentially fail for many different reasons, and possibly in combination: It could be the result of incorrect, incomplete, or faulty design and manufacture of key components; various problems with the hardware or sensors; coding errors in the software being used—so-called computer bugs; and also problems arising from human interaction with these systems, including maintenance, updating, and upgrading.[28] Any of these issues could prove important—and even decisive— individually, but the real difficulties come when these problems are combined or play out in ways that nobody could have foreseen. Charles Perrow, the founding father of normal accidents theory, explains this further:

> No matter how effective conventional safety devices are, there is a form of accident
> that is inevitable. . . . No one dreamed that when X failed, Y would also be out of

order, and the two faults would interact so as to both start a fire and silence the alarm. Sometimes things just don't occur to designers. . . . We have produced designs so complicated that we cannot anticipate all the possible interactions of the inevitable faults; we add safety devices that are deceived, or avoided, or defeated by hidden paths in the system.[29]

Although Perrow was speaking broadly about various complex systems used across society, the same dynamics apply to nuclear weapons—indeed, some of these tensions might actually be exacerbated. As Paul Bracken puts it in terms of the vulnerability of global nuclear weapons and command and control infrastructure: "The massive redundancy inherent in a system as complex as the world's nuclear forces reduces the danger of war resulting from a single technical accident. It very likely mitigates the danger of war from even a handful of such isolated stresses. When the stresses occur close together in time, the situation is a bit more dangerous. The situation becomes very dangerous, however, when the stresses occur in the middle of an international crisis."[30] As Bracken continues, this means that "against the discrete accident, malfunction, or operator error, the total [nuclear weapon's] system is massively redundant; [but] . . . multiple errors or malfunctions are a different matter."[31] This concern is compounded by the inability to fully test a nuclear command and control system under real-world, highly stressed conditions (for obvious reasons).[32]

It is therefore entirely possible for nuclear weapons systems to function normally for years but then break down, malfunction, or produce erroneous information at the most inopportune moments due to problems buried deep inside their software that no one was aware existed.[33] This is particularly disconcerting because of the apparent lack of attention given to millions of lines of coding in various computer systems that are essential for nuclear operations.[34] For example, in 1991 a mistake in the computer coding used for US nuclear targeting was discovered, and this error—which had apparently remained undiscovered for months—would have meant that the weapon would not have been able to hit its intended target.[35] As is explained below, the importance of such "unknown unknowns" and the seeming inevitably of inherent mistakes within nuclear systems becomes particularly acute in periods where officials and commanders place increased strain on nuclear systems and when they incorporate new technologies into command and control or are adapting to more multifaceted and different missions.

The risk of accidents within and mistakes stemming from computerized nuclear systems can be traced back to the late 1950s and early 1960s as both US and Soviet officials wrestled to incorporate a spate of new technologies being designed for the nuclear mission into nuclear command and control (and particularly for early warning). In 1960, a radar unit connected to the US North American Aerospace Defense Command (NORAD) in Colorado mistook the moon for a massive incoming Soviet missile attack after a computer accidentally removed two zeros from the radar feed (this lapse changed the estimated range of the sighting from 250,000 miles to 2,500 miles).[36] The result was a level-3 warning.[37] That same year, a classified US military investigation found that a series of major power surges at one of the many nuclear control centers spread across the American Midwest could theoretically lead to the unintended launch of an entire fleet of fifty nuclear-armed ICBMs.[38] A few years later, in February 1971, an operator at NORAD accidentally transmitted an emergency message ordering all broadcasts off the air, creating the impression that the United States was preparing for a nuclear war. It took the operator 40 minutes to find the right code to cancel the message.[39]

But perhaps the most notable normal accidents are those that occurred at NORAD between 1979 and 1984—although this list is by no means exhaustive and is based only on available (primarily US) data. The first took place in October 1979, after computers at NORAD indicated that a missile had been launched from a submarine in the waters off the West Coast of the United States. Officials were suddenly confronted with a scenario that conventional wisdom and war planning led them to interpret as a Soviet nuclear attack designed to decapitate both the US nuclear command and control infrastructure and nuclear forces.[40] A low-level state of nuclear war was declared, and nuclear-armed missiles across the United States went on alert. The "attack" was later discovered to have been caused by a technician accidentally loading a war game training tape simulating a Soviet nuclear attack scenario into the computer at the operations center.[41] Also in October 1979, a submarine-launched ballistic missile radar installation at Mount Hebo, Oregon, picked up a low-orbit rocket body that was close to decay and generated a false launch-and-impact report.[42]

In June 1980, a faulty computer processor twice caused false attack indications at NORAD after it began writing data into warning messages that indicated a massive Soviet nuclear attack was under way. According to a report by the US Government Accountability Office (an agency that provides auditing, evaluation, and investigative services for the US government) written shortly afterward, "On June 2 and 6, 1980, missile warning system failures occurred when a faulty component in the communications system began writing numbers into blank spaces in the missile warning messages sent out live to various command posts. The blank spaces during an attack indicate the number of attacking missiles and usually contained zeros, but in this case the erroneous numbers generated by the computer indicated a mass attack."[43] Then again, in 1984, a computer malfunction indicated that a US nuclear-armed missile was about to fire.[44]

More recently, on October 23, 2010, the US Air Force lost contact with fifty ICBMs at F. E. Warren Air Force Base in Cheyenne, Wyoming, after a computer circuit card had been dislodged.[45] It has been suggested that this undermined security procedures to such an extent that the missiles could have been vulnerable to an unauthorized or accidental launch, possibly through cyber means.[46] In fact, the incident led to an investigation ordered by US president Barack Obama, which turned up further deficiencies and vulnerabilities, such as the possibility that hackers might interfere with the missiles' guidance systems—potentially rendering them unusable for days.[47]

Data for other nuclear-armed states is very limited, but it should be assumed that similar accidents and mistakes—perhaps due to computer problems—have taken place in other countries in the past as well. Although none of these accidents or mistakes resulted in nuclear use, pressures could easily have been compounded or exacerbated by other concurrent events, such as simultaneous failures in the warning systems of other states or a rash reaction by an individual.[48] Or perhaps worst of all, they could have happened in the middle of a crisis. As Shaun Gregory argued nearly three decades ago, but which remains highly pertinent to the nuclear context today: "These and similar events suggest that at least some of the safety systems designed to prevent an accidental nuclear detonation may fail and have failed. . . . The risk of an accidental nuclear detonation thus becomes a question of whether all the safety systems will ever fail at the same time or in an unfortunate or unanticipated sequence."[49]

Although a nuclear accident, detonation, or computer-induced mistake that leads to nuclear use remains at the far end of the high-impact/low-probability events scale, the risks of unexpected and undesirable outcomes and problems are only likely to grow as nuclear-armed actors come to rely more on computers and complex systems for nuclear weapons management and as systems become further commingled.[50] Moreover, given the nature of the challenge—nuclear command and control is characterized by its inherent complexity, multiple linked systems and sensors, unusual human–computer interaction, and likely short time scales for decision making—producing any sort of viable and quantifiable risk assessment or analysis will be very demanding, perhaps even impossible.[51] Worryingly, as former US secretary of defense Ashton Carter and colleagues noted a generation ago, this can sometimes discredit the risks of nuclear weapons accidents as subjects for serious study.[52]

Although nuclear weapons clearly represent the biggest risks, greater digitization and complexity of nuclear operations are likely to compound and exacerbate tensions right across the nuclear weapons enterprise. Indeed, and though many nuclear mistakes and accidents have involved command and control, particularly early warning systems and sensors, the same principle applies throughout the various component parts of the nuclear weapons infrastructure. For example, data from the UK Atomic Weapons Establishment were accidentally rerouted though Ukraine for five days in 2015. During the transit of these data outside the United Kingdom, it may have been possible for employees at Vega (a Ukrainian telecommunications provider), or others, to monitor or tamper with the data.[53] Although the data would almost certainly have been encrypted, the fact that sensitive nuclear information could potentially be intercepted by others outside the United Kingdom demonstrated the considerable problems states face with nuclear information security (and, for that matter, with secure communications in general).[54]

As is explained in the next two chapters, poor practices, human error, and mistakes—not least through software bugs and zero-day exploits—represent a significant part of the cyber-nuclear challenge.

US and Soviet officials spent decades fine-tuning the principally analogue computer hardware and software used for nuclear command and control systems in the first nuclear age, and the list of mistakes, accidents, and near misses due to these systems is considerable. Even with these relatively unsophisticated systems, it took time, the gradual growth of expertise and understanding, and no small amount of luck to avoid some sort of nuclear accident or catastrophe. The worry is that the digital possibilities of today—not to mention the increase in the number of nuclear actors—will magnify these risks considerably. Specifically, the development and adoption of ever more high-technology systems for the nuclear mission are likely to be far harder to understand; will contain more vulnerabilities, hidden problems, and flaws; and will perhaps be much more difficult to maintain, let alone diagnose and fix glitches in a timely manner.[55] To paraphrase Edward Skoudis, computer complexity is very much the enemy of nuclear security.[56] These dynamics are equally applicable to established nuclear powers and to newer members of the nuclear club—and will be particularly acute, it seems, during periods of technological change, heightened threat perception, or shifting system requirements.

Ultimately, in the incipient digitized global context, states that develop complex nuclear arsenals and associated command infrastructure, and keep their weapons systems highly alerted, will be more accident prone than those that keep them simple.[57] As a result, a key part of the cyber challenge for nuclear systems security will be intrinsic, and not involve any attackers at all. Perhaps more important, the history of accidents and the growing awareness of inherent vulnerabilities within nuclear command and control systems also provides an interesting insight into how these systems might be hacked. This is because, as the computer scientist Peter Neumann notes, "If an event can happen accidentally, it often could be caused intentionally."[58] Thus, by implication, more sophisticated systems will not only be more accident prone but are also likely to become much more susceptible to cyberattacks or interference. This is examined in more detail below.

New Vulnerabilities to Be Exploited: Positive and Negative Attacks

A growing reliance on computers, code, and digital software for all aspects of nuclear weapons management—from early warning, through the protection, collation and analysis of data, up to authorizing and firing the weapons—is also creating new ways in which nuclear systems might be exploited or attacked by hackers. Such attacks may come in numerous different guises and could involve, for example, (1) the degradation or severing of communications links between early warning sensors, control centers, and commanders; (2) data manipulation or corruption inside command and control infrastructure or the weapons themselves; (3) the failure of weapons to operate as intended; (4) the potential destruction or sabotaging of nuclear weapons and associated systems; and (5) the launch of a nuclear weapon or the explosion of a nuclear device.[59] Therefore, though reliance on ever more complex systems is increasing the chances of accidents and mistakes within nuclear weapons and their subsidiary control systems, these same dynamics are also creating new vulnerabilities that attackers might seek to exploit.

One of the biggest challenges here is the natural and inherent problems and bugs that are contained in ever more sophisticated and complex software and coding—such as that used for nuclear command and control and other nuclear operations.[60] Complex systems—particularly computer-based systems—are likely to contain more bugs, problems, and unforeseen errors than their more basic analogue predecessors, especially those that rely on complex code, link multiple functions and hardware, and must make accurate computations quickly. As Martin Libicki explains, "Unfortunately, complexity is bad for security. It creates more places for bugs to lurk, makes interactions among software components harder to understand, and increases the flow rate of packets well past where anyone can easily reconstruct what happened when things go wrong."[61]

These "bugs," as they are known colloquially, are also one of the primary means that allow hackers to break into systems and circumvent their security mechanisms. Such vulnerabilities—and particularly "zero-day exploits" (i.e., vulnerabilities that are yet to be discovered or patched)—can now be purchased on the informal international market.[62] Stuxnet, for example, relied on five of these zero days in order to penetrate and attack the Iranian enrichment plant at Natanz.[63] Although this is clearly a fundamental threat to the highly sensitive components of nuclear command and control (e.g., the weapons, warning systems, targeting plans, and communications), it also has significant implications for the wider nuclear weapons enterprise, and particularly the security of sensitive nuclear-related data and information and the people that operate these systems. As Bruce Berkowitz explains,

> There is a hidden "data component" in virtually every US weapon system deployed today; this component may be in the form of targeting information that must be uploaded into a munitions guidance system or a "signature" description that tells the guidance sensor what to look for on the battlefield (for example, the distinctive infrared emission that a particular type of tank produces from its exhaust). If this information is unavailable or corrupted, even the smartest bomb regresses into stupidity.[64]

Moreover, some experts suggest that security holes in software are so common that the problem is likely to be growing faster than it can be addressed.[65]

Although nuclear systems, especially those used for command and control, will of course be among the best protected against cyber threats—and almost certainly air-gapped from the wider internet (an "air-gapped" system is one that is physically isolated and separated from external and unsecured networks—e.g., the control system at Natanz in Iran) and protected by firewalls (security protocols that prevent certain unauthorized access to systems)—they are by no means invulnerable. There are essentially six main ways to get in: (1) via an insider, perhaps the most common and easiest method; (2) through remote maintenance and dial-in ports, that is, by hacking; (3) by developing and accessing built-in backdoors remotely (these may have been deployed while the system was being manufactured); (4) by jumping the air gap via other electromagnetic tools; (5) by wiretapping; and (6) by intercepting radar and other insecure communications.[66] Malware may also be introduced during the procurement stage, left dormant, and then activated only later, either remotely or automatically, when certain conditions are met.[67] Such attacks could involve exploiting a known vulnerability (the most likely); discovering and exploiting new vulnerabilities (harder but not impossible); or by creating new vulnerabilities (probably only the preserve of the most sophisticated cyberattacker, and the option that would take the most time).[68] Attacks may also be indirect, corrupting, or disrupting information and data that systems and operators rely on, along with attacking the systems directly.

The possibility that hackers could initiate nuclear use or disable weapons and systems; indirectly spoof warning sensors into believing an attack was under way; jam or interfere with information flows or communications to prevent orders reaching the weapons; or access and utilize highly sensitive information about weapons systems and operational procedures is therefore real and growing. This is the natural result of an increase in the number of vulnerabilities in this software that could be exploited by a would-be attacker, both directly, within nuclear command and control systems, and indirectly, inside the various systems and infrastructure that support nuclear weapons management. Such vulnerabilities could either facilitate access to a system or enable the deployment of a payload—or, indeed, both. Of the two, increased vulnerabilities and "ways in" to operational software and the systems used for nuclear command and control are clearly the more serious—although hacking into weapon software directly and deploying malware would probably be very difficult (but by no means impossible).[69] For example, though the former head of the US Strategic Command, Gen. Robert Kehler, has remarked that he "is confident that US command and control systems and nuclear weapons platforms 'do not have significant vulnerability'" that cause him to be concerned,"[70] he later remarked in different interviews that "we don't know what we don't know,"[71] and that there was a growing concern that "adversaries might seek to undermine US nuclear weapons and command and control infrastructure using cyberattacks."[72] Other experts have also suggested that it must be assumed that nuclear systems could be vulnerable to cyberattackers.[73] In fact, in May 2017, a group of hackers known as the Shadow Brokers threatened to release information purportedly stolen from the US National Security Agency, which allegedly detailed computer vulnerabilities in Chinese, Iranian, North Korean, and Russian nuclear and missile systems.[74]

The concern is twofold. First, hackers might seek to compromise or retard nuclear systems through *disabling attacks*, such as by jamming and interfering with communications so that "go-codes" cannot be transmitted to weapons; by spoofing early warning systems, radar, or satellites so that an enemy cannot see what is really happening; or by sabotaging the weapons systems directly so they do not work or at least do not work as expected. The concern here is that attackers will seek to undermine systems by exacerbating tensions and procedures established for the *negative control* of nuclear forces. Hackers might also seek to combat these systems indirectly through espionage, particularly by stealing information on how they work and the various protocols and algorithms on which they rely and employ. Second, attackers might seek to facilitate a launch or explosion through *enabling attacks*, perhaps by spoofing early warning systems and sensors into believing that an attack was under way, or directly by hacking into targeting plans, programs, and launch control systems to cause an explosion, sending go codes, or otherwise seeking to facilitate a launch. The threat here is that attackers will try to exacerbate tensions and procedures established for *positive control*— that is, those that are designed to ensure nuclear use. Thus, though one would hope that computer systems used in nuclear weapons management are among the best protected of any critical infrastructure, the central paradox of nuclear command and control means that weapons will never be invulnerable and will always be susceptible to attackers (of any kind) seeking to undermine either positive or negative control. This is particularly the case with tightly coupled systems, where errors and problems can be amplified due to time pressures for complicated processes. The differences between *disabling* and *enabling* attacks are further explained in figure 2.2.

The major challenges for nuclear weapons management in the new cyber context—and particularly the risk of interference, disablement, or attack—stem from, primarily build on, and utilize the tensions and inherent problems of nuclear weapons management. Although nuclear systems have always been at risk, the cyber context, and particularly a mounting reliance on complex systems, are magnifying the intrinsic problems and creating new vectors for meddling, disruption, and attack. Indeed, the inherent risks of relying so heavily on complex, often incomprehensible systems that operators are increasingly unlikely to understand or really comprehend for nuclear weapons management is creating a worrying security paradox. Very few of those in charge of the ultimate weapon are likely to be trained as computer technicians or be able to fully understand the coding and systems on which the weapons rely, and this will make it much harder to keep them safe and secure. As the eminent scientist Carl Sagan put it, "It is suicidal to create a society dependent on science and technology in which hardly anybody knows anything about the science and technology."[75] This could hardly

Enabling	*Disabling*
Directly hack into weapons or command and control and cause a launch or explosion.	Sabotage weapons and systems so they do not work or do not work as expected.
Send "go codes" to weapons and commanders.	Jam communications and early warning systems so that orders or "go codes" cannot be received and commanders do not know what is happening.
Spoof early warning systems into believing that an attack is under way. Distort the nuclear information space.	Undermine nuclear systems by stealing information on how they work.
Terrorists and nonstate actors?	State-based actors?

Figure 2.2 Positive and Negative Command and Control

be more acute than when it comes to nuclear weapons. Thus, though the substance of the overall nuclear management challenge may not have changed significantly from previous eras, the overarching context—and therefore the tools, dynamics, and methods that may be used both against nuclear systems and in order to protect them—has indeed changed. This situation is explored in the chapters that follow.

Conclusion: The Cyber-Nuclear Nexus

Nuclear weapons systems have always been susceptible to accidents and mistakes, and at the same time they have been vulnerable to attackers seeking to interfere or disrupt processes, or even to those intent on causing unauthorized or inadvertent nuclear use. The historical record also suggests that risks appear to be magnified during times of tension and crisis as well as technological or operational transition and flux. But the proliferation and diversification in methods of attack in the increasingly digitized second nuclear age has been reflected in the new challenges facing those responsible for the security and defense of nuclear-related computer systems, networks, and data. These challenges are both *active*, such as from the types of threats and methods that might be employed by attackers, and *passive*, due to the increasing complexity of modern systems and software code, and from a combination of the two. The net result is a new set of vulnerabilities that must be understood and secured against. Indeed, it is the central tensions between the need for weapons to be reliable and ready to use but at the same time safe and secure that has underpinned many of the problems in the past and that resides at the heart of the cyber-nuclear challenge today.

The challenges posed by spoofing and inherent computer errors or problems, along with the more serious risks of both indirect and direct cyberattacks, seem likely to be far more difficult to protect against and mitigate in today's complex digital environment than perhaps the cruder analogue challenges were in the past. The cyber threat and cyber risk of course vary across nuclear actors and systems, and less sophisticated systems are likely to be less vulnerable to cyberattack. But cyber operations are fast becoming an increasingly important component of what has always been a difficult endeavor, especially as states seek to modernize their nuclear command structures and as reliance on computers and complex systems continues to grow.[76] As is explained in the following chapters, these new challenges—and the risks associated with both the emerging digital global security environment and the resulting growth of cyber capabilities, operations, and threats—therefore have considerable implications right across the nuclear weapons enterprise and for the global nuclear order more broadly.

Notes

1. For an interesting overview of how this developed in the United States, see Redmond and Smith, *From Whirlwind to MITRE*.
2. Anderson, *Security Engineering*, 427.
3. Corera, *Intercept*, 71–72; and Yost, "Interview Conducted with Roger Schell."
4. Ibid., 72. See also Anderson, "Computer Security Technology Planning Study."
5. Gartzke and Lindsay, "Thermonuclear Cyberwar," 3.
6. Feaver, "Command and Control," 163.
7. Bowen and Wolven, "Command and Control Challenges," 25.
8. See Sagan and Waltz, *Spread of Nuclear Weapons*, 74.
9. See National Security Archive, "First Documented Evidence."
10. On this, see Thompson, "Inside the Apocalyptic Soviet Doomsday Machine"; Rosen, "Spherical Bunker"; and Blair, "Russia's Doomsday Machine."
11. See Bender, "Russia May Have an Automated Nuclear Launch System."
12. For a good discussion of these measures, see Born, Gill, and Hänggi, *Governing the Bomb*.
13. See, Johnson, "Safety, Security, and Control of Nuclear Weapons," in *Technology*, ed. Blechman, 145.
14. Caldwell and Zimmerman, "Reducing the Risk of Nuclear War with Permissive Action Links," in *Technology*, ed. Blechman, 152.
15. For a detailed overview of this, see Drell, "Designing and Building Nuclear Weapons to Meet High Safety Standards," in *Nuclear Enterprise*, ed. Shultz and Drell.
16. Feaver, *Guarding the Guardians*, 26–28.
17. Ibid., 23.
18. Peurifoy, "A Personal Account of Steps toward Achieving Safer Nuclear Weapons in the US Arsenal," in *Nuclear Enterprise*, ed. Shultz and Drell, 67.
19. Cotter, "Peacetime Operations," in *Managing Nuclear Operations*, ed. Carter, Steinbruner, and Zraket, 52.
20. Feaver, *Guarding the Guardians*, x.
21. Gregory, *Hidden Cost*, 47.
22. Perrow, *Normal Accidents*.

23. Bracken, "Instabilities in the Control of Nuclear Forces," in *Breakthrough*, ed. Gromyko and Hellman, 23.

24. Sagan, *Limits of Safety*, 3.

25. The best overviews of nuclear accidents and near misses are provided by Gregory, *Hidden Cost*; and Schlosser, *Command and Control*. See also Lewis et al., *Too Close for Comfort*.

26. Sagan, *Limits of Safety*, 45, 267.

27. Raushenbach, "Computer War," in *Breakthrough*, ed. Gromyko and Hellman, 47. This theme is also examined in some detail by Hayes, "Nuclear Command and Control."

28. Borning, "Computer System Reliability and Nuclear War," 33.

29. Perrow, *Normal Accidents*, 3, 4, 11.

30. Bracken, "Instabilities," 30.

31. Ibid., 24.

32. Berkowitz, "Warfare in the Information Age," in *In Athena's Camp*, ed. Arquilla and Ronfeldt, 270.

33. Gregory, *Hidden Cost*, 76.

34. Brewer and Bracken, "Some Missing Pieces," 457.

35. Gen. Lee Butler, quoted by Gartzke and Lindsay, "Thermonuclear Cyberwar," 2.

36. Ibid., 156.

37. Jacobsen, *Pentagon's Brain*, 79–81.

38. Schlosser, "Neglecting Our Nukes."

39. Gregory, *Hidden Cost*, 170.

40. Sagan, *Limits of Safety*, 228.

41. Broad, "Computers," 1183.

42. US Government Accountability Office, "NORAD's Missile Warning System."

43. Ibid., 13.

44. Gregory, *Hidden Cost*, 97.

45. Schlosser, "Neglecting Our Nukes."

46. Ibid.; Blair, "Could Terrorists Launch America's Nuclear Missiles?"

47. Blair, "Could Terrorists Launch America's Nuclear Missiles?"

48. Sagan, *Limits of Safety*, 235–37.

49. Gregory, *Hidden Cost*, 97.

50. See Lee and Preston, *Preparing for High-Impact, Low-Probability Events*.

51. Stubbs, "Interplay between Cultural and Military Nuclear Risk Assessment," in *Nuclear Enterprise*, ed. Shultz and Drell, 228.

52. Carter, "Sources of Error and Uncertainty," in *Managing Nuclear Operations*, ed. Carter, Steinbruner, and Zraket, 612.

53. Russia Today, "'Innocent Mistake.'"

54. Quoted in ibid. See also Madory, "UK Traffic Diverted."

55. Skoudis, "Evolutionary Trends in Cyberspace," in *Cyberpower*, ed. Kramer, Starr, and Wentz, 157.

56. Ibid.

57. This draws on the thoughts of Sagan in *Spread of Nuclear Weapons*, by Sagan and Waltz, 169.

58. Neumann, *Computer-Related Risks*, 126.

59. US Department of Defense, Defense Science Board, *Task Force Report: Resilient Military Systems*, 28.

60. Libicki, *Conquest in Cyberspace*, 40.

61. Ibid., 293–94.

62. Greenberg, "Shopping List."

63. Murchu, "Stuxnet."

64. Berkowitz, "Warfare in the Information Age," in *In Athena's Camp*, ed. Arquilla and Ronfeldt, 270.

65. McGraw, "Cyber War Is Inevitable," 116.

66. Libicki, *Conquest in Cyberspace*, 75–79.

67. Lynn, "Defending a New Domain," 101.

68. US Department of Defense, Defense Science Board, *Task Force Report: Resilient Military Systems*, 2.

69. This threat is addressed in some detail by Global Zero Commission on Nuclear Risk Reduction, "De-Alerting and Stabilizing the World's Nuclear Force Postures."

70. Quoted by Sternstein, "Officials Worry."

71. Quoted by Schlosser, "Neglecting Our Nukes."

72. Quoted by Austin and Sharikov, "Preemption Is Victory," 4.

73. See, e.g., Blair, "Why Our Nuclear Weapons Can Be Hacked."

74. Feng, "Hacking Group That Leaked NSA Secrets."

75. Quoted by Jacobsen, *Pentagon's Brain*, 423.

76. For an interesting overview of the new problems for nuclear command and control, see Hayes, "Nuclear Command and Control."

PART II

> What Might Hackers Do
> to Nuclear Systems?

3

⫸ Stealing Nuclear Secrets

THE POSSIBILITY that an adversary might steal nuclear secrets—whether weapon designs and capabilities, operational plans and procedures, or private information about nuclear personnel—has always been a major challenge for nuclear-armed states. Indeed, the importance of nuclear espionage can be traced as far back as the early 1940s, when Soviet spies sought and acquired information on the Manhattan Project and early US nuclear bomb designs; ever since, all aspects of nuclear spying, nuclear intellectual property theft, and nuclear information security have remained a constant challenge.[1] However, the spread of computers, networks, and digitally stored, shared, and transmitted data has created an array of new problems for nuclear secrecy and has changed, expanded, and diversified the methods available for nuclear espionage. Digital computer systems therefore represent a trade-off; though they certainly allow organizations to work more efficiently and effectively than ever before, they have also made it far more straightforward to access information and steal secrets.[2]

Although nuclear information security may not be as sexy as cyber sabotage, cyberwarfare, or the so-called *WarGames* scenario, where a hacker causes a nuclear launch, it is of intrinsic and substantial importance to the greater cyber-nuclear challenge. In fact, the clear majority—and, arguably, some of the most important—cyber operations against nuclear systems of the past two decades have involved espionage rather than damage, sabotage, or war.[3] Vast amounts of sensitive nuclear-related data are stored and shared on computers and networks, and large amounts of information reside outside direct government control in the systems of contractors, laboratories, and researchers. Indeed, it is often far easier to target the systems of those outside direct military control and to acquire the information that they produce and utilize than it is to carry off a more complex cyberattack with a physical effect. Hacking into the facilities of the US Department of Energy or associated organizations and searching for bomb designs might therefore be a much more attractive option for potential US foes or competitors such as Russia, China, North Korea, and Iran (not to mention terrorist groups) than the much more difficult task of hacking directly into the weapons and their command and control systems, for example.⁴ As this chapter explains, both the new cyber context and the consequent spread of diverse cyber capabilities, and particularly the threat of computer network exploitation, are creating numerous new challenges for nuclear information security with considerable—and far-reaching—implications for how nation-states secure their most sensitive nuclear secrets.

The main aims of this chapter are to outline the new challenges posed by the emerging digital global security context for the protection of sensitive nuclear secrets; to explain the nature and dynamics of the burgeoning threat from exploitation; and to highlight the very diverse possible consequences of cyber-nuclear espionage. As is described below, attackers and attacks can have very different intentions and goals, although different cyber operations can look very similar and are often difficult to distinguish in practice, and could well be conflated and lead to misunderstanding.⁵ The chapter proceeds in three sections: The first charts and analyzes the new challenges posed to nuclear information security by the current information technology era, explains how attackers might seek to gain access to nuclear secrets, and shows how the problem of nuclear information security has changed over time. The second section provides an overview and description of the numerous (at least those that are known about) cases of cyber-nuclear espionage against nuclear weapons systems that have occurred during the past few decades. And the third section examines and explains the very different and differentiated implications and threats posed by the cyber espionage challenge, which range considerably in their possible impact on state security policies, nuclear proliferation, and the global nuclear order.

Nuclear Espionage: What Is New?

When we consider the cyber threat to nuclear weapons, it is easy just to focus on direct attacks on nuclear command and control systems and on the weapons themselves. But, arguably, a far bigger challenge (at least in terms of scale and frequency) to the broader nuclear weapons enterprise is posed by those seeking to acquire information on various nuclear systems, processes, and the personnel involved in operating them. In fact, the security of sensitive nuclear information is perhaps the biggest part of the challenge facing nuclear-armed states in the burgeoning cyber context—although, of course, the essence of this challenge is not new. It is often far easier to steal information or learn about systems than it is to sabotage or destroy them through cyber means, even though in some instances the result and effect could be equally as dramatic and important (and such operations might look the same to the victim). Although the safeguarding of sensitive nuclear secrets has always been a central challenge for nuclear weapons management, both for reasons of security and nonproliferation, this is being transformed by the cyber context in numerous different ways and thus provides a multitude of challenges for information security that must be met and mitigated. As is explained later in this chapter, stealing details about nuclear systems, processes, and even personnel can have many far-reaching effects and implications.

Espionage is often referred to as the second-oldest profession, and commercial, intellectual, and military secrets have been trading back and forth between nations for generations.[6] But the advent of the nuclear age in 1945 brought considerable new pressures to bear on acquiring and safeguarding highly sensitive military information. Espionage had now attained potentially existential importance, as states raced first to build the atomic bomb and then to keep up with or even outpace their adversaries in nuclear weapons technologies. A considerable portion of early nuclear proliferation was facilitated through espionage; in addition to the theft of nuclear secrets from the United States by the Soviet Union, it is thought that China, Pakistan, and North Korea all relied on espionage to help establish their nuclear weapons programs. And ever since, the perceived need to acquire sensitive intelligence on nuclear systems, procedures, and personnel has dominated strategic relations. Perhaps the most famous are the secrets stolen by communist spies in the 1940s, which led directly to the Soviet atom bomb in 1949;[7] the data stolen by China on the neutron bomb from the Lawrence Livermore National Laboratory in the United States in the 1970s (known as Tiger Trap);[8] the information passed to the Soviet Union by the John Walker spy ring in the 1980s about US nuclear submarines and their launch procedures, missile defenses, cruise missiles, and other technologies;[9] the documents taken by Robert Hanssen detailing US survival of government plans in case of nuclear attack, again passed to the Soviet Union;[10] and the technical details of the United States' use of lasers to simulate thermonuclear explosions in 1985, which allegedly were leaked to China by the Los Alamos National Laboratory scientist Peter Lee.[11]

A few years later, in the 1990s, the Los Alamos National Laboratory scientist Wen Ho Lee was accused of stealing secrets and the legacy codes (i.e., coding for older systems) used to simulate detonations for the US W88 thermonuclear warhead, and of passing these to China. The associate director for nuclear weapons at Los Alamos, Stephen Younger, later argued that "PRC [People's Republic of China's] official documents obtained by the CIA [US Central Intelligence Agency] proved beyond any doubt that the Chinese had acquired secret information about American nuclear warheads."[12] This information almost certainly helped facilitate the development of miniaturized Chinese thermonuclear warheads for use on intercontinental ballistic missiles in the 1990s.[13]

In 2004, the nuclear smuggling network led by the Pakistani scientist A. Q. Khan (which began when Khan stole secrets from the European nuclear fuel agency URENCO[14]) was revealed. Khan's nuclear proliferation network had played a key role in facilitating the Iranian, Iraqi, Libyan, North Korean, and Pakistani nuclear programs.[15] This list is merely indicative but gives a taste of the scale of the challenge in the pre–cyber age, despite considerable efforts to guard

and protect sensitive information. It also demonstrates that not simply government or military systems will be targeted; both contractors and researchers
provide a lucrative—and often easier—target for attackers, as opposed to better-
protected government and military systems.[16]

However, though the protection of nuclear secrets has always been a major
endeavor, and fraught with difficulties, this challenge has been transformed by
countless developments as part of the emerging cyber context. For almost all the
years of the first nuclear age—that is, the period between 1945 and the end of the
Cold War in, roughly, 1990–1991—the greatest nuclear espionage risks were
posed by human spies or "moles" with direct access to the most highly classified
state nuclear secrets, and not from attacks on networks or computer systems (notwithstanding the importance of signals intelligence).[17] Although the first case of
"cyber" espionage can be traced all the way back to an East German spy in 1968,
the expanding role of computers and networks in nuclear information storage and
sharing has concurrently changed how this information might be vulnerable to
attackers and spies during the coming years.[18] This is particularly true for the so-
called second nuclear age (1991–) in which we are now living. As the BBC security correspondent Gordon Corera explains, over the years, "espionage transformed
from waiting for information to be communicated, to accessing the information
at rest."[19] Corera continues, "During the intervening decades, computers went
from being a tool for espionage—by breaking codes and collecting data—to a
target of espionage—because they held valuable information—and finally to
being the means of espionage itself; because they could talk to each other, one
machine could steal another's secrets."[20]

In this way, the rise of computers has created two new sets of challenges. The
first is the ability to access and steal huge amounts of data that are stored on
computers, networks, and other digital media (perhaps now also including "the
cloud"[21]). And the second, and arguably bigger development, is the potential to do
this remotely, from far away, and without being noticed. Where a human spy once
might have had to gain access to a secure building or room, and then copy by
hand, photograph, or risk physically removing documents, it is now theoretically
far easier to copy and share information on a small digital device—such as a
Universal Serial Bus (USB) stick or thumb drive, a compact disk, or another type
of mobile hardware—and to attack this information remotely over networks.[22] A
good example of this challenge occurred in 2006, when a contractor working at
the Los Alamos National Laboratory in the United States was discovered to have
inadvertently transferred a large cache of classified information to a USB drive,
which he was then able to remove from the laboratory without anyone noticing.[23]
That said, in certain circumstances, paper could still sometimes be the easiest way
and least traceable method of stealing secrets (particularly as digital security processes are tightened—such as by banning the use of portable storage devices and
removing plug-in ports from computers).[24]

The first key development for nuclear espionage is that the ever-increasing reliance on digital computers to store sensitive data has made this information—even protected information—easier to access. Large amounts of scientific and technical material on nuclear testing, research, and development; weapons designs; and military structures, doctrine, and policies are now stored on computers, which makes them particularly attractive and therefore susceptible to attackers. According to the former US deputy secretary of defense William Lynn (writing in 2010), thousands of very sensitive files have been stolen from US computer networks, some of which contain technical details of weapons designs and blueprints, encryption techniques, operational plans, and other important military data.[25] Even if these computers are air-gapped from the wider internet and from unsecured networks, they are nevertheless susceptible to insider threats and from attackers in situ. In fact, as is demonstrated below, a significant proportion of cyber-nuclear espionage operations have involved insiders gaining access to poorly secured systems, principally by utilizing traditional methods of attack. The Wen Ho Lee case mentioned above and the subsequent security breaches at the US nuclear laboratories during the past two decades are indicative of this challenge.[26] As a result, and though the insider threat may not be new, the challenge for nuclear secrets appears to have grown exponentially, and the threat has diversified considerably.

Although the extent of the cyber-nuclear espionage challenge may vary between nation-states that are more "open" and those that are more "closed," the threat is real and growing for all actors involved. Part of the problem has been the sluggish approach toward cyber security and cyber hygiene adopted by those in charge of many very sensitive parts of the nuclear weapons infrastructure. An investigation by the US President's Foreign Intelligence Advisory Board in 1999 into the major findings of the Cox Report regarding alleged Chinese nuclear espionage provides a good example of this. When they published their findings, the investigators reported their shock and dismay at the "cavalier attitude" shown by officials and the "particularly egregious" failures to enforce cyber security measures by those in charge of safeguarding the nation's most important nuclear weapons design information.[27] The board even went on to say that "computer systems at some DOE [Department of Energy] facilities were so easy to access that even Department analysts likened them to automatic teller machines, [allowing] unauthorized withdrawals at our nation's expense."[28] The US Department of Energy is unlikely to be the only organization for which such practices represent a significant security risk. Indeed, and although one would hope that nuclear information security practices have improved since that time, the reality is that information will remain vulnerable, and the threat will be ever changing as new hardware and software are incorporated into these systems.

The second key development is the ability to target these secrets *remotely* and over networks. This may be achieved in several different ways, most notably through phishing attacks, by exploitation of a vulnerability, or in ways facilitated by an insider. Although copying files digitally in person may go undetected (as opposed to physically having to remove documents), conducting attacks remotely and over the internet reduces the risks of espionage even further so that no human agent necessarily needs to be placed in immediate danger. As Thomas Rid points out: "Espionage is changing: Computer attacks make it possible to exfiltrate data without infiltrating humans first in highly risky operations that may imperil them."[29] Malware may also then be placed to ensure continued access to this information—a so-called back door—or even to act as a beacon, sending the desired data back to the attacker.[30] The list of remote attacks on nuclear information and those involved in nuclear research and development is growing (the threat of social engineering is dealt with later in this chapter), and it is unknown just how much sensitive information on nuclear systems has been stolen. This challenge is clearly exacerbated in nuclear-armed states where research and development on the nuclear mission is carried out by nongovernment contractors, and may even be "semiprivatized" in some cases.

The nature of the challenge is therefore not simply hacking into highly sensitive and protected systems and downloading and copying information over the internet and from remote locations, although this is of course a key aspect of the problem, but also the importance of computer and information security in those systems that may already be air-gapped or separated from the internet, or that provide a bridge between the two. As such, though technical fixes and digital security will clearly be part of any response to the threats posed by cyber spies, it will also be about humans, and particularly good cyber hygiene (i.e., general good practice and safety around computers), as well as an awareness of the ever-present threat from malicious insiders.[31] In this way, humans are also a fundamental— and sometimes overlooked—part of the challenge for the nuclear enterprise.

Finally, the economies of scale offered by cyber espionage are also allowing for widespread espionage attacks—known as hoovering—that attempt to steal as much information as possible about all types of phenomena, along with more targeted attacks on specific and specialized information. In the words of Gordon Corera, "Cyber espionage facilitates spying on a scale previously unimagined and at a distance, changing the calculus of risk that had previously inhibited its use."[32]

Notable Cases from the 1980s to Today

In the 1970s, the Soviet Union ran a clandestine electronic spying project against the United States by bugging typewriters in its Moscow embassy with small digital recording devices. The operation, which became known as Project Gunman, probably marks the beginning of what we might think of as the cyber-nuclear espionage age—or at least demonstrated the potential for electronic operations against highly sensitive systems.[33] But it was not until a decade later, in the mid-

1980s, as computers and networks gradually expanded throughout (particularly US) defense and military establishments, that the challenge really began to manifest. More concretely, it can probably be traced to the 1986 Cuckoo's Egg episode. Cuckoo's Egg refers to the discovery by a systems administrator at the Lawrence Berkeley National Laboratory in California, Clifford Stoll, that a German hacker named Markus Hess had breached numerous research and military computers in the United States in order to acquire information on nuclear weapons and the Strategic Defense Initiative.[34] It later transpired that Hess had been working for the Soviet KGB, which had been desperate to find out about the initiative and the Reagan administration's nuclear plans. Apparently, Hess "had been inspired by seeing the film *WarGames* on German television and wanted to imitate the character in it by getting into NORAD."[35] Stoll discovered Hess due to a discrepancy in the accounts for computer usage at the laboratory, and his early efforts to trace the attacker essentially laid the foundations for intrusion detection that would become widely adopted over the next three decades.[36]

Since that time, the volume and scope of cyber-nuclear espionage have expanded exponentially. In the 1980s, hackers from the group known as 414—also allegedly inspired by *WarGames*—broke into supposedly secure systems at the Los Alamos National Laboratory, where classified work toward the design of US nuclear weapons was being conducted.[37] In 1991, it was feared that a group of Dutch hackers that had gained access to US military networks were searching for nuclear secrets and missile data to sell to Iraqi dictator Saddam Hussein before Operation Desert Storm (Saddam apparently refused the information, believing it to be a hoax).[38] In 1998, the Cox Report mandated by the US government accused China of stealing a considerable hoard of highly sensitive military secrets from the United States over a number of years (between 1983 and 1995).[39] Chinese hackers were believed to have acquired details of seven different types of US nuclear warheads,[40] notably the W88 thermonuclear warhead, the most sophisticated weapon in the US arsenal, and the one deployed on the Trident D5 submarine-launched ballistic missile.[41] Writing shortly afterward, James Risen suggested that US officials had been concerned for some time that secret information about US nuclear weapons could be copied from air-gapped and secure computers and then emailed out through an unclassified network.[42] In the wake of the report, US Secretary of Energy Bill Richardson suspended all scientific work on computers containing America's most sensitive nuclear secrets until security had been improved.[43] Matthew McKinzie, a senior scientist at the Natural Resources Defense Council, later remarked that it was an "unprecedented act of espionage. . . . The espionage in the Manhattan Project [would] pale in comparison."[44] This incident became known as Kindred Spirit.[45]

Later that same year, an American teenage hacker broke into India's Bhabha Atomic Research Centre (known as BARC) near Mumbai and downloaded the passwords and emails of its scientists and operators.[46] In 1999, the thousands of files stolen and the extent of the infiltration of the Moonlight Maze attack—

believed to emanate from Russia (partly because the attacks occurred during normal Moscow working hours)—on the Pentagon and sensitive information held by other US government departments was revealed.[47] It is believed that the attackers broke into systems at the US Department of Defense and US Department of Energy and their associated research institutions and laboratories, and acquired thousands of files on all manner of sensitive military information.[48] It was later ascertained that this coordinated attack designed to steal technical military and scientific information had actually been going on since the mid-1990s.[49] A *Newsweek* editorial written shortly afterward suggested that the perpetrators may have even gained "root-level" access to some systems—the highest authority or privilege given to a user working with an operating system or another control program.[50]

This trend has continued, and in fact it has deepened during the last two decades. In 2005 hackers believed to be linked with the Chinese People's Liberation Army infiltrated numerous US military computer systems searching for nuclear secrets—among other defense information—in an operation dubbed Titan Rain.[51] According to William Hagestad, sensitive information held at the Pentagon's research laboratories and by various defense agencies—such as the US Army Space and Strategic Defense Command, the Defense Information Systems Agency, and the Naval Ocean Systems Center—were directly targeted.[52] Highly sensitive information relating to missile navigation, submarines, and other strategic weapons systems was believed to have been stolen.[53]

In 2006 the Israeli Mossad planted a Trojan horse in the computer of a senior Syrian government official, which revealed the extent of the suspected Syrian nuclear weapons program. The information recovered—including photographs and construction plans—suggested that a suspicious building in the Deirez-Zor region of eastern Syria was likely a top-secret plutonium nuclear reactor.[54] According to Eric Follarth and Holger Stark, operatives were able to install the malware after the official left his laptop in an upmarket hotel room in the Kensington borough of London while he went out. The Israelis were then able to steal data at will.[55] A similar operation was purportedly carried out in March 2007 by Mossad agents against Ibrahim Othman, the head of the Syrian Atomic Energy Commission.[56] Later in 2007, these actions led directly to Operation Orchard, whereby Israel attacked and destroyed the suspected Syrian nuclear facility.

In 2008 an infected USB stick believed to have been deliberately left in a parking garage at a US military base in the Middle East led to Operation Buckshot Yankee (the name given to the defense against the attack), whereby US classified networks were breached and the air gap was jumped. The agent.btz malware was allegedly designed by staff members, probably "crack cyberspooks," at the Russian Academy of Sciences—a government-supported organization that interacts with Russia's top military laboratories—to steal military secrets, and it contained a beacon to allow mass data exfiltration.[57] As Karl Grindal explains:

In the summer of 2008, an infected thumb drive, possibly dropped in a parking lot or slipped into a briefcase, was inserted into a US military laptop on a base in the Middle East. The technically advanced virus stored on the USB stick penetrated the air gap that separates the military's secure networks from the internet at large, infecting both classified and unclassified networks. Once beyond the gap, the malware rapidly replicated throughout the network by infecting additional thumb drives, leading personnel to unintentionally spread the virus further.[58]

The agent.btz malware, which targeted the Windows-based operating system used by the US military, was one of the only known cases of classified Department of Defense networks that were separated from the wider internet being breached, and put at risk some of the military's most sensitive and important secrets.[59]

In recent years, the cyber espionage threat has diversified to include all manner of nuclear-related systems. In February 2011, an information-stealing Trojan, using an email that appeared to originate in the White House, was discovered that was aimed at contractors involved in building the UK Trident nuclear-armed submarine force.[60] In the words of the *Guardian* newspaper's security editor, Richard Norton Taylor, "A malicious file posing as a report on a nuclear Trident missile was sent to a defence contractor by someone masquerading as an employee of another defence contractor, [UK foreign secretary William] Hague told an audience of Western officials and businessmen. Security meant that the email was detected and blocked, but its purpose was undoubtedly to steal information relating to our most sensitive defence projects."[61]

In April 2011, Oak Ridge Nuclear Laboratory in Tennessee was hacked, and Web access was shut down—though officials believed that the attack was isolated from the most sensitive information held on their computers.[62] A month later, Iran was accused of hacking the International Atomic Energy Agency (IAEA), looking for secrets regarding the monitoring of its nuclear program, and possibly allowing them to identify "and potentially punish—people assisting the inspectors or evade the agency's probes."[63] It is possible that the SIM (subscriber identification module) cards in the inspectors' mobile telephones were manipulated or replaced in order to achieve this hack.[64] In August 2011, the Shady RAT malware targeting US government agencies, defense contractors, and numerous other high-technology companies was discovered.[65] A year later, in November 2012, the members of the group Anonymous claimed to have hacked the IAEA and threatened to release the agency's "highly sensitive data," including detailed satellite imagery of the Israeli nuclear program that they had allegedly seized, if the IAEA did not investigate "Israel's unofficially acknowledged nuclear program."[66] Also in 2012, hackers from China were accused of trying to steal classified information held on Indian naval computer systems at the Indian Eastern Naval Command in Visakhapatnam, which oversees the testing of India's ballistic missile submarines. This attack was possibly facilitated by an operator connecting an infected flash memory drive containing malware that allowed data from sensitive naval computers to be transmitted back to China.[67]

US nuclear laboratories and defense contractors have remained a primary target for at least the last decade,[68] and in 2013 hackers believed to be from the group Deep Panda linked with the Chinese People's Liberation Army, targeted the computers of US nuclear researchers directly by exploiting a zero-day vulnerability in an Internet Explorer browser.[69] Hackers have also sought to attack nuclear-related systems, perhaps most notably the US and Israeli ballistic missile defense programs, and are suspected of stealing important and secret data.[70] This apparently included systems such as Patriot, Thaad, and Aegis—all of which are key components of the regional ballistic missile defense architectures deployed in Asia, Europe, and the Persian Gulf.[71] As James Adams, former chairman of the Technology Advisory Panel at the US National Security Agency, noted more than a decade ago, "Missile defense, for example, will not be worth the billions it will cost if digital attacks undermine its software or infrastructure."[72] Adams continued: "Opponents of missile defense could handicap the system at the development stage by attacking the technology at its source—breaking into the computer networks of the corporations that design the system and making slight modifications that ensure huge costs and long delays."[73] The same thing clearly also applies to nuclear weapons systems.

Although many of the nuclear espionage operations (that we know about) involve activities directed against the United States, Operation Olympic Games—the program that would produce Stuxnet—began life primarily as an intelligence gathering and espionage operation against the Iranian nuclear program.[74] Likewise, both the Flame and Duqu cyberattacks (which probably came later) were designed to gain intelligence on systems and infrastructure—most likely as precursors to a possible future physical attack or sabotage on the Iranian nuclear program.[75] Duqu was a remote-access Trojan (or RAT) intended to find out as much as possible about the industrial systems controlling the Iranian nuclear enrichment machinery, in preparation for a future cyberattack against them.[76] As Kim Zetter explains, "As for Duqu's intent, it was pretty clear it wasn't a saboteur like Stuxnet, but an espionage tool. . . . Duqu appeared to be a forward scout, send out to collect intelligence for future assaults." That said, Zetter also noted that the security firm Symantec "suspected it was the precursor to another Stuxnet-like attack."[77] Flame, conversely, was designed to map out Iranian computer networks and send back all relevant data that might be pertinent to a future attack. The malware, which allegedly consisted of some 650,000 lines of code,[78] could "activate computer microphones and cameras, log keyboard strokes, take screen shots, extract geolocation data from images, and send and receive commands and data through Bluetooth wireless technology."[79] It did this by masquerading as a routine Microsoft update.[80] An incident at Iran's Fordow uranium enrichment plant in 2012—where a suspected monitoring device, disguised as a rock, blew up—suggested that the United States and Israel have continued to spy on the Iranian nuclear program through advanced cyber means. The remains of this device, which was purportedly capable of intercepting data from computers based inside the enrichment plant, were reportedly found in the rubble.[81] A similar program of cyber espionage operations is almost certainly a key part of US actions against North Korea's nuclear program.[82]

This list is by no means exhaustive (and is very United States–centric), and it is highly likely that many more cyber espionage and exploitation attacks have taken place that we do not know about. Moreover, and though the Pentagon has purportedly begun sharing classified cyber threat intelligence with some contractors, as with banks and other financial institutions, national security organizations are *very* reluctant to reveal when they have been compromised or attacked, and much less to share the details of these attacks.[83] As Dana Liebelson quipped, "One would like to think that nuclear weapons infrastructure would be ahead of the curve, but apparently, that is too much to ask."[84]

Nuisance, Proliferation, and Sabotage: Myriad Possible Nuclear Implications

Although the volume and scope of cyber spying and the attempted theft of a wide variety of nuclear secrets have expanded exponentially in recent years, the implications of this are mixed, and much like cyber threats in general, cyber-nuclear espionage is far from being a homogeneous challenge. Consequently (as is discussed earlier in this book), it is important to differentiate between threats posed by various actors, and particularly between their intentions, even though in some cases this may be very difficult to achieve in practice. It is also important to differentiate between attempts to seize data *resident* in a particular computer system or network, and attempts to steal data *about* that system and how it works—that is, in order to attack it later.

At the lower end of the scale, cyber-nuclear espionage is primarily about gaining access to nuclear information systems. The intention might simply be to show that it can be done—and acquire the kudos of breaching the supposedly most secure national security systems. Hackers might also wish to delete or corrupt files to cause a nuisance or minor damage inside certain computer networks to show that they can be penetrated—perhaps as a warning. This is the easiest and least sophisticated thing that can be done, as the former National Security Agency and CIA director, Michael Hayden, explains: "It is far more difficult to penetrate a network, learn about it, reside on it forever, and extract information without being detected than it is to go in and stomp around inside the network causing damage."[85]

It might also be about acquiring knowledge and intelligence on what a certain state or actor is doing or planning—such as was reportedly the case when North Korean hackers accessed US war plans in the event of rising tensions and a possible nuclear conflict in early 2017.[86] Or hackers could seek information about the relative capabilities of key weapons programs (particularly those in development) or related processes and protocol. This was certainly the case during the Cold War, and likely remains the case today as many nuclear-armed states seek to modernize their nuclear forces or develop new and exotic weapons systems with strategic potential. Cyber espionage could come in the form of a stand-alone attack—or, perhaps more likely, operations may be ongoing, with systems and information being monitored over an extended time frame. It might also take a prolonged period of time to discover that systems have been breached. To illustrate this point, it took 18 months before technicians at BAE discovered that hackers had breached its most sensitive networks looking for technical and design information on its latest weapons systems, such as the Joint Strike Fighter aircraft, and also monitoring meetings and emails.[87] This approach is also likely to be used for states seeking information on possible future nuclear proliferation. For example, Pakistan reportedly became a key target for UK cyber spies in the 1990s as concerns grew about overt weaponization;[88] and, as David Sanger and Martin Fackler have pointed out, the nuclear weapons program was clearly the primary target when US hackers first gained access to North Korean networks and computers, purportedly back in 2010.[89] That said, a large percentage of these operations are intended to steal commercial secrets and intellectual property—though these can also have military implications in some cases.[90]

Cyber espionage operations may also be conducted to find out more information about the people who are directly involved with nuclear processes, including political actors, military personnel, or those working on or with the weapons systems. So-called social engineering is a serious and growing risk within the nuclear weapons enterprise, particularly because all those involved are spending more time and revealing personal data online, particularly on social media. As the cyber security expert Jeffrey Carr explains, "Social networks are ideal hunting ground for adversaries looking to collect actionable intelligence on targeted government employees, including members of the armed forces."[91] Cyber capabilities, not to mention the ubiquitous use of social media by those involved in nuclear operations, have enabled information gathering on personnel, profiling, and targeting to an unprecedented extent. This is particularly worrying, for example, given that a simple search of Facebook reveals several hundred US Air Force employees who have listed themselves as "Minuteman missileers." By way of another example, in 2012 it was discovered that top-secret UK Ministry of Defence systems were hacked, and high-ranking officials reportedly left themselves vulnerable after accepting invitations from a spoof Facebook account purporting to be NATO's top commander.[92] Such operations may be designed for blackmail purposes, to steal information, or possibly to exert influence or subvert systems in some other manner. In this way, the computerized nuclear context also transforms and exacerbates the traditional insider threat and issues of personnel reliability (either wittingly or not).[93] The 2015 theft of millions of confidential staff records from the US Office of Personnel Management, including detailed background information related to security clearances, is another good example of this challenge.[94]

On the next level, nuclear secrets may be targeted to help combat or defend against certain systems or to provide a better idea of operational procedures. For example, this might involve finding out details about a nuclear submarine—such as about its stealth, or about the design or specifics of a warhead or missile—or it might be about the capabilities of an aircraft or even the broader nuclear command structure. Other examples of this are the recent attempts to steal Israeli and US missile defense information and the attacks on US defense contractors and research laboratories detailed above. The Israeli attack on the suspected nuclear site at Al Kibar in Syria in 2007 is another good illustration of how cyber espionage can facilitate broader nuclear goals—in this case, counterproliferation.[95] The intention of cyber-nuclear espionage could therefore be to acquire information that could be used to compromise, undermine, or neuter the key systems currently being used, or are being developed by an enemy for use in some future conflict. Even the perception of this could raise perceived costs, and might well drive instability and uncertainty at the global strategic level, as is discussed later in this book. That said, an adversary that gains a greater understanding of its rival's nuclear capabilities through cyber espionage, particularly if these capabilities are stronger or more sophisticated than previously thought, may be forced to consider policies that minimize escalation and enhance the credibility of deterrence.[96] In this way, the knowledge gained through cyber espionage could paradoxically also potentially help facilitate nuclear stability.

Of equal concern is the fact that nuclear secrets are stolen to aid proliferation, either vertically, by a state wishing to building more or better weapons, or horizontally, by acquiring a weapon, and either by states or nonstate actors. A good example here is China, which is believed to have stolen US weapons designs from Los Alamos National Laboratory, enabling a significant leap in its own nuclear weapons capability.[97] As a result, China successfully tested smaller thermonuclear warheads between 1992 and 1996 before announcing a moratorium on testing.[98] Of perhaps even greater importance is the threat that nuclear weapons designs could be traded on informal global nuclear markets to states or nonstate actors looking to acquire nuclear capabilities.[99] As the full scale of the A. Q. Khan nuclear smuggling network began to unravel in the mid-2000s, for example, it was discovered that nuclear warhead blueprints and other weapons designs had been transferred to digital formats that could be easily sent to any computer in a matter of seconds. No one is entirely sure where all these files went or who has access to them now. This probably marked the first overt case of cyber proliferation, and it is unlikely to be the last.[100]

The advent of three-dimensional printing and additive design have also transformed the scope of this challenge considerably, and might potentially reduce the challenges involved in moving between stages of nuclear development in the future.[101] Such hacking operations could also be used to facilitate thefts or other types of attacks on nuclear materials. For example, the US Nuclear Regulatory Commission's computers were frequently targeted between 2011 and 2014, and officials were baited by phishing emails linked to malicious software.[102] Hackers might have been seeking access to information on critical infrastructure vulnerabilities (e.g., at a nuclear power plant) or the security procedures surrounding the protection of other nuclear materials.[103] In fact, according to its website, the UK Nuclear Decommissioning Authority, which manages retired nuclear power plants and used fuel, "is subject to 30,000 automated cyberattacks or scans every day."[104] The unholy trinity of three-dimensional printing, cyber proliferation, and global terrorism represents a serious nuclear security concern.

Conversely, these same dynamics may offer the potential for counterterrorism through cyber means, and particularly the opportunity to provide false (nuclear) information to would-be proliferators. Cyber counterterrorism might be achieved by changing data inside a terrorist network or by providing operatives with false information about weapons designs. As Peter Singer and Allan Friedman note, this has possibly already taken place at the conventional level, where "in one case, online bomb making instructions were changed so that the attacker would instead blow himself up during the construction of the device."[105] It is conceivable that such methods could be used in the nuclear realm, perhaps even against nation-states. In fact, in 2000 the *New York Times* reporter James Risen revealed a secret CIA plan to use a Russian nuclear scientist to hand over flawed blueprints and bomb designs to his unsuspecting Iranian contacts.[106]

A final scenario is that these attacks are used as precursors to sabotage and physical destruction, and are principally designed to find out about nuclear systems and their vulnerabilities, "map" sensitive networks, implant logic bombs, and ensure access to these systems in the future. Operation Olympic Games is the classic example of this, but it is feared that other attacks—notably, Moonlight Maze—may also have been designed with a similar purpose in mind.[107] Winslow Wheeler explains this worry further: "If they got into the combat systems, it enables them to understand it to be able to jam it or otherwise disable it. . . . If they've got into the basic algorithms for the missile and how they behave, somebody better get out a clean piece of paper and start to design all over again."[108]

A big part of the problem, of course, is that it is very difficult to ascertain exactly what an attacker is trying to achieve because both the methods and malware used in cyber operations can often look very similar (and may be difficult to discover, unpack, and understand). In fact, to borrow from nuclear parlance, attackers may use the same "delivery vehicles" to transport very differently coded "warheads" or "payloads." Equally, espionage might escalate into sabotage without warning, or may be interpreted as such—and this is a far greater challenge for cyber spying than it was in the past, because the main dynamics of traditional espionage were arguably far better understood.[109] This in turn creates a legal gray area. As Kim Zetter points out, "Under international law and US policy, espionage is not an act of war. But since espionage could be the prelude to a destructive attack, as it was with Stuxnet and the spy tools the attackers used to collect intelligence for that operation, could the discovery of spy tools on a system indicate an intention to conduct an armed attack?"[110] This also has broader strategic implications for escalation and nuclear crisis management (which are discussed later in the book).

Conclusion: The Importance of Nuclear Information Security

Information security has always been a fundamental component of nuclear security, policy, and strategy, but this challenge is being transformed as we move further into the cyber age, and especially as more and more data are stored, shared, accessed, and processed by computers, networks, and interlinked digital systems. In this respect, information, coding, and software might even be becoming as important to the nuclear mission as the weapons, warheads, and hardware themselves. But the challenge is diverse and includes various types of data, information on personnel, and details of key processes and operations, as well as sensitive secrets about the weapons and associated systems—all of which could be invaluable to either an enemy or would-be proliferator. In fact, the cyber espionage threat against nuclear systems and sensitive information in its many different guises probably represents more than 90 percent of the cyber challenge that we currently face in the nuclear realm. However, the implications of this are clearly mixed and will require a suite of tailored responses—ranging from better cyber hygiene to enhanced security and defense, law enforcement, and possibly to legal prohibitions or moratoriums.

Perhaps one of the biggest challenges posed by cyber exploitation in the nuclear realm is that it may often not be clear to those being attacked (assuming they are able to discover the intrusion and attack) what the intention of their opponent and the malware is, and thus the level of the threat they face. The difficulty of distinguishing between types of attacks provides a real problem for policymakers and strategists alike, and this has undoubtedly clouded debates over the respective roles of defense and deterrence in dealing with the challenge. Ultimately, we will probably need to accept that some type of espionage—cyber or otherwise—against nuclear information and systems is a gray area, is probably inevitable, and thus cannot be entirely prevented. To some extent, it will therefore need to be tolerated and managed rather than eradicated.

Notes

1. On this, see, e.g., Rossiter, *Spy Who Changed the World*.
2. Singer and Friedman, *Cybersecurity and Cyberwar*, 92.

3. Healey, *Fierce Domain*, 20.
4. Quoted by Koebler, "US Nukes Face up to 10 Million Cyber Attacks Daily."
5. Libicki, *Crisis and Escalation in Cyberspace*, xix.
6. Elwell, "Cyber War!"
7. On this, see, e.g., Holloway, *Stalin and the Bomb*.
8. Kan, *China*, 2; see also Wise, *Tiger Trap*.
9. Sulick, *American Spies*, 104.
10. Ibid., 216.
11. Kan, *China*, 2.
12. Cited by Sulick, *American Spies*, 249. See also, Loeb and Pincus, "Los Alamos Security Breach Confirmed."
13. Risen and Gerth, "Breach at Los Alamos."
14. URENCO is a nuclear fuel company that operates several uranium enrichment plants in Germany, the Netherlands, the United States, and the United Kingdom.
15. On the A. Q. Khan network, see Corera, *Shopping for Bombs*.
16. Manson, "Cyberwar," 126.
17. Corera, *Intercept*, 94.
18. See Warner, "Cybersecurity," 784.
19. Corera, *Intercept*, 80.
20. Ibid., 8–9.
21. See, e.g., McGoogan, "Ministry of Defence Switches to the Cloud."
22. Wilson, "Cybercrime," in *Cyberpower*, ed. Kramer, Starr, and Wentz, 425.
23. See US Government Accountability Office, "Nuclear Security."
24. When I visited the UK Atomic Weapons Establishment at Aldermaston in 2013 to give a talk, all portable devices (including laptops and USB drives) were forbidden to be brought into the facility by guests.
25. Lynn, "Defending a New Domain," 97–98. See also Adams, "Virtual Defense," 99.
26. See, e.g., Russia Today, "American Atomic Secrets at Risk."
27. President's Foreign Intelligence Advisory Board, Special Investigative Panel, "Science at Its Best, Security at Its Worst," 6.
28. Ibid., 21.
29. Rid, *Cyberwar Will Not Take Place*, xiv.
30. Adams, "Virtual Defense," 100.
31. Kramer, "Cyberpower and National Security," in *Cyberpower*, ed. Kramer, Starr, and Wentz, 4.
32. Corera, *Intercept*, 13.
33. See US National Security Agency, "Learning from the Enemy."
34. For the best overview of this, see Stoll, *Cuckoo's Egg*.
35. Corera, *Intercept*, 184.
36. Stoll, *Cuckoo's Egg*.
37. Ibid., 87.
38. Denning, *Information Warfare and Security*, 3–4.
39. More formally, US House of Representatives, "Report of the Select Committee on US National Security and Military/Commercial Concerns with the People's Republic of China."
40. In addition to the W88, these included the W87, which was used on the peacekeeper intercontinental ballistic missile (ICBM); the W78, which was used on the Min-

uteman III ICBM; the W76, which was used on the Trident C-4 submarine-launched ballistic missile; the W70, which was used on the Lance short-range ballistic missile; the W62, which was used on the Minuteman III ICBM; and the W56, which was used on the Minuteman II ICBM. Kan, *China*, 9.

41. Ibid.

42. Risen, "Energy Department Halts Computer Work."

43. Quoted in ibid.

44. Quoted by Loeb and Pincus, "Los Alamos Security Breach Confirmed."

45. On this, see Stober and Hoffman, *Convenient Spy*; Trulock, *Code Name Kindred Spirit*; and Kan, *China*.

46. Penenberg, "Hacking Bhabha."

47. Elkus, "Moonlight Maze," in *Fierce Domain*, ed. Healey, 155.

48. Ibid., 152, 155.

49. Corera, *Intercept*, 174.

50. *Newsweek*, "We're in the Middle of a Cyberwar."

51. Hagestad, *21st-Century Chinese Cyberwarfare*, 12.

52. Ibid.

53. Boulanin and Ogilvie-White, *Cyber Threats*, 4.

54. Makovsky, "Silent Strike."

55. Follarth and Stark, "Story of Operation Orchard."

56. Makovsky, "Silent Strike."

57. *Newsweek*, "We're in the Middle of a Cyberwar"; Grindal, "Operation Buckshot Yankee," in *Fierce Domain*, ed. Healey, 208.

58. Ibid., 205.

59. Ibid.; and Nakashima, "Cyber-Intruder Sparks Massive Federal Response."

60. Dunn, "UK Government under Targeted Cyber Attack."

61. Norton-Taylor, "Chinese Cyber-Spies Penetrate Foreign Office Computers."

62. See Munger, "Lab Halts Web Access after Cyber Attack"; and Sternstein, "Attack on Energy Lab Computers Was Isolated."

63. Crawford, "UN Probes Iran Hacking of Inspectors."

64. Ibid.

65. Hagestad, *21st-Century Chinese Cyberwarfare*, 12.

66. Kelley, "Anonymous Hacks Top Nuclear Watchdog Again to Force Investigation of Israel."

67. Global Security Newswire, "Indian Naval Computers Targeted in Chinese Cyber Attack."

68. See, e.g., US Government Accountability Office, "Nuclear Security"; or, more recently, Sternstein, "Attack on Energy Lab Computers Was Isolated."

69. Russia Today, "US Nuclear Weapons Researchers Targeted with Internet Explorer Virus."

70. Global Security Newswire, "Chinese Hacking Targets US Missile Defense Designs"; Ghoshal, "China Hacking Iron Dome, Arrow Missile Defense Systems"; Futter, "Hacking Missile Defence."

71. Nakashima, "Confidential Report Lists US Weapons System Designs Compromised by Chinese Cyberspies."

72. Adams, "Virtual Defense," 100.

73. Ibid.

74. Zetter, *Countdown to Zero Day*, 321.

75. Morton, "Stuxnet, Flame, and Duqu: The Olympic Games," in *Fierce Domain*, ed. Healey, 219–21.

76. Ibid., 229.

77. Zetter, *Countdown to Zero Day*, 259.

78. Ibid., 279–80.

79. Morton, "Stuxnet, Flame, and Duqu," 221.

80. Nakashima, Miller, and Tate, "US, Israel Developed Flame Computer Virus to Slow Iranian Nuclear Efforts."

81. Mahnaimi, "Fake Rock Spying Device Blows Up Near Iranian Nuclear Site."

82. See Sanger and Broad, "Trump Inherits a Secret Cyberwar against North Korean Missiles."

83. Dharapak, "Pentagon Gets Cyberwar Guidelines."

84. Liebelson, "Are US Nuke Secrets Vulnerable to Cyber Attack?"

85. Quoted by Nakashima, Miller, and Tate, "US, Israel Developed Flame Computer Virus to Slow Iranian Nuclear Efforts."

86. See, e.g., Murdock, "North Korea Hackers Accessed 'War Plans' Detailing US Military Response to Conflict."

87. Healey, *Fierce Domain*, 166.

88. Corera, *Intercept*, 159.

89. Sanger and Fackler, "NSA Breached North Korean Networks before Sony Attack."

90. US Department of Defense, "Department of Defense Cyber Strategy."

91. Carr, *Inside Cyberwarfare*, 93.

92. Tomlinson, "Ministry of Defence Top Secret Systems Hacked, Head of Cyber Security Reveals."

93. A good recent example is Edwards, "Trident Whistleblower William McNeilly 'Discharged' from Royal Navy." Also see Williams, "Britain's Trident."

94. Hirschfeld Davis, "Hacking of Government Computers Exposed 21.5 Million People."

95. Follarth and Stark, "Story of Operation Orchard."

96. Caylor, "Cyber Threat to Nuclear Deterrence."

97. Risen and Gerth, "Breach at Los Alamos."

98. Kan, *China*, 9.

99. See Collins and Frantz, "Down the Nuclear Rabbit Hole."

100. Ibid.

101. For a discussion of this, see Kroenig and Volpe, "3-D Printing the Bomb?"

102. Sternstein, "Exclusive: Nuke Regulator Hacked by Suspected Foreign Powers."

103. Quoted in ibid.

104. See UK Nuclear Decommissioning Authority, "New Cyber Security Requirements."

105. Singer and Friedman, *Cybersecurity and Cyberwar*, 105.

106. Quoted by Lake, "Operation Sabotage."

107. Arquilla and Ronfeldt, "Cyberwar Is Coming!"

108. Cited by Nakashima, "Confidential Report Lists US Weapons System Designs Compromised by Chinese Cyberspies."

109. Brown was quoted by Zetter, *Countdown to Zero Day*, 405.

110. Zetter, *Countdown to Zero Day*, 402.

4

> Could Cyberattacks Lead
> to Nuclear Use or Stop
> Systems from Working?

MUCH LIKE nuclear information security and espionage, nuclear weapons and associated systems have always been vulnerable to different types of attack or sabotage. This is true both for attackers seeking to undermine nuclear weapons systems and stop them from working as planned, and also for attacks by those seeking to cause a launch or explosion, or to facilitate nuclear use in some other way. But a growing reliance on computers for all aspects of nuclear weapons management, and the concurrent growth of cyberattack capabilities globally, is creating significant new challenges—albeit many that build on rather than transform established vulnerabilities and concerns across the nuclear weapons enterprise.

In fact, the risk that the computers used to manage nuclear weapons might be interfered with by malicious attackers can be traced back as far as the 1970s, when then–US Air Force colonel Roger Schell warned that an enemy of the United States could potentially compromise operational plans or targeting for nuclear-armed missiles by penetrating the computer systems on which they rely. He went on to argue that "*the* opportunity for hostile exploitation of these vulnerabilities is increasing markedly, both because of the increased use of computers and the lack of a meaningful security policy controlling their use" (emphasis in original).[1] In fact, Schell raised these concerns with the US Strategic Air Command and refused to sign off on the system as being secure, maintaining that it was "vulnerable to subversion." His superiors, however, assured him that there was no risk.[2]

Although nuclear forces and their associated systems are, of course (we hope), among the best protected against any type of outside interference—cyber or otherwise—they are not foolproof. Moreover, as is explained in more detail below, the types of threats and challenges range considerably in terms of scale, attack vectors, and trajectories, as well as with regard to the intentions of the potential perpetrators. The cyber threat in the nuclear realm is therefore inherently multifaceted. Attackers might seek to compromise or interfere with nuclear weapons systems in several different ways, but the key differences are between attacks designed either to *enable* or *disable* nuclear systems, and attacks on these systems that are *direct* or *indirect*. The cyber threat spectrum therefore includes both attacks designed to cause a launch or explosion—either directly, by hacking into nuclear systems, or indirectly, by spoofing warning sensors or precipitating mistaken use in some other way. In addition, attacks may be designed to prevent systems from working as planned—either by jamming or interfering with communications and sensors, or by directly targeting command and control and weapons systems.

It is also important to be clear about *intentions* and *capabilities*. States are likely better equipped to carry out sophisticated cyber operations directly, but—barring some type of false flag or third-party attack—are unlikely to wish to precipitate nuclear use. Terrorists or nonstate hackers, conversely, may be less well equipped but more interested in causing a crisis, explosion, or launch. This—generally— means that *direct* attacks on nuclear systems are likely the preserve of nation-states, whereas *indirect* attacks would be easier for nonstate actors. But this does not mean that terrorists will not attempt to attack directly, or that nation-states will not pursue indirect attacks to further their goals.

The main aim of this chapter is therefore to explain the different types of cyber threats and challenges to nuclear weapons systems, and particularly the possibility that hackers could stop systems from working as planned, or in a worst-case scenario cause inadvertent or unauthorized nuclear use. In order to do this, the chapter proceeds in three sections. The first considers the growing potential for cyberattackers intending to compromise and disable early warning systems, manipulate the nuclear information space, and interfere with the information required by nuclear weapons systems and their operators to function properly; the second examines the possibility that cyber operations could be used to disable or damage nuclear weapons systems directly and prevent them from working as intended; and the third considers the prospect of a direct cyberattack on nuclear weapons and associated systems designed to cause nuclear enablement, either with an explosion or a launch, and either by a nonstate or unauthorized actor.

Manipulating the Nuclear Infosphere: Spoofing and Contaminating Information

The first key challenge is that attackers could target the information or the information space on which nuclear weapons systems and their operators depend to function—that is, the data that nuclear planners collect through sensors and on which they base their decisions, as well as the information already within these systems that is central to their proper functioning. Attempts to jam electronic communications or to deceive an adversary by providing false or misleading information have long been key components of warfare, and the use of the electromagnetic spectrum for operations will undoubtedly remain a key part of the cyber challenge. But the nature and implications of these operations is changing in the cyber age, and the incipient digital context is providing new possibilities to deceive or compromise nuclear systems. This challenge is effectively twofold. First, sensors and systems—such as those used for early warning radar, communications networks, and defense satellites—could be spoofed into believing either that something is happening that is not (a false positive), or could be prevented from knowing about something that is happening (a false negative). This is very similar to the age-old techniques of *misinformation* (i.e., duping an adversary into believing what is incorrect) or *disinformation* (i.e., causing an adversary not to believe what is genuine). Or, second, hackers might gain access to nuclear support systems and directly manipulate the information with the intention of contaminating or corrupting the data and information flows within these networks. Taken together, it should be assumed that the inability to fully understand what is happening in a future nuclear crisis will be the inevitable result of this new digitized security context.

There is perhaps no better example of attackers seeking to directly corrupt or manipulate information than the alleged use of the Suter computer program by Israel against Syrian air defense radar in 2007. This operation purportedly allowed Israeli jets to bomb a suspected nuclear site at Al Kibar with virtually no resistance. Instead of simply attempting to jam radar signals using electronic warfare methods (which would probably have been noticed and possibly counteracted), the Suter program is believed to have interfered with the Syrian air defense system allowing it to "see what enemy sensors see and then to take over as systems administrator so sensors can be manipulated into positions so that approaching aircraft can't be seen."[3] As the technology expert David Fulghum explains, the Suter system may have worked by "locating enemy emitters with great precision and then directing data streams into them that can include false targets and misleading messages algorithms that allow a number of activities including control."[4] A good analogy would be the way that bank robbers in Hollywood films often take over closed-circuit television cameras and play back prerecorded footage instead of a live feed, in order to break in undetected. As a result, the nonstealthy F-15 and F-16 Israeli airplanes used in the attack remained unnoticed and were able to bypass the Syrian air defense system and bomb the suspected complex unhindered. It remains unclear exactly how the Suter system was delivered to the target, but it is possible that the code could have been beamed into the radar from above as Fulgham suggests; the system may have been compromised using an unmanned aerial vehicle or drone; it had been hacked or breached electronically in another way before the attack; or that the fiber-optic cable linking the radar with central command computers had been spliced by agents.[5] Whichever of these is true, the attack was most likely carried out by Unit 8200, the secret Israeli cyberwarfare bureau.[6] The Syrian radar system was probably purchased from Russia and is currently being used by several other states—among them, reportedly, Iran—which raises serious questions about the susceptibility of others to a similar attack in the future.[7]

Although this attack was limited, it nevertheless provides a stark warning about new types of cyber-induced vulnerability, particularly for key nuclear communications and early warning systems. In fact, the Obama administration apparently considered employing cyber capabilities against air defense systems in both Syria in 2010 and Libya in 2011 preceding conventional air strike hostilities. This might have involved introducing malware into the air defense networks through both cyber and electronic methods—in some cases, attacking the radar units directly by feeding them false or destructive information—in order to prevent these systems from working as intended.[8] As Eric Schmitt and Thom Shanker explain, a concomitant goal would have been to "break through the firewalls of the Libyan government's computer networks to sever military communications links and prevent the early warning radars from gathering information and relaying it to missile batteries aiming at NATO warplanes."[9] The United States also allegedly had a plan (code-named Nitro Zeus) to disable Iranian air defenses if a strike against the much-disputed nuclear program was deemed necessary (i.e., if the diplomatic initiative to agree on a nuclear deal in 2015 had failed). At its height, Nitro Zeus is said to have involved thousands of US military and intelligence personnel working to break in and lace Iranian computer networks with malware to "prepare the battlefield" for future hostilities.[10]

The idea of attacking early warning and air defense radar in this way is nothing new. The United States had compromised Iraqi early warning and command and control systems with malware before the 2003 Operation Iraqi Freedom (although, apparently, the order to execute these cyberattacks was not granted until it was too late).[11] The United States may also have tried to attack Serbian air defense networks in 1999 during the Kosovo War—tricking the computers controlling Serbian radars into believing that airplanes were attacking from a different direction, thus making the task of shooting them down far more difficult.[12] The aim of the attack was to cause just enough interference so the Serbian operators would blame mechanical failures and glitches rather than raise their suspicion that the systems had been attacked.[13] This operational logic would be repeated a decade later with Stuxnet. Finally, there are also rumors that the US National Security Agency built a custom integrated circuit chip containing a computer virus that could have shut down Iraqi air defense systems in January 1991 at the start of Operation Desert Storm.[14] There is some debate as to whether this was merely a hoax—the code name of the malware being "AF/91" or "April Fools 1991"—but either way, it seems that the plans to hack into Iraqi air defense systems were rejected by Gen. Norman Schwartzkopf, who along with many others at the time was apparently concerned about establishing a dangerous precedent.[15]

Although the extent and implications of these actions have been debated, just knowing that sensitive nuclear-related systems may have been breached and might have been compromised, regardless of the extent and nature of the attack, leads to suspicion, concerns, and a lack of confidence in these systems when they are required.[16] It seems almost inevitable that a future conflict will begin with electronic and cyber operations against key warning, communications, and command and control systems. As Richard Stiennon notes, "Communicating secretly, reliably, and without tampering is key to waging war. Disrupting command and control is a primary goal of cyberwar in support of full-scale war."[17] This is also the case with operations that might involve nuclear weapons.

Although there are ways to protect and ensure against such attacks (particularly against electronic attacks)—for example, digitization; sophisticated algorithms; frequency hopping; code-division, multiple-access waveforms; and ultra-wideband signaling can protect against jamming[18]—nuclear communications and early warning systems more broadly represent an obvious target in any future crisis, both for states and terrorist groups.[19] In fact, there is evidence that hackers attempted to compromise the extremely low-frequency communications networks used by the US Navy to send orders to nuclear-armed submarines (including missile launch orders) from a radio transmitter in Maine in the mid-1990s.[20] Once the US Navy discovered this vulnerability and back door, it quickly drafted in a specialist private company (Mountain State Information Systems) to assess the extent of the challenge.[21] The Navy reportedly then soon altered its communications systems so commanders would never accept a single order to fire without any other warning.[22] Submarine communications links might also be targeted in other ways, such as by attacking or corrupting the regular weather updates they receive, which are then used in the Fire Control System. In theory, as John Ainslie explains, "Those messages could be used to send covert on/off signals to the computers on Royal Navy [nuclear-armed] submarines," causing confusion and possibly preventing the weapons from being used.[23]

Although nuclear weapons systems based on land are likely to be hardwired and point-to-point hardened (i.e., linked by underground cables),[24] in 2013 a workshop convened by the Union of Concerned Scientists warned that they were far from invulnerable in practice, particularly to attacks via code stored on portable media (e.g., compact discs [CDs] or Universal Serial Bus [USB] drives).[25] Likewise, increased reliance on satellite and space assets for early warning and command and control also represents a growing vulnerability in any future conflict. In fact, the computer expert Lucian Constantin suggests that researchers have discovered various computer vulnerabilities that could potentially allow attackers access to systems on board the satellite, and possibly even to take control of its key functions.[26] Hacking into satellites during a crisis and essentially "turning off the lights" could create considerable escalatory pressures. More broadly, there seems to be a misplaced assumption that communications will remain intact once a nuclear crisis escalates and hostilities begin. This is summed up well by the apocryphal order: "Inform the troops that the communications are down."[27]

With all states relying more and more on complex digital technologies for nuclear weapons management—and particularly for early warning, situational awareness, and communications—the risk that an attacker may hack in and corrupt, manipulate, or jam this type of information appears to be increasing. Attacking the information on which nuclear systems and their operators rely is perhaps the most straightforward threat vector for those wishing to interfere with nuclear operations or deepen a crisis; but it is also, particularly in times of relative peace and stability, likely to be the easiest to guard against. That said, the fear that an opponent (or a third-party actor) could fundamentally undermine the ability of key decision makers to communicate and understand what is happening in a future crisis is a real concern for all nuclear-armed states, and one that will undoubtedly have implications for crisis stability. This problem is summed up well by former US National Security Agency director Mike McConnell: "If attackers want to interrupt communication or contaminate information, they need only find one-way in. But if we want to defend against an attack, we have to defend the whole system from penetration."[28] Arguably, the most important aspects of this challenge are encryption, attribution, and the integrity of data—particularly when it comes to the order to fire nuclear weapons. Problems with any one of these could potentially lead to either unauthorized launch orders being transmitted, an inability to launch, or even hitting the wrong target(s).[29] Unfortunately, as the cryptography pioneer Whitfield Diffie points out, "The growth of communications has outrun the protection of communications for all human history."[30]

Last, attackers might seek to manipulate the nuclear information space—that is, the information required by planners and systems to function properly, such as credible data on threats, warnings, communications with forces, and general situational awareness, and therefore to target the operation of nuclear systems and their operators *indirectly*. The risk of "spoofing" remains ever present in this respect. In July 2014, for example, an Israeli military Twitter account was hacked, and an erroneous report was published that the top-secret nuclear facility at Dimona had been attacked by rockets and had caused a "radiation catastrophe." The tweet read: "Warning: possible nuclear leak in the region after 2 rockets hit Dimona nuclear facility."[31] A year earlier, the Twitter account of the Associated Press was hacked, and a tweet was sent reporting a bomb attack on President Obama (this caused the Dow Jones to plunge 146 points).[32] Such indirect attacks and interference might be very attractive to cyberterrorists seeking to deepen or exacerbate a crisis.

Although both these examples were of course manageable at the time, if either one had occurred during a crisis (but particularly the Israeli example)—perhaps combined with a denial-of-service attack or other attempts to cloud the information space—the impact and reaction could have been quite different. Current concerns about the proliferation of "fake news" (not to mention a US president keen to use Twitter as a key communication tool) are indicative of this rising challenge. Equally, an attacker might seek to flood the information space with cyber "noise," obscuring the signal and message intended to be sent and reducing the actual information flow.[33] With nuclear-armed states relying more and more on computer-enabled situational awareness for military strategy and perhaps also nuclear operations—particularly those states that are in close geographical proximity—the risk of causing or exacerbating a crisis in this way is a serious and growing concern. This is particularly the case for interference by third-party actors, which could seek to precipitate or deepen a clash, crisis, or conflict.

Ultimately, control of and confidence in the nuclear information battlespace is likely to be a fundamental part of any future nuclear confrontation, and the risk that hackers might send or somehow introduce false data intended to mislead commanders or operators or distort the nuclear infosphere will continue to be a major challenge when it comes to ensuring the veracity of any information coming from computers. A good example of this occurred in the 1990s during a coalition war game, when red-team hackers from the US Defense Information Systems Agency's Coalition Vulnerability Assessment Team took over the American commander's personal computer, "sending him fake emails and false information, thus distorting his view of the battlefield and leading him to make bad decisions, which in a real war, could have meant defeat."[34]

The Risk of Cyber Disablement and Destruction

The second major concern is that cyber capabilities will be used to disable, disrupt, or destroy nuclear and associated systems, with the main intention being to prevent these systems from working as planned, or from working at all. This risk is, however, far from new. Even as far back as the 1970s, Roger Schell had warned of the considerable risks posed to US nuclear weapons by the reliance on support programs for the nuclear mission built on unclassified machines by people without security clearances.[35] Likewise, as part of Operation Eligible Receiver (a US government "red-team" cyber security exercise in 1997, more than two decades ago), the US National Military Command Center—the facility that would transmit orders from the US president in wartime, including emergency action messages to nuclear launch centers—was hacked.[36] More worrying still, most of the officers manning those servers apparently did not know that they had been compromised.[37] The attackers received no advanced intelligence about these networks and used only commercially available equipment.[38] But despite these examples, it has only been recently, with the exponential increase in the computer requirements for modern nuclear systems, that the threat of cyber disablement of nuclear weapons systems has reached public and perhaps even military consciousness.[39]

Sabotage can come in many guises: It could involve the physical alteration of hardware components so that they do not work or at least do not work as expected; the introduction of malware, or "doctored" coding, to change a software process; or even the implanting of malware to allow access to a particular component within the system in order to control, disturb, or destroy it in the future. Although it is probably possible to gain remote access to nuclear weapons systems (e.g., by interfering with the radio receivers on a nuclear missile silo), it is more likely that attackers will target the supply chain and procurement process, or target systems that are being updated and patched. As the systems security expert Ross Anderson suggests, "The moral is that vulnerabilities can be inserted at any point in the tool chain, so you can't trust a system you didn't build yourself."[40] That said, even protecting systems built "in house"—as is almost certainly the case with nuclear weapons and their control systems—is not straightforward, and some vulnerabilities may simply be the result of accidents, bugs, or unanticipated circumstances. In fact, it is estimated that regular program maintenance and updates have perhaps a 20 to 50 percent chance of introducing new errors and bugs into computer systems.[41]

The procurement of nuclear-related software and components and the need to update and replace critical systems presents a serious challenge for the nuclear weapons complex. The main threat here is that vulnerabilities, problems, logic bombs, software and hardware Trojans, and other malware or faults can be inserted into software, systems, or components at the manufacturing, supply, and maintenance stages.[42] Moreover, as a former US deputy secretary of defense, William Lynn, has pointed out, "The risk of compromise in the manufacturing process is very real and is perhaps the lowest understood cyber threat. . . . Tampering is almost impossible to detect and even harder to eradicate."[43] A successful breach of key systems in their manufacturing phase could potentially complicate all aspects of military strategy (including nuclear operations), crashing parts of the network, providing false or misleading information, and generally undermining confidence in the veracity of all the systems being used.[44] A good example of this emerged in 2012, when British researchers discovered that Chinese-manufactured computer chips used in military weapons systems and vital infrastructure all over the world contain a secret "backdoor" that could facilitate remotely disabling or reprogramming the chip.[45] It is at least possible that such computer chips—or something similar—have found their way into, and are being used in, nuclear weapons and related systems.[46]

Moreover, and irrespective of how well systems might be protected against outside interference when they have been deployed, they will almost certainly need to be updated and upgraded; fueled with new data, instructions, and software; and regularly patched and repaired.[47] The supposedly air-gapped nuclear-armed submarine provides a good example in this regard. As a former vice chairman of the US Joint Chiefs of Staff, William Owens, and his colleagues explain: "Under some circumstances, an access path may be intermittent. For example, a submarine's on-board administrative local area network would necessarily be disconnected from the internet while underwater at sea, but might be connected to the internet while in port. If the administrative network is ever connected to the on-board operational network (controlling weapons and propulsion) at sea, an effective access path may be present for an attacker."[48] This makes the nuclear acquisition process, supply chain, and particularly maintenance and updating procedures particularly susceptible to attackers—and especially for systems that will likely be air-gapped in the future when deployed.

The threat of disruption or interference has always been a central nuclear risk, but the first known examples of cyber sabotage can be traced back to the 1980s. Specifically, it probably started when the US Central Intelligence Agency began an extensive operation to feed modified designs, software, and technical and computer-related equipment to the Soviet Union. In January 1982, White House policy adviser Gus Weiss proposed to William Casey, then the Central Intelligence Agency's director and a close friend of President Ronald Reagan, to put in place a vast plan for sabotaging the Soviet economy by transferring false information to the Soviet KGB's spies.[49] This was made easier by the fact that the KGB had in place a major operation—carried out by operatives of "Line X"—to steal sensitive US secrets (the Line X operatives were dramatized in the US television drama *The Americans*). According to Weiss, under what became known as the Farewell Dossier ("Farewell" was the code name given to Col. Vladimir Vetrov, who was working for French intelligence, and who was the main go-between), a wide range of doctored computer chips, software and high-technology components, incorrect drawings, and designs and blueprints relating to the most advanced US weapons programs found their way into the most sensitive areas of the Soviet military–industrial complex.[50] Former US Air Force secretary Thomas Reed would later claim that the huge explosion of a Russian gas pipeline in the summer 1982 (the first nonnuclear explosion to be seen from space) was a direct result of the Farewell Dossier.[51] According to Reed, the pipeline software was altered so that the pumps, turbines, and valves would begin to run out of sync, causing the pipeline's joints and welds to come apart and then explode.[52] Reed's testimony has, however, been disputed by former KGB officer Vasily Pchelintsev, who suggested that the explosion was caused by "poor construction, not planted software."[53] It is not known whether the operation had any direct effect on Soviet nuclear weapons or strategic systems, but it is at least possible.

The second example is the rumor that the US intelligence community formulated a plan during the 1980s to target Soviet high-frequency command and control communications networks through electronic (cyber) attacks.[54] The main aim of Canopy Wing—as the plan was known—was to find new ways of attacking the key Soviet weapons and control systems through what was then labeled "electronic warfare"—but which we would more correctly think of now as "cyber operations"—so that these systems could be targeted and compromised in the event of nuclear war between East and West.[55] In this way, it was likely part of the Reagan administration's broader interest in the possibility of achieving victory, or a "prevailing strategy," in an East–West nuclear exchange. East German spymaster Markus Wolf is believed to have passed details of Canopy Wing on to his Soviet handlers, resulting in significant improvements and upgraded security at sensitive command and control nodes across the Soviet Union.[56] Although the extent and success of the operation remain unknown, by the early 1990s, the Russians—and particularly the Russian Navy–had learned to fear technology as a tool for sabotage and had grown increasingly concerned about possible vulnerabilities, malware, and trapdoors in military hardware and software.[57]

The Farewell Dossier and Canopy Wing provided the intellectual and tactical foundation for the possibilities of cyber operations and attacks that would follow (albeit nearly two decades later). In March 2007, the US Department of Energy's Idaho Laboratory in Idaho Falls undertook an experiment whereby an electric power generator was attacked through cyber means and caused to self-destruct.[58] The US Department of Homeland Security later confirmed that "the experiment involved controlled hacking into a replica of a power plant's control system. Sources familiar with the test said researchers changed the operating cycle of the generator, sending it out of control."[59] This would become known as the Aurora Generator Test, and it seemed to mark the beginning of a new era for physical disablement or destruction from cyberattacks.[60] However, though Aurora demonstrated the possibilities of sabotage through cyber means, only a handful of cyberattacks have caused publicly known physical destruction, and only one—Stuxnet—has caused direct damage to a nuclear facility.

The Stuxnet worms (there were at least two versions, and possibly more, according to Kim Zetter[61]) were designed to attack the Iranian uranium enrichment program based at Natanz in central Iran—specifically, the supervisory control and data-acquisition control systems operating the gas centrifuges, which in turn would enrich the uranium. This attack would entail altering computer processes in order to damage the valves that manage the flow of uranium hexafluoride into the centrifuge, and later more directly by damaging the frequency converters themselves.[62] The thinking was that the Iranians would simply assume that the problems were the result of faulty parts and hardware, engineering deficiencies, or just incompetence.[63] In this way, the focus of the attack was as much the confidence of the Iranian leaders and their chief scientists in the equipment being used, and in themselves, as it was about causing significant physical damage.[64] It is believed that Stuxnet entered the air-gapped Natanz system through an infected USB drive or other media, and probably via an unwitting employee who had access to infection points.[65] But it is possible that it was achieved through a phishing attack, although no "dropper" (which surreptitiously installs malware on the target machine) has yet been found.[66] As the cyber security expert Ralph Langner, who ascertained the true purpose of the malware, explains:

> Rather than trying to infiltrate directly by crawling through fifteen firewalls, three data diodes, and an intrusion detection system, the attackers played it indirectly by infecting soft targets with legitimate access to Ground Zero: Contractors. Whatever the cyber security posture of contractors may have been, it certainly was not at par with the Natanz fuel enrichment facility. Getting the malware on their mobile devices and USB sticks proved good enough as sooner or later they would physically

carry those on site and connect them to the [fuel enrichment facility's] most critical systems, unchallenged by any guards.[67]

The success of Stuxnet was therefore also dependent on a considerable amount of prior monitoring and mapping of the system before any attack could take place. Specific information on the software, hardware, and processes being used, as well as the contractors and operators involved, was integral to its ability to work as planned.

Stuxnet has been credited with causing damage to centrifuges and delaying any Iranian bomb (albeit perhaps only temporarily[68])—but comprehensive destruction of the Nantanz facility was clearly not the main intention of the attack.[69] Nevertheless, Stuxnet demonstrated that it was possible to infect and damage physical systems in a different country—including those not connected to the internet—by accessing the computers and networks that control them, in this case first through espionage and second through good old-fashioned human error. Indeed, it is believed that engineers working on the Iranian nuclear program regularly connected their laptops to the air-gapped systems, or went away to work on updates and patches, providing the perfect "way in."[70] Or, in the words of one official, "There is always one idiot who doesn't think much about the thumb drive in his hand."[71] Either way, as Ralph Langner noted, Stuxnet represented "a clear turning point in the history of cyber security," not least because the technology and tactics "are generic and can be used against other targets as well."[72]

There are rumors of similar United States–led cyberattacks on the North Korean nuclear program,[73] possibly even involving an Olympic Games / Stuxnet-like operation, as well as cyberattacks that may have undermined North Korean ballistic missile tests.[74] But as the journalist Kim Zetter explains, introducing it would likely be much more difficult, even if the systems were found to be the same.[75] This is because the North Korean nuclear program is far more isolated from the outside world, and particularly outside contractors. More broadly, there is an increasing number of reports about other attacks that have caused physical destruction or disablement, and three in particular are worth noting. The first is the attack on Saudi Aramco in 2012, when attackers breached the networks of the Saudi national oil company and used the Shamoon virus—with a timed, disk-wiping payload—to destroy important data indiscriminately.[76] This self-replicating virus may have infected as many as 30,000 of the company's Windows-based machines.[77] The United States later blamed Iran for the attack.[78] The second attack was on a German steel mill in 2014—where control systems were manipulated so that the blast furnace could not be shut down, resulting in "massive damage."[79] The attackers are believed to have gained access to the corporate business network through a spear phishing attack, and then managed to penetrate the secured parts of the system that operate and control the plant's equipment.[80] Third, in December 2015, hackers—believed to be from Russia—successfully breached computers of three energy distribution companies in Ukraine, temporarily disrupting the country's power grid. A year later, the Ukrainian power grid was successfully hacked again. Though the impact of both attacks was temporary, and both outages lasted only a few hours, experts were fearful that it might simply have been a "dry run" and a "warning shot" of what could follow.[81]

It is also clear that a widespread sabotage campaign (including cyber operations) directed against the Iranian nuclear program has continued in the wake of Stuxnet.[82] This is in fact likely part of a much bigger and established program against Iran that has been ongoing for many years and has involved tampering with computer equipment as well as other clandestine operations.[83] In this way, the significance of Stuxnet was that it essentially transformed the approach from analogue to digital. During the 1990s, for example, the United States and Israel "modified" vacuum pumps purchased by Iran to make them break down;[84] in 2012, the Iranian lawmaker Alaeddin Boroujerdi accused the German company Siemens of planting tiny explosives inside equipment that Iran had purchased for its nuclear program;[85] in 2014, Iranian foreign minister Mohammed Javad Zarif blamed "the West" for attempting to sabotage the heavy water nuclear reactor at Arak by seeking to interfere with components of its control system;[86] and a huge explosion at the Parchin military base a few months later in October again raised the question of sabotage.[87] Such cyber or cyber-enabled operations might therefore also offer a good method of counterproliferation or counterterrorism—as the journalist Eli Lake points out, "The specific benefit of [cyber] sabotage is that it makes countries [and terrorists] wary of purchasing crucial [nuclear-related] materials on the black market."[88]

The moral of the story is that it is becoming increasingly possible to attack systems, and perhaps nuclear systems, directly through cyber means (both hardware and software) in order to prevent them from working as planned. In fact, it has probably been possible to do this for at least the last three decades—although only now, it seems, has the seriousness of this threat begun to be recognized. Both the required tools in terms of cyber capabilities as well as the necessary vulnerabilities within nuclear weapons systems themselves now exist to be attacked. It is particularly important that this is true for systems that are air-gapped, separated, and well protected—the main defense often used by those downplaying the potential threat. Although the effect of Operation Orchard, the Farewell Dossier, Canopy Wing, Stuxnet, and other known attacks has been limited, they nevertheless give a useful indication of future attack vectors, and they highlight the increasing problems and vulnerabilities that will need to be addressed throughout the nuclear weapons complexes of nuclear-armed states. As Kim Zetter has suggested, "As shocking as the revelations about Stuxnet, Duqu, and Flame were, they likely were just the shallow tip of a stockpile of tools and weapons that the United States and Israel had built."[89] This is also increasingly likely to be true for other nuclear-armed states. As is discussed later in this book, even the perception that these systems might be in some way compromised could be significant in a future crisis or conflict.

Cyber Enablement and Cyber-Nuclear Terrorism

The worst-case cyber threat in the nuclear realm is that an undeterrable terrorist group (or a rogue insider), hell-bent on causing mass destruction and panic, hacks into the systems that control nuclear weapons and seeks to cause a launch or explosion. Though there may be some debate as to the exact nature and particularly the seriousness of so-called cyber-nuclear terrorism, the systems that control nuclear weapons would appear to offer a very attractive target to these groups, and therefore the threat cannot be discounted.[90] Cyber-nuclear enablement might also be the goal of an unauthorized actor (the so-called Dr. Strangelove scenario—after the film of the same name, where a rogue US Air Force commander initiates an unauthorized nuclear attack against the Soviet Union). This is a threat that has never really gone away in the nuclear age, but is being recast and perhaps amplified in the cyber context.

There are three key things worth remembering when we think about this threat. The first thing to note about cyber enablement is that it is likely the preserve of nonstate actors, terrorists, and possibly also unauthorized insiders rather than nation-states. Although it is perfectly possible that a state actor could seek to do this, such actions seem far more likely to be the goal of nonstate actors or a terrorist group because it is hard to see a scenario where a state would want to cause, or would benefit from, a nuclear launch or explosion. The second thing to note is that though opinion remains split on just how serious the cyber-nuclear terrorist threat is, there is a growing recognition that these groups will one day achieve a certain "cyber sophistication," and that cyber operations against nuclear systems—both military and civilian—represent a much easier option than a nonstate actor building or even acquiring a nuclear device of their own.[91] Third, despite the confidence of many that nuclear systems will be virtually impossible to breach (e.g., the US National Nuclear Security Administration claims "that they are not aware of any viruses or malware that could remotely launch a nuclear warhead"),[92] nuclear weapons systems would appear to offer a very attractive target for terrorist groups and nonstate actors—and, perhaps more important, they *can never* be completely secure.[93]

Cyberterrorists—or other nonstate actors—might seek to target nuclear systems and their operators in three main ways. First, they could manipulate information and the information space, spoof systems into overreaction or incorrect outcomes, or exacerbate a crisis in some way, as discussed in this chapter's first section. This is perhaps the most likely and most pressing threat vector, and the easiest for nonstate actors to exploit. Second, hackers could somehow manipulate communications systems and maybe even acquire and send unauthorized launch orders to missile crews onboard submarines, or at Air Force bases or missile command centers. This might also include interfering with the systems used for targeting and war planning. Third, hackers (either outsiders or insiders) could directly attack the weapons and control systems and somehow cause an explosion or launch. This is perhaps the least likely scenario.[94]

However, there is reason to be worried. In 2013, a high-level report from the US Defense Science Board warned that "US nuclear weapons may be vulnerable to highly sophisticated cyber attacks"[95] and that "the resiliency of most US nuclear systems against a cyber strike is untested."[96] Moreover, former US Minuteman intercontinental ballistic missile (ICBM) launch officer Bruce Blair has revealed that many US nuclear weapons systems, and particularly communications networks that are supposed to be firewalled against malicious attackers, have been found to contain "glaring weaknesses."[97] Perhaps even more worrying, as US senator Bill Nelson (D-FL) has warned, it remains unclear whether other nuclear powers have safeguarded their nuclear command and control systems against hackers. It should probably be assumed that their nuclear strike capabilities could be vulnerable to outside interference that might lead to an unauthorized launch.[98] In fact, the former commander of the US Strategic Command, Gen. Robert Kehler, has cautioned that he "simply doesn't know" if Russia, China, or others could prevent hackers from launching one of their nuclear missiles through cyber means.[99] The risks may be even more serious in other nuclear-armed states.

The cyberterrorist threat seems particularly acute for states that retain their nuclear forces on high alert, and especially for those that keep warning and firing systems closely coupled. Indeed, the estimated 1,800 US and Russian heavily armed ballistic missiles that are kept on high alert, and are ready for prompt launch, may offer a very tempting target for terrorists or other actors intent on causing a launch or war.[100] Because both US and Russian missiles are currently being kept at such a heightened state of alert, where they are "wired to launch as soon as they receive a short stream of computer signals," Bruce Blair has suggested that the current condition is "a potential cyber vulnerability of the first order."[101] Though US nuclear-armed missiles are currently targeted into the open ocean, attackers could retarget these weapons with just a few keystrokes.[102] And given these alerted postures, particularly during any crisis, it is particularly important that a cyberterrorist attack or deception would potentially only need to be believable and successful for a relatively short period of time.[103]

It is also possible that a cyberattack on a nuclear early warning system could further degrade its performance and exacerbate the problem of inadvertent launch by a third party or terrorists.[104] In this way, nuclear command and control systems might not need to be hacked directly for terrorists to cause a launch.[105] An attacker could also utilize other types of electromagnetic interference—for example, by sending or beaming electrical impulses into nuclear weapons systems that might secretly arm or even detonate the devices.[106] In fact, Bruce Blair has warned that both the US ICBM missile silos' radio receivers and the hardened intersite system used to transmit messages and keep launch control centers in constant contact with missiles are potentially vulnerable to cyber or electronic attack. As

Blair explains, a 2010 incident at the F. E. Warren Air Force Base in Cheyenne, Wyoming, gives a good indication of how this could play out:[107]

> When the Wyoming rockets went offline on October 23 [2010], the remote underground launch centers that control them lost their ability to detect and cancel any unauthorized launch attempts. Such an attempt could have come moments before the blackout from a rogue or compromised underground crew. Or it could have come during the blackout from someone hacking into the ICBMs' radio receivers tuned to a backup launch-control aircraft. Or from someone splicing into the many thousands of miles of cabling that connect America's ICBMs to launch control. In such a situation, the rockets would have waited for a short period—30 minutes or so—to give the crews a chance to cancel an illicit command. But since the crews would have been unable to do so, the 50 rockets would have accepted the launch instruction, ignited their boosters, and risen out of their silos.[108]

The problem was caused by a circuit card installed in a weapons system processor that had been dislodged by routine vibration and heat. This also gives an indication of how an attacker might seek to disable these weapons. As Eric Schlosser later remarked: "The idea that a hacker could somehow disable 50 ballistic missiles—each of them armed with a nuclear warhead about seven times more powerful than the bomb that destroyed Hiroshima—seemed like the improbable plot of a Hollywood thriller."[109] Likewise, an attacker could possibly transmit a specifically engineered electromagnetic signal through the antenna or through the wire.[110] That said, cyberterrorists might also take advantage of old-fashioned techniques and use cyberattacks to facilitate or aid physical or kinetic attacks on nuclear systems.

The possibility that an unauthorized actor, rogue commander, or other insider might somehow cause nuclear use by interfering with nuclear weapons systems in some way is an equally troubling prospect. Notwithstanding the sophistication of Stuxnet and other possible advanced cyber threats, perhaps the easiest targets for cyberattackers, and the biggest risks, are still humans, operators, and officials (either acting on their own, at the behest of an adversary, or unwittingly).[111] The human threat is therefore both from malicious actors with immediate access to systems as well as those who may be duped into doing something to compromise the systems they work with. In this way, the Dr. Strangelove scenario from the analogue 1960s remains a fundamental challenge for the digital world of today.

Cyber-nuclear terrorism remains the worst-case, least-likely threat in the new cyber context, but this does not mean that it should be discounted or even ignored. A direct attack is possible and becomes particularly troubling during a crisis—especially when combined with attacks on warning systems, and for closely coupled nuclear forces. An indirect attack or third-party spoofing during a crisis could also create conditions that lead to inadvertent escalation or even unauthorized nuclear use. It is also possible, although outside the remit of this study, that terrorists would target other nuclear facilities, such as a nuclear power plant. In 2003, for example, the Slammer computer worm found its way into the Davis-Besse nuclear power plant in Ohio and disabled a safety monitoring system for nearly five hours.[112] In fact, this may prove to be a more attractive and easier alternative to attacking nuclear weapons systems, and could create an equally dramatic effect.[113] In terms of the radiation released, environmental damage, and threat to human life, a terrorist attack on a nuclear power plant could be equally as devastating as the detonation or launch of a nuclear weapon.[114]

Conclusion: Assessing Risks, Intentions, and Capabilities

It is certainly possible that cyber operations could be carried out against nuclear systems and the information on which they and their operators rely, but the vectors, intentions, and implications of this are mixed. The first risk is that nuclear warning sensors and associated systems could be indirectly spoofed in some way or flooded with misleading disinformation or misinformation. Next is the possibility that hackers could gain access to key information systems and cause them to operate differently, such as by contaminating data within nuclear planning and operating systems. Then there is the risk that hackers could break into command and control systems (including targeting software) for nuclear weapons—perhaps before they become operational, by implanting malware during the procurement phase—and prevent weapons or communications systems from working as planned when needed. Finally, the greatest risk—but perhaps also the least likely worst-case scenario—is that hackers could break into nuclear weapons systems and cause either a launch or explosion.

However, it is important to note the differences between the intentions and capabilities of the actors involved. Nation-states—particularly nuclear-armed ones—are likely to be more interested in disabling the nuclear and control systems of their opponent, and they are perhaps more likely to be able to deploy sophisticated cyber capabilities and weapons in order to do this. Cyberterrorists and other nonstate actors, conversely, are likely to be far more interested in operations designed to cause a nuclear explosion or launch, but may have to rely on less sophisticated and indirect methods to achieve this. Stuxnet-type attacks are probably beyond the reach of most terrorist groups for the moment, but it is certainly not impossible that nonstate hackers—perhaps facilitated by an insider—could breach nuclear systems in the future. Moreover, even if this worst-case scenario never becomes a reality, the secrecy and security that surround both cyber and nuclear capabilities mean that the perception that this could happen will remain an ever-present and pervasive concern. Ultimately, all nuclear-armed states will need to accept that the systems used to manage and secure nuclear weapons will never be 100 percent protected from cyberattacks.

Notes

1. Schell, "Computer Security," 1.
2. Quoted by Corera, *Intercept*, 71.
3. Fulghum, "Why Syria's Air Defenses Failed to Detect Israel's"; and Leyden, "Israel Suspected of 'Hacking' Syrian Air Defences."
4. Fulghum, "Why Syria's Air Defenses Failed to Detect Israel's."
5. Clarke and Knake, *Cyber War*, 6–8.
6. Kaplan, *Dark Territory*, 161.
7. Leyden, "Israel Suspected of 'Hacking' Syrian Air Defences."
8. See Michaels, "US Could Use Cyberattack on Syrian Air Defenses."
9. Schmitt and Shanker, "US Debated Cyberwarfare in Attack Plan on Libya."
10. Sanger and Mazzetti, "US Had Cyberattack Plan."
11. Wilson, *Information Operations*.
12. Kaplan, *Dark Territory*, 113–14.
13. Ibid.
14. Schwartau, *Information Warfare*, 426; and Denning, *Information Warfare and Security*, 5–6.
15. Clarke and Knake, *Cyber War*, 8–9.
16. Kaplan, *Dark Territory*, 76.
17. Steinnon, *Surviving Cyberwar*, 130.
18. Libicki, *Conquest in Cyberspace*, 105.
19. Fritz, "Hacking Nuclear Command and Control."
20. Ibid.; and Blair, "Could Terrorists Launch America's Nuclear Missiles?"
21. Ainslie, *Future of the British Bomb*, 56.
22. Blair, "Why Our Nuclear Weapons Can Be Hacked."
23. Ainslie, *Future of the British Bomb*, 83.
24. US general Robert Kehler, quoted by Farnsworth, "Study Sees Cyber Risk for US Arsenal."
25. Union of Concerned Scientists and American Association for the Advancement of Science, "Workshop on US Nuclear Weapons Safety," 19.
26. Constantin, "Satellite Communications Systems."
27. Carter, Steinbruner, and Zraket, *Managing Nuclear Operations*, 217.
28. McConnell, "Cyberwar Is the New Atomic Age," 74–75.
29. Corera, *Intercept*, 129.
30. Quoted in ibid., 133.
31. Global Security Newswire, "Hacked Israeli Military Twitter Account."
32. Segal, *Hacked World Order*, 16.
33. Libicki, *Conquest in Cyberspace*, 51.
34. Kaplan, *Dark Territory*, 65–66.
35. Yost, "Interview Conducted with Roger Schell."
36. See Kaplan, *Dark Territory*, 68–69.
37. Ibid.
38. Adams, "Virtual Defense," 100–101.
39. Hayes, "Nuclear Command and Control," 9.
40. Anderson, *Security Engineering*, 645.

41. Borning, "Computer System Reliability," 34.

42. Lynn, "Defending a New Domain," 101.

43. Ibid.

44. Gompert and Libicki, "Cyber Warfare," 11.

45. Curtis, "Cambridge Researchers Uncover Backdoor in Military Chip."

46. Van der Meer, "Cyber Warfare," 1.

47. Singer and Friedman, *Cybersecurity and Cyberwar*, 63.

48. Owens, Dam, and Lin, *Technology*, 87.

49. Kostin and Raynaud, *Farewell*, 283.

50. Weiss, "Duping the Soviets," 125; and Reed and Stillman, *Nuclear Express*, 274.

51. See Reed, *At the Abyss*.

52. Ibid., 269.

53. Medetsky, "KGB Veteran Denies CIA Caused '82 Blast."

54. See Fischer, "Canopy Wing," 439.

55. Ibid. See also Gartzke and Lindsay, "Thermonuclear Cyberwar," 3–4.

56. Wolf, *Man without a Face*, 329–30.

57. Corera, *Intercept*, 160; and Kaplan, *Dark Territory*, 13.

58. Quoted by Meserve, "Mouse Click."

59. Ibid.

60. Ibid.

61. Interview with the author.

62. Zetter, *Countdown to Zero Day*, 302–3.

63. Sanger, *Confront and Conceal*, 188.

64. Kaplan, *Dark Territory*, 208.

65. Lindsay, "Stuxnet," 381.

66. Interview with Zetter.

67. Langner, "To Kill a Centrifuge," 20.

68. For a detailed discussion of this, see Albright, Brannan, and Walrond, "Did Stuxnet Take Out 1,000 Centrifuges?"

69. Langner, "To Kill a Centrifuge," 15.

70. Sanger, *Confront and Conceal*, 196.

71. Quoted in ibid., 196.

72. Langner, "To Kill a Centrifuge," 4.

73. See Rodriguez, "US Tried, Failed to Sabotage North Korea Nuclear Weapons Programme"; and Sanger and Broad, "Trump Inherits a Secret Cyberwar against North Korean Missiles."

74. See, e.g., Ryall, Smith, and Millward, "North Korea's Unsuccessful Missile Launch 'May Have Been Thwarted by US Cyber Attack.'"

75. Zetter, "Could Stuxnet Mess with North Korea's New Uranium Plant?"

76. See Bronk and Tikk-Ringas, "Cyber Attack on Saudi Aramco."

77. Ibid., 81.

78. Perlroth, "In Cyberattack on Saudi Firm, US Sees Iran Firing Back."

79. See Zetter, "Cyberatttack Has Caused Confirmed Damage."

80. Ibid.

81. Greenberg, "Crash Override."

82. Quoted by Lake, "Operation Sabotage."

83. Langner, "To Kill a Centrifuge," 15.

84. Sanger, *Confront and Conceal*, 194.

85. *New York Times*, "Iran Says Nuclear Equipment Was Sabotaged."

86. Sanger, "Explosion at Key Military Base in Iran Raises Questions about Sabotage."

87. Ibid.

88. Lake, "Operation Sabotage."

89. Zetter, *Countdown to Zero Day*, 294.

90. See, e.g., Green, "Myth of Cyberterrorism."

91. McConnell, "Cyberwar Is the New Atomic Age," 76.

92. Koebler, "US Nukes Face up to 10 Million Cyber Attacks Daily."

93. See, e.g., Green, "Myth of Cyberterrorism."

94. Gady, "Could Cyber Attacks Lead to Nuclear War?"; and Fritz, "Hacking Nuclear Command and Control."

95. Quoted by Farnsworth, "Study Sees Cyber Risk for US Arsenal."

96. Quoted by Sternstein, "Officials Worry."

97. Blair, "Could Terrorists Launch America's Nuclear Missiles?"

98. Quoted by Sternstein, "Officials Worry."

99. Quoted by Schlosser, "Neglecting Our Nukes."

100. Global Zero Commission on Nuclear Risk Reduction, "De-Alerting and Stabilizing the World's Nuclear Force Postures," 16.

101. Blair, "Lowering the Nuclear Threshold," 4.

102. Ibid.

103. Fritz, "Hacking Nuclear Command and Control."

104. Global Zero Commission on Nuclear Risk Reduction, "De-Alerting and Stabilizing the World's Nuclear Force Postures," 20.

105. Fritz, "Hacking Nuclear Command and Control."

106. Gregory, *Hidden Cost of Nuclear Deterrence*, 72.

107. Blair, "Why Our Nuclear Weapons Can Be Hacked." See also Reed, "Keeping Nukes Safe."

108. Blair, "Could Terrorists Launch America's Nuclear Missiles?"

109. Schlosser, "Neglecting Our Nukes."

110. On this, see Fryer-Biggs, "DoD Looking to 'Jump the Gap.'"

111. Rid, *Cyberwar Will Not Take Place*, 58.

112. Poulsen, "Slammer Worm Crashed Ohio Nuke Plant Network."

113. See, e.g., Masood, "Assessment of Cyber Security Challenges"; and Sprenger, "Q&A."

114. Rothkopf, "Where Fukushima Meets Stuxnet."

PART III

> The Cyber-Nuclear Nexus
> at the Strategic Level

5

> Cyberdeterrence, Nuclear
> Weapons, and Managing
> Strategic Threats

MOST CYBER ACTIVITIES—such as general hacking, crime, exploitation, and espionage—clearly fall well below the level of warfare and should not be thought of as strategic or as requiring a concerted national response, at least not a military one. But there is growing recognition that a sophisticated cyberattack against either critical national infrastructure and society (which might be thought of as countervalue) or, more discretely, on nuclear and conventional forces and associated systems (counterforce) is an increasing possibility and is fueling a public debate about how to respond.[1] Although a full analysis of the broader societal cyber threat is beyond the scope of this book, such attacks—particularly if they lead to substantial disruption, destruction, and even loss of life—nevertheless raise significant questions about how such actions might be defended against or deterred.[2] Direct attacks on nuclear systems are likely to be far more acute in their implications and clearly have far more immediate consequences for defense and deterrence policies and for strategic balances. However, both sets of challenges require thinking about how security, defense, and deterrence (both through denial and punishment), as well as cross-domain and asymmetric responses, can be combined, and about the types of threat that will make deterrence credible.[3] This naturally leads to questions about the possible role of nuclear weapons in deterring "strategic" cyberattacks, which in turn requires an examination of the relationship between nuclear and cyber weapons.

The relationship between "cyber weapons" (itself a contested term) and nuclear weapons is complicated. This is at least partly because though we have come to understand just how powerful and destructive nuclear weapons are during the past seventy years, the same cannot yet be said for the diverse range of threats posed by the much newer cyber challenge.[4] In fact, and despite a tendency to conflate the two, cyber weapons and nuclear weapons are fundamentally different, and it is not clear that cyber threats will fit neatly into the established paradigms and thinking about defense, security, arms control, deterrence, or warfare that form the canon of nuclear studies. Indeed, such attempts may even hamper the development of new norms, rules of the road, and policy planning frameworks.[5]

Nevertheless, the emerging computerized global security environment will require that all nuclear-armed states reflect on the particularly problematic questions of when cyberattacks or attacks on key information systems might become "acts of war" and, perhaps above all, whether and when such attacks can ever be attributed with sufficient confidence to elicit a response—cyber, kinetic, or even nuclear. Ultimately, though cyber threats and nuclear threats may be qualitatively and quantitatively different, any attacker must be cognizant that conducting a large-scale cyberattack on a nuclear-armed state, and especially against an opponent's nuclear weapons infrastructure, runs the risk (however slight) of a nuclear response.

The main aim of this chapter is therefore to analyze the link between nuclear weapons and cyber threats, and to consider how the two entities relate to each other in both theory and practice. Accordingly, this chapter proceeds in three parts: The first section seeks to compare cyber and nuclear weapons, highlights the many fundamental and important differences between the two, and explains why cyber weapons are unlikely to supplant nuclear weapons any time soon. The second section explains why different cyber threats will require different responses and how deterrence will therefore include both denial and punishment, before unpacking the problems of attribution and considering the best mechanisms to make deterrence threats credible and viable. The third section then goes on to consider the shape and form that this cyberdeterrence strategy might take, particularly the debate about the wisdom and efficacy of ever using nuclear weapons to deter a strategic cyberattack.

Comparing Cyber and Nuclear Threats—Bombs and Bytes

The rise of the cyber challenge has necessarily led to comparisons with other forms of weaponry, previous so-called revolutions in warfare, and particularly with nuclear weapons.[6] It has also naturally led to attempts to superimpose the frameworks and thinking used for previous weapons systems and warfare, including nuclear weapons and nuclear strategy, on the cyber challenge. However, even if one discards the significant amount of cyber activity that falls way below what one might conceive of as strategic (or involving weapons)—and notwithstanding the importance of the broader cyber context—there are many notable and important differences between the two, and these are differences that have implications for how the cyber threat is understood and might be responded to. Unfortunately, it seems that many high-ranking officials (and others) often adopt a misplaced analogy between nuclear and cyber weapons, and use this flawed understanding as a basis for policy and debate.[7] The aim of this section is therefore to unpack this comparison and look more deeply into how the relationship between the two should be understood in both the academic and policy worlds.

To be sure, some parallels can be drawn between cyber weapons and nuclear weapons. Joseph Nye points to five notable similarities: (1) Cyber offense appears to trump defense, (2) the use of cyber capabilities may be tactical or strategic, (3) first- and second-use scenarios share resemblances with nuclear strategy, (4) both cyber and nuclear operations might involve automated responses and unintended consequences, and (5) there is a belief that these weapons are "great equalizers," and offer asymmetric advantages against a stronger opponent.[8] Both types of weapons can often have a distinct delivery vehicle and a payload or warhead. There are also a number of similarities in how both nuclear and cyber weapons have been developed and used: (1) Both have been developed due in part to a fear that they might be developed by others; (2) the effects and implications of developing and using these weapons are poorly understood; (3) scientists and engineers warn about the weapons' inherent dangers and call for international agreements and arms control; and (4) the US government and others are moving ahead anyway, without public discussion or a concrete understanding of its implications for international security.[9] However, when one digs slightly deeper, it becomes apparent that nuclear and cyber weapons, though sharing some similarities, are intrinsically different, particularly regarding the level of destruction they might cause. As William Owens, former vice chairman of the US Joint Chiefs of Staff, and colleagues point out, "Many questions asked regarding nuclear conflict are relevant to cyberattack, even though the answers to those questions will be very different in the two cases."[10]

Perhaps the most obvious difference is the extent of the damage that might be caused by either nuclear or cyberattacks. In terms of the scale and nature of the threat, even the most sophisticated cyberattacks are highly unlikely to cause the enormous physical destruction, damage, and death that just one nuclear bomb can and has caused.[11] About 200,000 people died as a result of the two atomic bombs dropped on Hiroshima and Nagasaki in 1945, and millions would potentially die in even a limited exchange of much more powerful modern thermonuclear weapons. So far, no one has died as a direct result of a cyberattack, and cyber operations are usually lethal only when they unleash the power already inherent in the system being attacked (e.g., a dam or a nuclear power plant).[12] For this reason, it can be difficult to think of cyber weapons as being strategic or lethal or, for that matter, of their use as constituting an act of war—at least on their own. Because of this, Thomas Rid and Peter McBurney have suggested that cyberwar is perhaps best thought of as a metaphor rather than a statement of what has taken place in cyberspace so far.[13] Even the most severe cyberattacks—such as on a banking system (the Hollywood plotline in films such as *Die Hard 4.0: Live Free or Die Hard*) or power grid (e.g., in Ukraine in 2015)—would probably only be temporary and would be unlikely to directly cause casualties or deaths.[14] The most serious cyberattacks could of course be burdensome and nasty, and cause expensive damage, but things would probably return to normal fairly quickly—but the same is clearly not true in the wake of a nuclear exchange.[15] Or, as Joseph Nye eloquently explains, "Destruction or discontinuation of cyber systems could return us to the economy of the 1990s—a huge loss of GDP—but a major nuclear war could return us to the Stone Age."[16] In this way, cyber weapons are perhaps better thought of as weapons of mass *disruption* rather than as weapons of mass *destruction*, and more often as force multipliers rather than stand-alone capabilities—although this could of course change in the future.

Part of the reason for this is that the intended targets of cyber and nuclear attacks tend to be different. Although it is theoretically possible to have a limited or focused nuclear attack, nuclear weapons are generally seen as indiscriminate and are intended to cause widespread damage to large urban areas. In contrast, even the most threatening cyberattacks, and particularly the use of sophisticated cyber weapons, are likely to be highly specialized and target very specific systems or machines—notwithstanding the use of denial-of-service cyberattacks, such as those directed against Estonia in 2007, Georgia in 2008, and purportedly by Iran against US banks in 2013.[17] Put simply, to be effective, high-end cyber operations often require very exact prior knowledge of the system being attacked.[18] Cyberattacks are usually designed against specific targets. Indeed, details of a target system's construction and internal subsystems determine not only its susceptibility but also what the effects are likely to be for such cyberattacks.[19] This is not the case with nuclear weapons, at least not to the same extent. Nuclear strikes, conversely, even on hardened counterforce targets such as missile silos, require relatively little specific knowledge of the target beforehand, other than its geographic location. Somewhat paradoxically, however, it is often very difficult to have precision in cyber operations—particularly regarding aftereffects, though the consequences of a nuclear blast and damage have been calculated and are generally well understood.[20]

Another set of differences involve the rules and conventions that govern the use and operation of nuclear and cyber capabilities. In particular, the notions of mutually assured destruction and cyberdeterrence are inherently complicated in cyberspace, and there is no established tradition of cyber nonuse or a cyber taboo.[21] In fact, some forms of cyber operations are ongoing pretty much all the time.[22] As James Adams explains, "Unlike during the Cold War, when the nuclear standoff produced its own understandable rules of the game that included a sophisticated deterrence mechanism, no legal or de facto boundaries inhibit cyber aggressions. Instead, information warfare is a free-for-all, with more and more players hurrying to join the scrimmage."[23]

This, in turn, clearly has implications for the possibility of legally binding structures required to govern cyber operations, and particularly for any notion of cyber arms control—especially arms control frameworks that draw on previous nuclear experiences and involve established mechanisms such as inspection regimes, transparency, and verification.[24] As the *Newsweek* reporters Michael Riley and Ashlee Vance put it, "Deterrence and arms treaties are but philosophical concepts when invisible weapons are involved."[25] Traditional notions of arms control therefore do not necessarily translate well into the cyber realm. States tend to lack clearly defined cyber strategies, and the secretive and intangible nature of cyber capabilities, and the pace at which they change, are likely to make comprehensive cyber verification and transparency virtually impossible.[26]

In fact, there is a considerable difference in the importance of transparency (and, therefore, in the ability to verify) in cyber and nuclear operations. Put simply, disclosing or revealing cyber capabilities is likely to almost instantly undermine its coercive power (adversaries will rush to protect against these new threats by patching systems or changing processes), while revealing a nuclear capability is unlikely to have much effect other than bolstering the current balance of power by making nuclear threats seem more credible. This is because most cyber operations rely on deception and secrecy, whereas nuclear strategy relies on clear and overt communication.[27] This is what Erik Gartzke and Jon Lindsay refer to as the "military commitment problem" inherent in cyber operations.[28]

Essentially, a state can demonstrate its conventional or even nuclear weapons capabilities by conducting tests, training, and exercises; through conspicuous deployments; or even as part of military parades. Many of these munitions can also be observed and even quantified to some extent through an adversary's "national technical means"—that is, overhead surveillance and other forms of spying. In stark contrast, cyber capabilties may be almost entirely invisible and cannot be tested, paraded, or deployed before use in any meaningful way. Indeed, revealing cyber capabilities would very likely undermine their future value and use. Unlike traditional components of military force, the extent of a foe's cyber capabilities can therefore probably only be guessed at and estimated (leaving some doubt about their effectiveness).[29] These dynamics often help to drive worst-case thinking when it comes to an opponent's cyber capabilities.

The perception that an adversary can and will be able to respond to an attack is a fundamental part of deterrence, as is the ability to accurately convey both intentions and capabilities. Unfortunately, a key principle of cyber operations is precisely the opposite. Instead, cyber operations seek to undermine confidence in data, prevent an enemy from making an informed strategic judgment, and conceal the weapons that you have and might want to use.[30] The net result is that using nuclear weapons as a model for cyber operations is flawed, although some have suggested that biological or chemical weapons,[31] or even airpower during the two world wars, might provide a better basis for comparison.[32]

Notwithstanding the specter of nuclear terrorism, nuclear weapons have also traditionally been the preserve of nation-states, and thus the main actors in the nuclear game have been national governments.[33] This is partly due to the enormous cost and undertaking involved in producing, managing, and fielding nuclear weapons (and maintaining their support and other subsystems)—and this has meant that it has been pretty clear where the danger comes from and who is ultimately responsible for any threat or attack. Although sophisticated cyber weapons might also require a concerted effort carried out over a prolonged period of time, the differences are stark. As the investigative journalist Fred Kaplan explains, "Unlike the atomic bomb or the intercontinental ballistic missile, . . . a cyber weapon didn't require a large-scale industrial project or a campus of brilliant scientists; all it took to build one was a roomful of computers and a small corps of people trained to use them."[34] It is therefore probably much easier for a state, or perhaps even a nonstate actor, to acquire a powerful cyberattack capability than a nuclear or even sophisticated conventional weapons system. Such cyber weapons would also in theory be much easier to get hold of through illicit networks and informal global markets (and perhaps through cyber espionage), or might even be custom-built from scratch by a skillful programmer. The fact that every cyber weapon essentially carries its own blueprints makes this threat even more acute.[35]

What this suggests is that despite the belief held by some that cyber weapons are somehow equivalent to nuclear weapons (or might even supersede them) and that the frameworks and thinking that underpinned the nuclear era might somehow be transported into the cyber realm, the challenges posed by cyberattacks and nuclear weapons are very different. Even if we discard the considerable range of cyber operations that should not be classified as strategic, cyberattacks still lack the considerable destructive power of nuclear weapons. In fact, the range of new dynamics that are evolving under the cyber moniker might even necessitate a rethinking of how we evaluate, conceptualize, and define the term "weapon" more broadly (perhaps in a similar manner to what has happened during the last two decades with the concept of security).[36] Thus, the task is to move beyond the allure of relatively uncomplicated nuclear-based frameworks (largely developed in the pre-cyber era) and to begin to unpack how the strategic cyber challenge needs to be met, and consider whether there might be a role for nuclear weapons in managing these new threats.

Deterrence by Denial and Deterrence by Punishment

Given the considerable dissimilarities between nuclear and cyber weapons, and the vast range of different operations that fall under the cyber moniker, the response to the cyber challenge will naturally be multifaceted. Any strategy to address these challenges will therefore need to start with (1) a consideration of the possibilities of cyber defense and security, (2) the potential to limit new threats through arms control and other frameworks, and (3) the applicability of deterrence by punishment in the cyber realm. It will also almost certainly involve consideration of how these might be best combined and balanced; just like the threat, the tools required to address the cyber challenge will not be homogeneous.

The management of cyber threats will therefore be split into two components: (1) defense (including possibly active defense) against attackers seeking to steal secrets, interfere with systems, and cause disruption and (2) defense *and deterrence* against strategic attacks intended to cause damage and destruction—the focus here. Because the cyber challenge is not uniform, it will require a suite of different types of responses, which will need to be tailored to specific actors and threats. This will necessarily involve both deterrence *by denial* as well as *deterrence through punishment*, and perhaps also other tools.[37] Part of the problem with the cyberdeterrence debate has been the tendency to conflate the two challenges (and responses), which often results, in the words of a former director of the Los Alamos National Laboratory, Siegfried Hecker, in "straw man comparisons" when considering the possibilities of applying "nuclear-style deterrence in cyberspace."[38] In essence, this is because cyberdeterrence is likely to be far less about punishment than is the case with nuclear deterrence.

The first thing to note is that a significant part of what is labeled "the cyber challenge" is best addressed through deterrence by denial—that is, with better computer network defense, good practices, and enhanced security that deny any benefits (or at least raise the costs) to a would-be attacker.[39] As has been explained earlier in this book, the clear majority of cyber operations occur at a relatively low level and involve nuisance, crime, espionage, and exploitation—and they therefore clearly fall well below what one would consider for deterrence through punishment and especially the use of military force.[40] Strong defenses, as well as robust cyber hygiene, will create costly barriers for any would-be attacker, and may be particularly useful in deterring terrorists or criminals, who will potentially opt for easier options.[41] Deterrence by denial also clearly has a role to play against more serious, strategic cyber challenges, and it is not hindered by the problems of attribution—discussed below—in the same way as is deterrence by punishment.[42] As Patrick Morgan notes, this essentially represents a reversal of Cold War nuclear thinking: "For cyberattacks, the deterrence supplied by defense must now compensate for the limits of deterrence based on retaliation."[43]

However, cyber security and defense, and the broader notion of deterrence by denial, are far from panaceas—even for supposedly air-gapped, highly redundant, and well-protected systems (e.g., those used for nuclear command and control), and particularly against states with advanced cyber offensive capabilities. There are three main reasons for this. First, complete isolation of computer systems—even those used to control nuclear weapons—is rarely practical given the need to access and update these systems and the information that they contain and the subsequent expansion of attack vectors for a hacker to exploit that this provides.[44] Second, the most credible types of defense in cyberspace might entail active defense—that is, where a potential adversary's networks must be breached before any action or conflict takes place. Active defense is, however, a problematic concept, with links to strategies of preemption and prevention. Third, because it is difficult to classify different cyber capabilities in the same way that one might do with nuclear or conventional weapons systems, it is difficult to devise direct defensive mechanisms. In a sense, the growth and diversification of cyberattack methods and weapons appears to be outpacing the ability and structures required to manage them.[45] As a result, a significant component of any strategy to engage the cyber threat will probably need to include deterrence by punishment and through the threat of retaliation. However, deterring cyberattacks through the threat of punishment raises other significant questions and complications. These are discussed below.

The first key question raised by the necessity of cyberdeterrence by punishment is whether attacks can be attributed with enough confidence to elicit a response—the so-called attribution problem. The concern here is that it is far harder to know for sure who has carried out a cyberattack and who is ultimately responsible than it is with other forms of strategic weapons—particularly nuclear weapons. The logic is that if one cannot credibly and confidently attribute attacks to a particular actor, then it becomes far harder to dissuade an opponent from conducting such actions through the threat of some sort of retaliation; deterrence through punishment and retaliation only work when you know who your attackers are—or at least, when attackers believe that there is a reasonable chance that they will be identified.[46] A report into a simulated cyberattack in 2010 gives some idea of this problem: As the authors explain, "No one could pinpoint the country from which the attack came, so there was no effective way to deter further damage by threatening retaliation. What's more, the military commanders noted that they even lacked the legal authority to respond—especially because it was never clear if the attack was an act of vandalism, an attempt at commercial theft or a state-sponsored effort to cripple [in this case] the United States, perhaps as a prelude to a conventional war."[47]

Attribution is also likely to be complicated by third-party interference, which, particularly during a crisis, could potentially lead to misattribution because the natural response would be for leaders to assume that an attack had been carried out by the opponent with which it was already in conflict.[48] This also becomes problematic if one includes attacks by hackers who are based in a particular country but who are not necessarily working for—or authorized by—its government. State-based nuclear or conventional attackers have historically had a "return address" and are therefore theoretically "deterrable" through the threat of unacceptable punishment. But it is not always clear who has carried out a cyberattack, or whether they were authorized to do so, making any threat of retaliation inherently complicated, and perhaps in some cases essentially hollow.

Stable deterrence in both the nuclear and conventional realms also depends largely on information and certainties about weapons and capabilities, military doctrine, and command and control; but this does not appear to apply quite so easily in the inchoate, ambiguous, and intangible realm of cyberspace.[49] Indeed, both cyber operations and the incipient cyber context are likely to blur even more the intelligence picture regarding intentions and capabilities. Each of these problems—particularly when time is limited—has made understanding who is responsible and how threats can be deterred far more difficult than it was in the past. As Martin Libicki explains, "In the Cold War nuclear realm, attribution of attack was not a problem; the prospect of battle damage was clear; the 1,000th nuclear bomb could be as powerful as the first; counterforce was possible; there were no third parties to worry about; private firms were not expected to defend themselves; any hostile nuclear use crossed an acknowledged threshold; no higher levels of war existed; and both sides always had a lot to lose."[50] That said, sophisticated strategic cyberattacks are likely to be the preserve of a handful of nation-states (specifically, China, Russia, the United Kingdom, the United States, and perhaps a few others[51])—which should in theory make some high-level cyberattacks much easier to attribute.[52]

It is, therefore, perhaps better to think of levels of attribution rather than view the problem in plain black and white. For example, any large-scale attack is unlikely to happen without a political purpose,[53] or within an indicative political/strategic context—and may even be done overtly for the purposes of coercion.[54] This is particularly the case for counterforce cyberattacks where weapons systems are targeted directly.[55] Attribution is also likely to be far easier when time is available to conduct an investigation and carry out "cyber forensics"—although this might also make subsequent retaliation more difficult politically (i.e., if it takes place some time after the initial attack).[56] Moreover, even if the problem of attribution cannot be confidently solved, it is unlikely that any state would assume that it could conduct a large-scale cyberattack out of the blue and simply get away with it.[57] Ultimately, as Thomas Rid and Ben Buchanan note, "The quality of attribution is a function of (1) available resources; (2) available time; and (3) the adversaries' sophistication."[58] It is therefore likely to be different in different situations, and not, as conventional wisdom often suggests, an either-or phenomenon.

Second, there is a question as to what form this response might take if it is to be credible, proportional, legal, and viable—not to mention timely.[59] It is certainly possible that the victim of a cyberattack may wish and be able to "respond in kind." Indeed, it is thought that the United States responded to the hacking of Sony Pictures in late 2014—believed to have been carried out by North Korea—by launching a comparable response. As Nicole Perlroth and David Sanger explain, "While perhaps a coincidence, the failure of the country's computer connections began only hours after President Obama declared Friday that the United States would launch a 'proportional response' to what he termed an act of 'cybervandalism' against Sony Pictures."[60] But in most situations, it seems far more likely that a state would simply utilize the most appropriate tools available. Responding in kind would mean assuming that the victim had the capability to do so—such as having already laced an opponent's computer systems with malware, having the requisite cyber capability or weapon at hand, and having confidence that the attack would not—perhaps inadvertently—lead to escalation or have other indirect effects.

This, in turn, leads to a discussion of whether cyber operations should be considered separately or as part of a broader (cross-domain) deterrence strategy that also involves other forms of military and political power.[61] The notion of a war fought purely in cyberspace is problematic, and it is much more likely that we will see *war involving cyber* rather than cyberwar (as is discussed later in the book). Thus, the notion of deterring cyberattacks with corresponding cyber threats has probably limited applicability—particularly the higher up the scale of severity that the attack takes place.[62] If a cyberattack leads to significant damage or death—or achieves similar effects to an attack with conventional weapons—then it would naturally lead to consideration of retaliation in the most appropriate way, an idea known in the US military as "equivalence."[63]

As such, a cyberdeterrence strategy may also include threatening the use of conventional weapons (as well as other nonmilitary means) and a recognition that some types of cyberattacks might require an asymmetric response, including kinetic military force, as part of a cross-domain deterrence strategy.[64] Or, as one US military official put it rather more succinctly, "If you shut down our power grid, maybe we put a missile down one of your smokestacks."[65] Although this may seem problematic and disproportional at first glance, the key would be the level of damage, destruction, or even death caused. Essentially, the more strategically significant the attack is, and the more disruption or damage it causes, the closer it becomes to operations conducted with traditional forms of military power.[66] It is also likely that states will adopt a certain degree of ambiguity of response to compensate for any perceived lack of credibility in the cyber realm.[67] As Joseph Nye explains, "A response to a cyberattack need not be by cyber means any more than a response to a land attack need be by the army rather than naval forces."[68] Depending on the objective of the attack, it is also likely that cyber capabilities would be used alongside conventional forces. In this way, it might make more sense to think about the cyberdeterrence problem in broader terms—that is, as part of an overall concept of deterrence that includes all levers of national and particularly military power as responses to all types of strategic attacks,[69] a so-called combined arms strategy.[70] That said, even this broader cross-domain deterrence approach will probably need to be tailored to specific threats and circumstances.[71]

The natural cyberdeterrence balance is therefore likely to include both deterrence by denial (defense, security, prevention, better cyber hygiene, and raising the costs for would-be attackers) and deterrence by punishment (utilizing all means of military and nonmilitary force to threaten retaliation), with the former comprising the major part of the response to low-level cyberattacks and the latter forming the main components of a strategy against strategic attacks. When viewed in this way, it is possible to see a role for deterrence in countering cyber threats, albeit along a spectrum, and including both denial and punishment in different combinations. However, as Erik Gartzke and Jon Lindsay explain, this could result in a cross-domain "version of the stability/instability paradox, where deterrence works at the high end but is not credible, and thus encourages provocation at the lower end."[72] Cyberdeterrence through punishment will likely have less utility than with other weapons systems in the past—particularly nuclear weapons—but it will still play a role in countering more serious state-based threats and in cross-domain operations. This is also likely to hold true for more compli-cated extended deterrence guarantees.[73] But deterrence will need to be reinforced with different mechanisms of protection and engagement, possibly some sort of more nuanced arms control, and with the establishment of norms at different levels of the cyber challenge.[74] Consequently, the applicability of deterrence in cyberspace is not simply an either-or question but is entirely contingent on what and who is being deterred, and how.[75]

Is There a Role for Nuclear Weapons in Deterring Cyber Threats?

If the deterrence of strategic cyberattacks, and more problematically attacks that involve cyber operations and weapons, must be tailored to the specific types of threats and activities being undertaken—and must be proportional and legal—this raises the question of what types of responses might be required. Strategic cyberattacks may come in two guises: As countervalue attacks that are targeted against civilian infrastructure, such as power plants, financial centers, dams, or other critical national infrastructure or as counterforce attacks, which are tar-geted at military forces, including possibly nuclear weapons and associated sys-tems. But both could potentially fall under the rubric of warfare or be conducted as part of a strategic attack involving conventional weapons—and perhaps even as part of a nonnuclear disarming first strike. Although future warfare involving cyber operations is perhaps more likely than pure cyberwarfare, both, therefore, have strategic implications. This, in turn, necessarily raises questions about the costs and benefits of including nuclear threats as part of a broader cyberdeter-rence policy.

Whether publicly or not, all nuclear-armed states will be thinking about the role that nuclear weapons might play in deterring strategic attacks involving cyber operations, or a full-scale cyberwar with potentially existential implications (if such a scenario were ever to be manifest in the future). The United States has made it pretty clear that all necessary means—including "diplomatic, informa-tional, military, and economic" ones—are on the table when responding to cyber threats as part of the 2011 International Strategy for Cyberspace.[76] And this was strengthened considerably in the updated 2015 version of the strategy, which announced that "the United States will continue to respond to cyberattacks against US interests, at a time, in a manner, and in a place of our choosing, using appropriate instruments of US power and in accordance with applicable law."[77] Although these policy proclamations have been relatively ambiguous about what role, if any, nuclear weapons might play in US cyberdeterrence strategy, a 2013 report by the US Defense Science Board suggested that there could be a role for nuclear weapons in anchoring US deterrence strategy in the event of a cyber-attack of an existential nature. As the report suggested, "There is no silver bullet that will reduce [the Defense Department's] cyber risk to zero. While the problem cannot be eliminated, it can and must be determinedly managed through the combination of deterrence and improved cyber defense. Deterrence is achieved with offensive cyber, some protected conventional capabilities, and anchored with nuclear weapons."[78]

The report did not suggest that nuclear weapons would be used against all types of cyberattacks—as many commentators and newspapers reported at the time. But it did make it clear that threatening a nuclear response may make sense in the most extreme cases,[79] and that nuclear weapons should—either explicitly or not—"remain the ultimate response and anchor the deterrence ladder."[80] Though there is less publicly available evidence, it seems likely that Russia would adopt a similar position. In fact, according to Stephen Blank, most Russian writing on information warfare appears to suggest that Moscow would respond to a strategic cyberattack in the same way that it would a conventional or nuclear attack—that is, with any strategic weapons in its arsenal, including nuclear weapons.[81] None of the other nuclear weapons states has explicitly ruled out a nuclear response to a major cyberattack. Ultimately, therefore, though cyberattacks and nuclear attacks may be very different, if the impact of a cyberattack (or an attack involving cyber operations) were considered a strategic threat, and perhaps even an existential threat, this would necessarily raise questions about the role of nuclear forces as a deterrent and perhaps as a response.

There is certainly some logic in including nuclear forces as part of a cross-domain cyberdeterrence strategy—especially given the problems of cyber defense. As Elbridge Colby—one of the few to publicly express this view—explains,

If Russia and China knows that we [the United States] would never consider using nuclear weapons in response to even a massive cyberattack, then that gives them a strong incentive to try to exploit that advantage—even implicitly—by using cyber as a way to deter and even coerce the United States and our allies. . . . A military strategy relying only on defenses against cyberattacks is a recipe for failure. This makes sense—the problems of attribution, the costliness of cyber defenses, and affordability of cyber offenses all make the contemporary cyber domain a classic offense-dominant arena, one in which the attacker has huge advantages and which can be very unstable unless the offense dominance is backed by a credible threat of retaliation. . . . A major cyberattack's effect on our conventional or nuclear forces could mean that, without our nuclear forces in equilibrium, the United States might well find itself with no serious riposte to a massive cyber assault.[82]

However, most analysts have questioned the logic of commingling nuclear and cyber weapons in this way.

We can probably think of three main problems of using nuclear weapons to deter cyber operations: (1) That the majority of cyberattacks lack the destructive and existential threat of nuclear weapons, therefore a nuclear response to a cyberattack is unlikely to be either proportional in terms of international law, or very credible in an adversary's eyes, in most cases; (2) cyberdeterrence through punishment in general is difficult to achieve (for the reasons discussed above); and (3) adopting such a policy would provide a new rationale for nuclear proliferation and a further barrier to arms control.[83] Indeed, the former US government officials Steven Andreasen and Richard Clarke have made it clear that seeking to deter cyber operations with nuclear weapons is not only illogical but is also highly likely to be counterproductive. As they argued forcefully back in 2013, shortly after the Defense Science Board report was released,

> Integrating the nuclear threat into the equation means making clear to any potential adversary that the United States is prepared to use nuclear weapons very early in response to major cyberattack—and is maintaining nuclear forces on "prompt launch" status to do so. . . . It's hard to see how this cyber-nuclear action/reaction dynamic would improve US or global security. It's more likely to lead to a new focus by Pentagon planners on generating an expanding list of cyber-related targets and the operational deployment of nuclear forces to strike those targets in minutes.[84]

Andreasen and Clarke continue:

> US cyber vulnerabilities are serious, but equating the impact of nuclear war and cyberwar to justify a new nuclear deterrence policy and excessive Cold War–era nuclear capabilities goes too far. It diminishes the unique threat of national devastation and global extinction that nuclear weapons represent, undermines the credibility of nuclear deterrence by threatening use for lesser contingencies, and reduces the urgency for focused action to lessen nuclear dangers. Excessive rhetoric on the threat of cyberwar from the United States and blurring the distinction between cyber and nuclear attacks just makes progress toward cyber peace more difficult.[85]

However, and notwithstanding these points, it seems highly likely that the relationship between cyber operations, cyberwarfare, and nuclear weapons will become more acute and more important rather than less.

Given the existing nature of the cyber threat, it is probably fair to say that nuclear weapons are not currently a good option for addressing and deterring cyber challenges—and linking the two "domains" would appear to offer few benefits and numerous problems, at least theoretically. However, whether we like it or not, they are of course intrinsically linked, and if the nature of the cyber threat changes and evolves—which it arguably will—then it is certainly not impossible that nuclear weapons could have a role to play in the future, if they ever became a proportionate response to a verified, attributed cyber assault. This would particularly be the case if hackers or malware were detected or discovered within nuclear weapons systems, and especially if an adversary were to carry out a serious attack that caused damage to the critical national infrastructure. It is not impossible that the result could be nuclear war.[86] Moreover, as the next chapter explains, a more likely scenario is that cyber capabilities and weapons would be used alongside other kinetic and possibly even nuclear forces, and this raises other questions about deterring attacks involving cyber operations and not just cyberattacks on their own.

Conclusion: Tailoring Policies to Threats

Despite the considerable differences between the nature and impact of nuclear weapons and cyber operations, and the desire by many to keep them separate, it seems almost inevitable that the two will become increasingly interlinked in both thinking and policy in the future. A nuclear-armed state must now reconsider the relationship between cyberattacks and nuclear weapons, what constitutes an act of war with or including cyber weapons, what type of response would be both proportional and legal, and how this might reconstitute the notions of nuclear deterrence and national security. Although finding the balance between nuclear and conventional deterrence was difficult in the past (i.e., establishing a threshold for nuclear use that appeared both credible and efficacious—and of course notwithstanding a growing nuclear taboo)—the addition of cyber forces appears likely to blur the distinction still further. The introduction of cyber weapons and dynamics into strategic balances—potentially as a force multiplier but also possibly to act as an asymmetric weapon against a more powerful foe—presents a further set of difficult choices that will need to be met by both policymakers and the scholarly community regarding declaratory policy, deterrence, and nuclear strategy. This choice is further complicated by the fact that a successful cyberattack might not involve any human casualties, or potentially any long-term physical destruction— as would most likely be the case with a conventional or nuclear attack.

Although it may not currently make much sense to officially declare that strategic cyberattacks might be met with a nuclear response, any would-be attacker runs the risk of a nuclear response if they carry out such attacks. Deterrence through punishment will have to play a role in managing more serious cyberattacks, and this will be anchored by the threat of a nuclear response from any state armed with such weapons, whether it is declaratory policy or not. As a result, all nuclear-armed states will have to reconsider and reevaluate their deterrence and nuclear use policies in light of growing worldwide cyber capabilities—and though this will certainly not be easy, it cannot simply be ignored. As the next chapter explains, this becomes particularly complicated when cyberattacks are conducted along with other kinetic attacks as part of an unfolding crisis or conflict.

Notes

1. Farnsworth, "Is There a Place for Nuclear Deterrence in Cyberspace?"
2. Glaser, "Deterrence of Cyber Attacks," 1.
3. Ibid. See also Nye, "Deterrence and Dissuasion."
4. Benedict, "Stuxnet."

5. Libicki, *Cyberdeterrence and Cyberwar*, xiii.
6. The heading of this section is adopted from Nye, "From Bombs to Bytes."
7. Cirenza, "Cyberweapons Aren't like Nuclear Weapons."
8. Nye, "Nuclear Lessons," 23.
9. Benedict, "Stuxnet."
10. Owens, Dam, and Lin, *Technology*, 293.
11. Krepinevich, *Cyber Warfare*, iii.
12. Rid, *Cyberwar Will Not Take Place*, 13.
13. Rid and McBurney, "Cyber-Weapons," 7.
14. Cyberattacks against critical infrastructure have become an increasing theme for Hollywood films in recent years. See also the films *Sneakers* (1992) and *Spectre* (2015).
15. Libicki, *Cyberdeterrence and Cyberwar*, 72.
16. Quoted by Nye, "Nuclear Lessons," 22.
17. See Nakashima and Zapotosky, "US Charges Iran-Linked Hackers."
18. Peterson, "Offensive Cyber Weapons," 121.
19. Libicki, *Conquest in Cyberspace*, 40.
20. Cavaiola, Gompert, and Libicki, "Cyber House Rules," 85.
21. See Tannenwald, *Nuclear Taboo*.
22. Krepinevich, *Cyber Warfare*, iii.
23. Adams, "Virtual Defense," 102.
24. See Meyer, "Cyber-Security," 22–27.
25. Riley and Vance, "Cyber Weapons."
26. Meyer, "Cyber-Security," 22; and Kello, "Meaning of the Cyber Revolution," 32.
27. Gartzke and Lindsay, "Thermonuclear Cyberwar," 9.
28. Ibid., 6.
29. Glaser, "Deterrence of Cyber Attacks," 2.
30. Blank, "Can Information Warfare Be Deterred?" 132.
31. Andres and Winterfeld, *Cyber Warfare*, 8; and Fidler, "Relationship between the Biological Weapons Convention and Cybersecurity."
32. Arquilla, "Deterrence after Stuxnet."
33. On this, see Allison, *Nuclear Terrorism*.
34. Kaplan, *Dark Territory*, 5.
35. Zetter, *Countdown to Zero Day*, 374–75.
36. See Brown, "Proposal for an International Conventional," 184.
37. Nye, "Deterrence and Dissuasion," 45.
38. Quoted by Cirenza, "Cyberweapons Aren't like Nuclear Weapons," 5n19.
39. Lynn, "Defending a New Domain," 99–100.
40. Lewis, "Cyber Attacks."
41. Nye, "Deterrence and Dissuasion," 7.
42. Ibid.
43. Morgan, "Applicability of Traditional Deterrence Concepts and Theory to the Cyber Realm," in *Proceedings of a Workshop*, ed. National Research Council, 58–59.
44. Kello, "Meaning of the Cyber Revolution," 17.
45. Ibid., 8.
46. Clark and Landau, "Untangling Attribution," in *Proceedings of a Workshop*, ed. National Research Council, 25.
47. See Markoff, Sanger, and Shanker, "In Digital Combat, US Finds No Easy Deterrent."

48. Glaser, "Deterrence of Cyber Attacks," 4.

49. Liff, "Cyberwar," 421.

50. Libicki, *Cyberdeterrence and Cyberwar*, xvi.

51. Breene, "Who Are the Cyberwar Superpowers?"

52. Quoted by Cirenza, "Cyberweapons Aren't like Nuclear Weapons," 5n19.

53. Glaser, "Deterrence of Cyber Attacks," 3.

54. Blagden, "Anonymity," 1.

55. Glaser, "Deterrence of Cyber Attacks," 3.

56. Cornish et al., *On Cyber Warfare*.

57. Rid and Buchanan, "Attributing Cyber Attacks," 28.

58. Ibid., 28–29.

59. For an interesting discussion of the possibilities of cyberdeterrence, see Rivera, "Achieving Cyberdeterrence and the Ability of Small States to Hold Large States at Risk," in *Architectures in Cyberspace*, ed. Maybaym, Osula, and Lindstrom.

60. Perlroth and Sanger, "North Korea Loses Its Link."

61. See Kramer, "Cyberpower and National Security," in *Cyberpower*, ed. Kramer, Starr, and Wentz, 15.

62. Owens, Dam, and Lin, *Technology*, 5.

63. Gorman and Barnes, "Cyber Combat."

64. Owens, Dam, and Lin, *Technology*, 5.

65. Quoted by Gorman and Barnes, "Cyber Combat."

66. Healey, *Fierce Domain*, 21.

67. Gartzke and Lindsay, "Thermonuclear Cyberwar," 6.

68. Nye, "Deterrence and Dissuasion," 46.

69. Kramer, "Cyberpower and National Security," in *Cyberpower*, ed. Kramer, Starr, and Wentz, 15; and Glaser, "Deterrence of Cyber Attacks," 5.

70. Wirtz, "Cyber Pearl Harbor."

71. Kugler, "Deterrence of Cyber Attacks," in *Cyberpower*, ed. Kramer, Starr, and Wentz, 310.

72. Gartzke and Lindsay, "Thermonuclear Cyberwar," 6.

73. On this see, Kramer, Butler, and Lotrionte, "Cyber, Extended Deterrence, and NATO."

74. Lewis, "Cross-Domain Deterrence," 5.

75. Nye, "Deterrence and Dissuasion," 68.

76. Office of the President of the United States, "International Strategy for Cyberspace."

77. US Department of Defense, "Department of Defense Cyber Strategy."

78. US Department of Defense, Defense Science Board, *Task Force Report: Resilient Military Systems*, 15.

79. Ibid., 32.

80. Ibid., 8.

81. Blank, "Can Information Warfare Be Deterred?" 122.

82. Colby, "Cyberwar."

83. Farnsworth, "Is There a Place for Nuclear Deterrence in Cyberspace?"

84. Andreasen and Clarke, "Cyberwar's Threat Does Not Justify a New Policy."

85. Ibid.

86. Libicki, *Cyberdeterrence and Cyberwar*, 70.

6

> A Cyber-Nuclear Security
> Dilemma, Nuclear Stability,
> and Crisis Management

DURING THE PAST decade or so, threats from hackers and cyberattacks have become an increasingly important and influential component of conflict around the globe, and this trend seems unlikely to abate any time soon. In fact, the wide gamut of threats and dynamics associated with the cyber challenge will probably become more rather than less important in the years ahead, and this will be particularly acute for nuclear-armed states. The new global cyber environment is likely to further muddy and complicate international nuclear relations; introduce different, often-unforeseen dynamics into conflicts and crises; and further distort and obfuscate the "fog of war."[1] This in turn may lead to a greater chance for misperception, misunderstanding, and poor communications and to an inability to signal between nuclear-armed adversaries, and therefore a greater chance of escalation, either unintended or caused by a third party.[2] As such, it is essential to consider how cyber operations, cyber weapons, and new perceptions of risk associated with the broader computerized global security context will manifest between nuclear-armed actors, and unfold as part of future interstate conflict.

The cyber dimension of future warfare may play out in several different ways, but each one will likely have considerable implications for risk assessments, threat perceptions, stability, and consequently for managing future nuclear crises. The impact of cyber operations on global nuclear relations and balances might manifest through some type of conflict that begins primarily in cyberspace, but then escalates to include a kinetic use of force in some hitherto-unforeseen manner, perhaps involving the use of cyber capabilities directly against nuclear weapons and associated systems. It might involve a conflict that begins in the conventional military domain and then escalates to include cyberattacks on civilian infrastructure—or vice versa. Or it might be from a conflict that includes both cyber and kinetic operations used together as force multipliers at the start—perhaps the most likely—but that also might escalate to the nuclear level. Each of these scenarios will have implications for strategic thinking and policy, where perceptions and fears—along with growing uncertainties and suspicions about an opponent's possible use of cyber weapons against critical systems, including nuclear systems—will have widespread and numerous implications for international nuclear relations.

The cyber challenge may be viewed by some as a distinct and separate "domain" from other forms of military power (at least theoretically), and thus as fundamentally different from nuclear weapons. But cyber operations will almost certainly become intertwined with other military spheres, environments, and dynamics in future conflict, and *will* therefore play a role in nuclear-related decisions and strategic balances. As such, an increased role for cyber operations, weapons, interference, and attacks—either on their own or, more likely, in concert with the use of traditional kinetic military force—is likely to have implications for the nature of warfare, strategic stability, and particularly future crisis management between nuclear-armed actors. In all probability, this will introduce a range of new destabilizing and unhelpful factors to what is already a complicated and delicate endeavor. The threat of direct attacks or indirect interference with nuclear systems, combined with the increased likelihood that cyber capabilities could lead to escalation in future crises, will therefore have implications for the role and perceived utility of nuclear forces, relations, perceptions, and risks, along with having potential implications for force multiplication. As Greg Austin points out, this might also "destabilize pre-existing agreements that constrain nuclear weapons deployment and possible use."[3]

In order to examine and analyze the impact of this burgeoning cyber context and the concurrent growth of cyber threats in international nuclear relations, this chapter proceeds in three sections: The first explains why cyberattacks will form a key component of future conflict, why the notion of cyberwarfare may represent a problematic concept, and why we might best characterize the challenge as future warfare involving cyber operations. The second section looks at the new challenges posed for crisis management and escalation (both within the military domain and from military to civilian domains and vice versa) and how the threat or use of cyberattacks might require a rethinking of established nuclear concepts, such as the escalation ladder and signaling. The third section focuses on how cyber threats and the potential use of cyberattack capabilities directly against nuclear systems might make an impact on strategic stability, arms control, and established nuclear notions such as mutually assured destruction between nuclear-armed powers.

Cyberattacks as a Key Component of Future Conflict

Future conflict between nuclear-armed adversaries will almost certainly include cyber operations, cyberattacks, and the use of digital weapons. It will also likely take place in an ever more complex digitized domestic and international security environment. As the documents leaked in 2013 by a former US government contractor, Edward Snowden, suggest, the United States military believes unequivocally that the next major conflict will involve widespread cyberattacks and possibly even take place in cyberspace.[4] And the same is likely to be true for other leading nuclear powers. Indeed, the United States, Russia, China, the United Kingdom, and other major nation-states are all developing doctrines for the use of cyber weapons in future conflicts, and are becoming increasingly explicit about the importance of cyber capabilities for military operations.[5] But what is far less clear is the shape that this cyber–military–nuclear interaction is likely to take. This is true both for the capabilities or weapons that might be deployed—or that an adversary fears could be used against them—and for the targets and intentions that would underpin their use. This also holds true for the rather ambiguous notion of "cyberwarfare"—a term that is often used by officials but is far less often elucidated. Consequently, it is important to unpack and begin to consider how cyber capabilities are likely to be used and become entangled in future conflicts between nuclear-armed actors.

Although the age of cyberattacks and cyberwarfare remains to some extent in its infancy, we have already seen how cyber capabilities and weapons might be used before or during a conflict. The United States is arguably the most developed country in this regard. As has been noted in previous chapters, there were rumors that cyberattacks had been considered and possibly used by the United States against Iraq in the Persian Gulf War of 1991;[6] were used in 1999 against Serbia during the Kosovo War;[7] were planned but not carried out as part of the Second Gulf War in 2003;[8] more recently, were conducted against Libya and North Korea;[9] and were also used in the now-well-known attacks on Iran in the 2000s. To give an idea of the importance of cyber operations for the US military, the multi-billion-dollar US Cyber Command was established in 2009 and now employs over 5,000 staff.[10] The United States is also allegedly seeking cyber weapons "strong enough for deterrence"[11] and has developed a formal structure of cyber capabilities, some of which are significant enough to require presidential approval before use.[12] These might even include cyber capabilities that could be used to attack nuclear weapons systems. In fact, in 2012, the *Washington Times* reported that Gen. C. Robert Kehler, the chief of the US Strategic Command, when "asked about the use of offensive cyberwarfare attacks on nuclear control systems," replied that "we need to be able to conduct offensive operations through cyberspace, just as we conduct offensive operations through other domains."[13]

However, Russia and China may not be far behind. Russia is accused of using cyber operations—specifically, distributed denial-of-service attacks against Estonia in 2007;[14] against the Georgian government and its communications infrastructure in 2008 (which Jeffrey Carr later described as "a perfect example of a combined kinetic and cyber operation"[15]); and against Ukraine in both 2015 and 2016,[16] both of which purportedly interrupted the Ukrainian power grid.[17] Some analysts even believe that Russia is way ahead of the United States in electronic warfare and cyber capabilities,[18] particularly in developing a broader Russian doctrine of "hybrid warfare."[19] China has been developing thinking on the use of cyber and information warfare capabilities for more than two decades. Indeed, the use of information technology and network-centric warfare by the United States and its allies in the 1991 Gulf War came as a wake-up call,[20] and would lead to the publication of *Unrestricted Warfare* by the Chinese People's Liberation Army colonels Qiao Liang and Wang Xiangsui in 1999—a blueprint for modern Chinese cyber operations.[21] China has also been very clear that cyber capabilities will be employed in any future conflict, likely against the United States.[22]

Israel is widely believed to have played a central role in Operation Olympic Games against Iran in the 2000s (and may have been the reason for its discovery[23]). Iran—which purportedly was behind the Saudi Aramco attacks in August 2012[24]—is also thought to have considered or even attempted to carry out cyberattacks against the United States and other countries, notably, on a dam in New York State in 2013.[25] North Korea may have been behind the "Sony hack" of 2014,[26] and has purportedly also conducted a range of other attacks against the United States and South Korea.[27] Pyongyang clearly sees considerable asymmetrical value in cyber capabilities. Elsewhere, at a 2014 summit in Wales, NATO classified cyberattacks as a separate domain of warfare that will be subject to its Article V declaration of collective defense.[28] Although a formal NATO policy on cyberdeterrence has yet to be agreed on, and it remains unclear how this threshold will be measured, the Wales declaration demonstrates how seriously the alliance takes the threat of cyberattacks against its members. The effect has been to create a sense of strategic ambiguity akin to that pertaining to nuclear weapons.[29] The United Kingdom formally declared that it was developing offensive cyber weapons in 2013, and though less explicit, it should be assumed that other nuclear powers—India, Pakistan, and France—will also be developing and perhaps deploying sophisticated cyber capabilities.[30]

This suggests that we should expect cyber operations in some capacity to play a part in all future conflicts between nuclear-armed states, at whatever level. It also suggests that nuclear-armed states should assume that an adversary will act in unpredictable ways and not necessarily play by the rules as they seek the perceived (often asymmetric) advantages many believe are offered by cyber operations.[31] In fact, as was discussed earlier in the book, a perceived requirement for "active defense"—that is, breaking into a possible adversary's systems before a conflict has begun to ensure access if and when it does—means that many of these operations might have already taken place. This approach can look a lot like cyber preemption, and will do little to aid stability and trust.[32]

What is less clear, however, is the shape that future cyber conflicts, conflicts involving cyberattacks, or fighting in a computerized global security environment will take. This uncertainty is driven in part by (1) the problems of viewing cyber capabilities as weapons and (2) the problematic concept of cyberwarfare itself. First, it is difficult to think of most cyber operations as involving weapons in the conventional sense. This is because most operations in cyberspace—such as espionage, hacking, and crime—fall well below what one might consider a traditional "use of force." Only those attacks that cause physical damage and harm, or even death (directly or indirectly)—and akin to conventional munitions—might be thought of as involving weapons.[33] Although such capabilities are conceivable, it is unclear that cyber weapons alone could constitute warfare, and, unless used alongside kinetic conventional munitions, are unlikely to be decisive.[34] This, in turn, has implications for how we might understand the notion of cyberwarfare more broadly. As Thomas Rid and Peter McBurney explain, "Cyberwar is a highly problematic, even a dangerous concept. An act of war must be instrumental, political, and potentially lethal, whether in cyberspace or not. No stand-alone cyber offense on record meets these criteria."[35]

To be considered as warfare, cyber operations would theoretically need to have some sort of physical impact—on people, systems, or infrastructure—similar to that posed by conventional weapons.[36] In part because of this, Maj. Gen. Jonathan Shaw, commander of the UK Ministry of Defence's Cyber Policy and Plans Team, has even gone as far as to suggest that "the word 'war' has lost all its meaning; it's now only relevant in political theory, not as an operational term."[37] That said, it is possible to envisage a use of cyber capabilities that does not meet a traditional definition of war but nevertheless justifies a proportionate noncyber response.[38] As the former senior legal counsel for the US Cyber Command, Gary Browne, points out, it is also possible to foresee the use of cyber capabilities being *misinterpreted* as acts of war.[39] Overall, however, it is difficult to conceive of cyberwarfare—or, at least, of a future conflict—where the primary, and perhaps only, theater of battle is cyberspace.

In part because of this, it seems unlikely that future cyber conflicts will remain isolated in the cyber domain or that cyber operations will be used remotely from other forms of military force.[40] This is particularly the case the more significant a crisis or conflict becomes. Instead, we should probably expect cyber capabilities to be used alongside other kinetic military forces as part of cross-domain operations. In the words of James Lewis, "Pure cyber war—'keyboard versus keyboard' or 'geek versus geek'—is unlikely. . . . No one would plan to fight using only cyber weapons."[41] Or, as Erik Gartzke puts it, "Notions that cyberattacks will themselves prove pivotal in future war are reminiscent of World War I artillery barrages that cleared enemy trenches but still required the infantry and other arms to achieve a breakout."[42] What seems most likely, therefore, are future conflicts where cyber operations are augmented by kinetic and other military capabilities—or *war that involves cyber* rather than *cyberwar*. For example, cyber capabilities might be employed to interfere with weapons and support systems, disrupt communications and early warning systems, or to flood the nuclear information space with misleading information. All this would help facilitate traditional conventional (and perhaps even nuclear) operations.[43] Cyber operations might also be particularly suited for attacks on likely less-well-protected critical national infrastructures, such as those for banking, transportation, and power systems. These attacks may well augment or even precede military operations.

This also suggests that cyber capabilities are arguably best suited for early use in any future conflict—indeed, they may be perfect "opening salvos," according to James Johnson[44]—increasing uncertainty and doubt, and perhaps also exacerbating the fog of war, as discussed above.[45] The idea here would be to retard or destroy the military systems on which an adversary relies to complete its military mission, or to cause mass disruption and widespread confusion by targeting critical national infrastructure. This makes the use of cyber capabilities perfect for a surprise attack and for use right at the start of any military conflict.[46] Indeed, the United States, Russia, and China all appear to be conceptualizing cyber capabilities in this way, despite the difficulties of calibration and execution.[47]

Cyber capabilities are therefore likely to be used as a precursor to kinetic conventional operations, and as part of future crises, conflict, of warfare between nuclear armed opponents. This could also include attacks (or at least the perception that attacks might be carried out) on command and control systems, the manipulation of important data, insider attacks, denial of service, misinformation and disinformation, and attacks on communications networks in all domains.[48] The objective of these operations will be to plant seeds of doubt in an adversary's mind about the veracity of its systems and the data that they contain, and also to interfere with and spoof early warning sensors and guidance and targeting systems, and even to keep stop-weapons systems from working altogether.[49] Cyber capabilities and cyberattacks are therefore most likely to be used alongside other military tools and as a force multiplier, as a facilitator, and perhaps even as a method of psychological warfare rather than as a weapon in its own right at both the strategic and tactical levels.

As such, it seems doubtful that there will be a cyberwar where nation-states fight each other on a digital battleground akin to some futuristic Hollywood science fiction movie, at least not in the near future. Instead, there will be a situation where cyber tactics, operations, and capabilities can and will be used in all future conflicts alongside—and in support of—kinetic weapons. All wars between advanced nations will also therefore be fought in a cyber context, where all combatants are likely to be vulnerable to enemy attacks against their sensitive computer systems and infrastructure (both military and civilian). As is discussed below, this may create a new set of escalatory pressures and produce a new suite of complications for nuclear crisis management and arms control.

Escalation, Signaling, and Nuclear Crisis Management

What, then, might this cyber-enabled conflict, or warfare involving cyber operations, look like? And how might these pressures involve thinking about nuclear weapons? The first thing to note is that even if nuclear systems are not targeted directly or are successfully guarded against malicious hackers, it seems very likely that the use—or even the threat of use—of cyber capabilities against an opponent during a crisis will raise tensions, concerns, and perceived vulnerabilities, and that this will make nuclear crisis resolution more complicated and perhaps more dangerous.[50] The second thing to note is that the use of cyber capabilities is likely to obfuscate and complicate the escalation ladder, and possibly lead to an inadvertent deepening of a crisis, perhaps even up to the nuclear level. It is likely to do this in different ways from those theorized in the past, and probably at a much greater speed. It could also, for example, include attacks in both civilian and military domains. Taken together, new cyber dynamics—both operations and context—might even necessitate a rethinking of these established nuclear concepts altogether.

Perhaps the most important thing to note about cyber operations in future crises and warfare is that they are likely to be offense-dominant. That is, in cyberspace the advantage will be held by the attackers rather than the defenders. Although this forecast is challenged by some, and is contingent on several variables—particularly the target and intention of the attack—it does have rather significant implications for the broader security dilemma, and especially for strategic stability.[51] Along with creating pressures for arms racing, this also makes cyber capabilities more likely to be employed early in a crisis, particularly given the policy of active defense mentioned above.[52] The result could potentially be greater insecurity for all, and possibly unintended, and in the worst-case scenario perhaps even unmanageable escalation. By way of an example, an Israeli war game conducted in 2013 demonstrated how the use and threat of cyberattacks might very quickly escalate a crisis, in this case bringing the United States and Russia to the brink of conflict in a possible Middle East war.[53] Such conflicts might begin and play out in a number of different ways, but all will likely create new pressures for crisis management.

First, during a crisis hackers could potentially disrupt or destroy communications channels, making it difficult to manage forces, including nuclear forces, and reducing commanders' confidence in their weapons systems and the ability of officials to communicate. Even a relatively small-scale attack could create considerable doubt about the security and reliability of communications, and particularly about the veracity of the information flowing from their computers.[54] Moreover, despite often-held beliefs to the contrary, many military communications systems—including even some used for nuclear command and control—utilize commercial infrastructure or are based on networks that could be vulnerable to an attack or disruption.[55] It must therefore be assumed that the linkages required for nuclear second-strike capabilities could also be unreliable, and possibly vulnerable to an opponents cyber operations.[56] Aggressors might also employ distributed denial-of-service attacks to prevent communication, hamper battle management systems, magnify confusion, and make it more difficult to identify what is happening and perhaps to conduct a coordinated response. Such attacks might be particularly acute for nuclear dyads that are in close geographical proximity—and therefore face limited decision-making time—such as India and Pakistan.[57]

Second, the use of cyberattack capabilities might inadvertently escalate a crisis—very much building on the model of "inadvertent nuclear escalation" developed by Barry Posen back in the early 1990s.[58] This might be due either to deliberate interference from a third-party actor—such as a terrorist group—or from an unauthorized insider, or by another state seeking to deepen the crisis through false flag operations (that is, operations conducted to look like they were carried out by someone else). Alternatively, it might involve accidentally targeting the wrong systems. This risk is amplified considerably in the cyber context because it is increasingly difficult to know which computer systems support which weapons and operations. For example, as Lawrence Cavaiola and his colleagues explain, "an attack [by the United States] on a Chinese system that is used to increase the readiness of tactical forces might also inadvertently degrade the readiness of Chinese strategic nuclear forces, with grave risks of misinterpretation and escalation, up to and including launch on warning."[59] Thus, a cyberattack on computer systems thought to control conventional weapons might be mistaken (and interpreted) as a direct attack on an adversary's ability to use its nuclear forces. Moreover, even if enemy cyberattacks are detected and mitigated, this could still lead to a "spiral of mistrust" and worst-case scenario thinking.[60]

Third, cyberattacks might reduce the ability to signal, causing flawed images of intentions and capabilities, or be used to "spoof early warning systems"—again, a particular concern given the possibility of false flag cyber interference by third parties. It is perfectly possible that the ability to clearly signal intentions could be one of the biggest challenges created by cyber operations for nuclear crisis management. The concern here is twofold. First, the cyber context will make communicating with an adversary (and your own forces) much more complicated. Second, it is far from clear that cyberattacks themselves offer a very useful way of signaling, and may in fact be worse than traditional methods. As Erik Gartzke and Jon Lindsay explain, this is because cyber operations "are complex, esoteric, and hard for commanders and policymakers to understand."[61] Previous methods of signaling—such as seeking to indicate intentions or red lines to an adversary through limited conventional action, already a complicated and delicate endeavor—will probably be even more difficult to implement when cyberattacks are also involved.[62] Moreover, given the difficulties of attribution—particularly when time is short, decision makers are under pressure, and third-party cyber activities abound—it may not be straightforward to ascertain when a conflict has actually stopped.[63] In this way, cyber operations are likely to further complicate and "muddy" signaling between adversaries during a crisis or conflict, either deliberately or inadvertently.[64] This would also, therefore, make the functioning of leadership far more complicated in any future nuclear crisis too.

Fourth, the use of cyberattacks might reduce the search for viable alternatives, thereby compressing—or at least muddying—the escalation ladder, particularly the steps between conventional and nuclear use. Once hostilities begin, leaders may not feel confident that the information they are receiving is genuine; the same might also be true for commanders in the field. Each decision would be underpinned by an uneasiness about the veracity of the information and data being used, possibly leading to different types of calculations and actions.[65] In addition to this, leaders would fear that cyber operations would be used early in a crisis to disable or retard their most important weapons systems and to prevent them from being used against an adversary. Unfortunately, this might create a spiral effect, and more pressure to "use them or lose them," when it comes to a state's most important military capabilities.[66]

In a worst-case scenario, these concerns might increase perceived time pressures to act or respond, and the option to act preemptively. Stephen Cimbala has even gone as far as to warn that a nuclear-armed state bombarded with cyberattacks—particularly on its command, control, communications, and early warning networks—might feel so vulnerable that it would opt for preemption, in the worst case with nuclear weapons.[67] This exacerbates the feeling that cyber operations could undermine the ability to threaten retaliation, and therefore to strike second, because cyber capabilities appear to augment conventional first-strike possibilities against key enemy systems and forces, including their nuclear weapons.[68] Taken together, these dynamics raise the likelihood of unintended and potentially uncontrollable escalation and make the management of such crises more complicated and dangerous.[69]

Perhaps the most likely future cyber-nuclear security dilemma is between the United States and China in the Asia-Pacific region, where both nations have been rather open and explicit about the importance of cyber capabilities and attacks on information systems in a future conflict.[70] The US Air-Sea Battle concept makes it very clear that Chinese kill-chain networks and other key types of digital military infrastructure will be targeted with cyberattacks in the event of a conflict.[71] The emerging US Third Offset Strategy, which will ostensibly replace Air-Sea Battle, appears to take this even further.[72] At the same time, the Chinese planners realize how important—if not fundamental—networks, communications links, and computer systems are to the United States' ability to carry out operations in the Western Pacific, and would almost certainly conduct cyber operations of their own against US forces.[73] This could have a considerable impact on the United States' ability to wage war. In fact, some analysts believe that China has acquired the capacity to asymmetrically challenge US conventional military superiority by utilizing operations in cyberspace.[74] As a result, the cyber operations conducted at the beginning of any future United States–China crisis could well be central to its conclusion. This also suggests that that a low-key, conventional conflict or skirmish could quickly escalate to the strategic level once cyber operations began.

But there is also a risk—particularly in China—that nuclear command and control and associated systems could be targeted or compromised, at least partly, through cyber means. This could well happen accidentally, and will become increasingly possible as China becomes more vulnerable as a result of its enhanced reliance on computer networks for its military operations.[75] This in turn is likely to have implications for China's No First Use nuclear posture, particularly when cyber operations are combined with US missile defense plans and advanced conventional strike capabilities.[76] In fact, the nature of a possible United States–China conflict involving the use of cyberattacks has already been explored in the futuristic novel *Ghost Fleet*—although in this case nuclear weapons systems were left unattacked.[77]

The second potential cyber-nuclear security dilemma, especially given their recent and obvious use of cyber capabilities, is likely to be between the United States, its NATO allies, and Russia.[78] As part of its Wales summit in September 2014, NATO clearly indicated that it sees cyberattacks as a major challenge and concern, and that cyber threats will now be subject to Article V of the Atlantic Charter. That is, the commitment to come to the defense of any member if it is attacked. As Sydney Freedberg put it, "NATO is now taking cyber threats as seriously as the Russian tanks and nuclear weapons it was created to deter."[79] A few months later, in November 2014, NATO held its largest-ever cyber war game just outside the city of Tartu in Estonia. A location and exercise that gave the impression that the exercise was principally about the possible threat from Russia, particularly given that it occurred in the wake of the crisis in Ukraine.[80] Although the exact threshold at which a cyberattack might trigger Article V remains unclear,[81] current NATO policy suggests that both cyber and conventional attacks that cause considerable destruction will be understood and treated in the same manner.[82] It is important to remember that NATO's deterrence thinking—and, for that matter, Russia's deterrence policy—remains anchored by nuclear weapons, and that a significant number of these weapons remain at a status of high alert.[83]

Above all, the main concern is that in the new cyber-nuclear environment, crises are unlikely to unfold in a uniform or predictable manner, and not necessarily in ways that they did, or at least were expected to, in the past. Although the increasing importance of cyber dynamics in strategic nuclear relationships does not necessarily mean that the next crisis will become unmanageable and lead directly to disaster, it clearly will make a safe and peaceful resolution more complicated. Thus, the use of cyber capabilities—or even the perception that cyberattacks could be employed against key systems and networks, and the broader computerized strategic environment—has myriad implications for how states manage a crisis, and ultimately will place extra pressures on nuclear strategy and thinking.

Strategic Stability, Arms Control, and Mutually *Un*assured Destruction

There is also a growing concern that states might directly target each other's nuclear weapons and associated nuclear command and control systems with cyberattacks. Although the idea—and perhaps the possibility—of hacking into an adversary's nuclear weapons systems and stopping them from working has been around for decades, the risk has become far more pronounced and far more "real" in the past few years. This is partly because of the exponential increase in cyber operations, and the growing public awareness of the risks that this poses. But it is also due to the revelation of sophisticated attacks such as Stuxnet, which have demonstrated the potential of what might be achieved using cyber capabilities. Again, the threat is diverse; it could involve direct attacks on weapons and delivery systems; or interference with various aspects of the nuclear command and control infrastructure, such as the ability to communicate; or attacks on early warning systems and other sensors. In extremis, nuclear weapons systems might conceivably be prevented from working, thus undermining the credibility of retaliatory deterrence postures.

Directly targeting nuclear command and control systems with cyber operations is clearly a move fraught with danger and represents the most serious cyber-nuclear risk. But there is evidence that one state (the United States) has begun to integrate such operations into its thinking and planning, and it is perfectly possible that others will follow suit. Given the nature of cyber operations—particularly, the fact that they are intangible, highly secretive, and difficult to verify—even the threat that certain states *could* develop, let alone carry out, such attacks is likely to be highly destabilizing. The creation of a norm in this regard is very troubling, and may well have widespread negative connotations. Indeed, it could potentially have considerable implications for strategic stability, deterrence based on a secure second-strike nuclear capability, and confidence in the efficacy of nuclear weapons systems more broadly. As a result, there is a perception that strategic nuclear stability is increasingly at risk and that the norms that underpin global nuclear order—especially mutually assured destruction (MAD)—may even need rethinking, as a result of developments in the cyber threat.[84]

The gravest concern in this regard is the inclusion of cyberattack capabilities as part of the US global strike concept—that is, the desire to be able to strike targets (e.g., a nuclear-armed missile being readied to fire) anywhere in the world at very short notice with whatever weapons are best suited for the task. Or, as Gen. James Cartwright, the former head of the US Strategic Command, puts it, this means the ability to hit targets anywhere in the world with conventional weapons in 30 minutes, and with cyber weapons in 300 milliseconds.[85] Although the global strike concept has been around for more than a decade, it is also increasingly becoming merged as part of a new US "full-spectrum missile defense" plan concept.[86] As Brian McKeon, the principal US undersecretary of defense for policy, testified to the US Congress in April 2016, "We need to develop a wider range of tools and that includes the efforts under way to address such threats before they are launched, or 'left of launch.' The development of left-of-launch capabilities will provide US decision makers additional tools and opportunities to defeat missiles. This will in turn reduce the burden on our 'right-of-launch' ballistic missile defense capabilities. Taken together, left-of-launch and right-of-launch will lead to more effective and resilient capabilities to defeat adversary ballistic missile threats."[87]

The idea appears to be to augment kinetic missile interceptors with new digital, "left-of-launch" information and cyber weapons as part of a revamped global prompt strike capability.[88] These new military capabilities are principally aimed at so-called rogue states, most notably North Korea and Iran. Indeed, revelations in 2017 suggested that the United States may have been employing a highly sophisticated suite of cyber operations against North Korea's nuclear and missile program for several years.[89] Some have even suggested that these operations have been responsible for missile test failures and other problems experienced by the North Korean military[90] (although this remains the subject of some debate[91]). It is also possible that South Korea has been developing "Stuxnet-like" cyberattack capabilities to use against the North's nuclear weapons infrastructure, and to prevent or at least delay any possible future nuclear launch.[92] Although there is clearly a marked difference between conducting cyberattacks against rogue states with nascent nuclear capabilities, and attacks against nuclear peer-competitors, this will almost certainly create concern for all nuclear-armed states.[93] Moreover, it is highly likely that other states have—or are at least contemplating—similar cyber tools and programs that could be used against the nuclear weapons systems of competitors and potential adversaries.

The problem for the United States, of course, is that it is very difficult to convince other states (in this case, Russia and China) that such capabilities will not—or could not—also be used against them, given the intangible, secretive, and unverifiable nature of cyberattack capabilities and weapons. There is also a growing risk that simply talking openly about such plans creates significant uncertainty and a highly destabilizing norm.[94] Indeed, evidence suggests that Russian planners may now see cyberattacks on their nuclear weapons systems as one of the greatest threats at the strategic level[95]—and this is particularly acute given recent problems with Russian nuclear early warning systems.[96] China is unlikely to view an expanded US missile defense plan with any great enthusiasm either. In fact, Richard Danzig has even gone so far as to suggest that in light of these developments, we may need to rethink certain parts of the global nuclear weapons edifice, and particularly reassess the supposed certainties of MAD.[97] Danzig suggests that the viability and sanctity of second-strike retaliatory nuclear forces could be questioned where states rely heavily on computers and complex systems for warning, communications, and operations—given the possibility that they could be interfered with.[98] Ultimately, the emergence of cyber risks to nuclear systems could mean that a world of MAD is replaced by a world of mutually unassured destruction, or MUD.[99] Although cyber-enabled MUD may be some distance away, growing perceptions of risk and worst-case scenario thinking are unlikely to aid international nuclear relations, and will probably create new problems and pressures to be dealt with. As such, it seems almost inevitable that nuclear-armed states will plan for the worst when it comes to a future conflict that involves cyber operations against their most sensitive systems.

This risk may play out in two ways. First, such attacks might be designed primarily as a warning shot—this is probably the case with the purported US cyberattacks against North Korea. Second, and far more worryingly, they might be used as a precursor to retard systems before conducting a strategic attack. Although it is unlikely that any state—at least for the time being—would feel sufficiently confident that its use of cyberattacks had fully disabled an adversary's nuclear command and control systems "to the point at which they can act with impunity," or for that matter be willing to carry out such a potentially catastrophic move in anything but the most extreme circumstances, the perception that systems could be compromised or undermined is raising the perceived level of risk.[100] The net result is that the development of cyber weapons that could be used against nuclear systems is creating a plethora of new challenges for the safe, secure, and reliable management of nuclear weapons for all nuclear-armed actors—including the United States.[101]

The potential implications of this increasing risk of cyber disablement are considerable. First, it reintroduces the possibility of carrying out preemptive (and perhaps even nonnuclear) strikes against an adversary's nuclear weapons and associated command and control systems.[102] Although this is perhaps most obvious for the United States–Russia relationship, it may become particularly acute or attractive for newer nuclear powers or those with a small or underdeveloped nuclear force or command structure. According to Greg Austin and Pavel Sharikov, "It is not unreasonable to posit that if military technology advances have made nuclear command and control systems of some states more vulnerable, then at least hypothetically, that may increase the propensity to resort to a first strike of some kind. . . . This incentive may be higher for states or nonstate actors with only a small number of nuclear weapons."[103]

Second, this clearly has implications for notions of MAD, the established process of nuclear deterrence by punishment (rather than denial), and therefore for future nuclear force structure, posture, and planning. Third, it will almost certainly have an impact on and undermine the likelihood of any future nuclear arms control or reductions agreement, and may even drive renewed vertical and horizontal proliferation. This is because though previous nuclear reductions can and should be seen as a positive development, any further reductions may increase the possible influence and significance of cyber threats. The move toward "minimum" nuclear deterrent postures, for example, might therefore compromise nuclear flexibility and the certainty that nuclear weapons can always be used if required in the face of enemy cyber operations.[104] Fourth, and finally, keeping nuclear weapons on high alert and/or tightly coupled with warning systems increases the risks of third-party interference, potentially by employing cyber capabilities, that could result in accidental, mistaken, or unauthorized nuclear use.[105]

Taken together, the notion that cyber weapons might be used directly against nuclear forces to interfere with, disrupt, or disable them is a serious and growing counterforce risk—not to mention another unhelpful, and largely incalculable, source of escalatory pressure. These risks seem set to increase markedly during a crisis, and particularly if cyber capabilities were to be used alongside other advanced conventional weaponry in a future strategic digital battlespace. As the Global Zero Commission on Nuclear Risk Reduction points out, we should assume that "at the brink of conflict, nuclear command and warning networks around the world may be besieged by electronic intruders whose onslaught degrades the coherence and rationality of nuclear decision making."[106]

The result might well be a gradual descent into a new era of "aggravated" nuclear instability, where it could become increasingly difficult to wait out a crisis or even an attack if a state fears that its second strike capability has been disabled by an adversary's cyber operations. It may also increase pressures to use all available nuclear forces in one go rather than keeping some back.[107] This could mean that nuclear-armed states acquire an increasingly "itchy keyboard finger," as Richard Clarke and Robert Knake put it, if they believe that an adversary has already hacked into their nuclear weapons infrastructure, implanted logic bombs, corrupted data, or is in a position to stop these systems—and broader war-fighting capabilities—from working as planned.[108]

Conclusion: Toward a Cyber-Nuclear Security Dilemma?

Nuclear weapons and cyber threats are becoming increasingly commingled in security thinking, theory, and reality, but this does not mean that we should be deliberately courting this linkage.[109] The pressures, vulnerabilities, and uncertainties stemming from the emerging cyber-nuclear context seem likely to significantly complicate and obfuscate decision making, both within and between nuclear-armed powers that are also known to possess cyberattack capabilities. The "use them or lose them" notion is particularly germane in this regard, given the likelihood that cyber capabilities and weapons will probably need to be used at the start of any conflict—or even before hostilities begin—and particularly perhaps by those seeking advantage against a more powerful opponent.

Because any future crisis is likely to include cyber operations and weapons in some capacity, nuclear-armed states must assume that their key national security infrastructure and possibly nuclear weapons and support systems would by targeted (either deliberately or inadvertently)—if not necessarily compromised—as part of the conflict. Although the intention behind these attacks might vary between those seeking to raise doubts about the efficacy of an adversary's systems (a dangerous game of psychological warfare) and attacks that actually compromise them so they do not work and in order to limit damage, the interpretation is likely to be the same.[110] The result may be a growing incentive for nuclear-armed states to adapt nuclear policy away from notions of deterrence by retaliation—which may or may not be assured any longer—in favor of preemptive deterrence based on denial. This in turn could signal a sea change in nuclear strategy and the axioms that govern global nuclear order. This may well necessitate a reassessment of the sanctity of nuclear norms such as MAD and deterrence based on retaliation.[111] Moves to bolster deterrence frameworks, pursue cyber arms control, or agree to certain prohibitive conventions may help to ease this, but such mechanisms and agreements will be very difficult to achieve and may not even be possible in any truly meaningful sense.

Notes

1. Farwell and Rohozinski, "New Reality of Cyber War," 114.
2. Posen, *Inadvertent Escalation*, 22–23.
3. Austin, "Costs of American Cyber Superiority."
4. Kulikova, "Is a Cyber Arms Race between the US and Russia Possible?"
5. See, e.g., Shinkman, "American Is Losing the Cyber War."
6. Clarke and Knake, *Cyber War*, 8–9.
7. See Kaplan, *Dark Territory*, 110–18.
8. Markoff and Shanker, "Halted '03 Iraq Plan Illustrates US Fear of Cyberwar Risk."
9. For Libya, see Schmitt and Shanker, "US Debated Cyberwarfare." For North Korea, see Sanger and Broad, "Trump Inherits a Secret Cyberwar against North Korean Missiles."
10. Kaplan, *Dark Territory*, 4.
11. Hennign and Bennett, "Pentagon Seeks Cyberweapons."
12. See Nakashima, "List of Cyber-Weapons Developed by Pentagon."
13. Quoted by Austin and Sharikov, "Preemption Is Victory," 4.
14. For a good overview of the Estonia attacks, see Davis, "Hackers Take Down the Most Wired Country in Europe."
15. Quoted by Matthews, "Russia's Greatest Weapon May Be Its Hackers."
16. See Geers, *Cyber War in Perspective*.
17. See Zetter, "Inside the Cunning, Unprecedented Hack of Ukraine's Power Grid."
18. *SC Magazine*, "Russia Overtaking US in Cyber-Warfare Capabilities."
19. See, e.g., Lanoszka, "Russian Hybrid Warfare."
20. McConnell, "Cyberwar Is the New Atomic Age," 77.
21. See Liang and Ziangsui, *Unrestricted Warfare*.
22. See Gompert and Libicki, "Cyber Warfare and Sino-American Crisis Instability."
23. Melman, "Exclusive: Israel's Rash Behavior Blew Operation to Sabotage Iran's Computers."
24. See Bronk and Tikk-Ringas, "Cyber Attack on Saudi Aramco."
25. Thompson, "Iranian Cyber Attack on New York Dam Shows Future of War."
26. *New York Times*, "Deterring Cyber Attacks from North Korea."
27. Szoldra, "North Korea Suspected in Hack of South Korea's Cyber Command."
28. See Freedberg, "NATO Hews to Strategic Ambiguity."
29. Ashford, "NATO to Adopt New Cyber Defence Policy."

30. James Blitz, "UK Becomes First State to Admit to Offensive Cyber Attack Capability."

31. US Department of Defense, Defense Science Board, *Task Force Report: Resilient Military Systems*, 5.

32. Kaplan, *Dark Territory*, 180.

33. Rid and McBurney, "Cyber-Weapons," 186.

34. Gompert and Libicki, "Cyber Warfare and Sino-American Crisis Instability," 12.

35. Rid and McBurney, "Cyber-Weapons," 7.

36. McGraw, "Cyber War Is Inevitable," 112.

37. Elwell, "MI5 Boss Reveals 'Astonishing' Number of Cyber Attack Secrets."

38. Kello, "Meaning of the Cyber Revolution," 26.

39. Quoted by Zetter, *Countdown to Zero Day*, 405.

40. Gartzke, "Myth of Cyberwar," 42.

41. Lewis, "Cyber Attacks."

42. Ibid., 57.

43. Owens, Dam, and Lin, *Technology*, 2.

44. Correspondence with James Johnson.

45. Lewis, "Cyber Attacks."

46. Libicki, *Cyberdeterrence and Cyberwar*, 143.

47. Correspondence with James Johnson.

48. US Department of Defense, Defense Science Board, *Task Force Report: Resilient Military Systems*, 5.

49. Ewing, "Pentagon's New Cyber Attack Plan."

50. Cimbala, *Nuclear Weapons in the Information Age*, 205.

51. See Gartzke and Lindsay, "Weaving Tangled Webs."

52. Kello, "Meaning of the Cyber Revolution," 32.

53. Opall-Rome, "Israeli Cyber Game Drags US, Russia to Brink of Mideast War."

54. Singer and Friedman, *Cybersecurity and Cyberwar*, 129.

55. See Blair, "Pre-Planned Operations," in *Managing Nuclear Operations*, ed. Carter, Steinbruner, and Zraket, 140.

56. Brewer and Bracken, "Some Missing Pieces," 463.

57. Fritz, "Hacking Nuclear Command and Control."

58. See Posen, *Inadvertent Escalation*.

59. Cavaiola, Gompert, and Libicki, "Cyber House Rules," 86.

60. Gartzke and Lindsay, "Thermonuclear Cyberwar," 9.

61. Ibid., 6.

62. Owens, Dam, and Lin, *Technology*, 308.

63. Libicki, *Cyberdeterrence and Cyberwar*, xi.

64. Cimbala, *New Nuclear Disorder*, 72.

65. Libicki, *Conquest in Cyberspace*, 71.

66. Cavaiola, Gompert, and Libicki, "Cyber House Rules: On War, Retaliation and Escalation," 81.

67. Cimbala, *Nuclear Weapons in the Information Age*, 206.

68. Gompert and Libicki, "Cyber Warfare and Sino-American Crisis Instability," 11–12.

69. Cimbala, *Nuclear Weapons in the Information Age*, 205.

70. See, e.g., US Department of Defense, "Department of Defense Cyber Strategy"; and Gompert and Libicki, "Cyber Warfare and Sino-American Crisis Instability."

71. Gompert and Libicki, "Cyber Warfare and Sino-American Crisis Instability," 16.

72. See, e.g., Bitzinger, "Why China Should Fear the US Military's Third Offset Strategy."

73. Ibid.

74. Manson, "Cyberwar," 122.

75. Gompert and Libicki, "Cyber Warfare and Sino-American Crisis Instability," 16.

76. See Fravel and Medeiros, "China's Search for Assured Retaliation."

77. Singer and Cole, *Ghost Fleet.*

78. For a discussion of this, see Cimbala and McDermott, "New Cold War?"

79. Freedberg, "NATO Hews to Strategic Ambiguity."

80. Jones, "NATO Holds Largest Cyber War Games."

81. Freedberg, "NATO Hews to Strategic Ambiguity."

82. Ashford, "NATO to Adopt New Cyber Defence Policy."

83. For a discussion of the problems of cyber threats during US–Russian crises, see Futter, "Cyber Threats and the Challenge of De-Alerting US and Russian Nuclear Forces."

84. Austin, "Costs of American Cyber Superiority."

85. Cartwright, "Whither the Forward-Basing of US Troops?" See also Futter, "Danger of Using Cyber Attacks."

86. Austin and Sharikov, "Preemption Is Victory," 4.

87. McKeon, "Statement before the Senate Armed Services Subcommittee."

88. For a discussion of this, see Futter, "Danger of Using Cyber Attacks."

89. Sanger and Broad, "Trump Inherits a Secret Cyberwar against North Korean Missiles."

90. Ryall, Smith, and Millward, "North Korea's Unsuccessful Missile Launch."

91. See, e.g., Schiller and Hayes, "Could Cyber Attacks Defeat North Korean Missile Tests?"

92. Keck, "S. Korea Seeks Cyber Weapons."

93. Libicki, *Cyberspace in Peace and War,* 293.

94. Ibid., 9.

95. Austin and Sharikov, "Preemption Is Victory."

96. See, e.g., Osborn, "Russia's Satellite Nuclear Warning System down until November."

97. Danzig, "Surviving on a Diet of Poisoned Fruit," 6.

98. Ibid.

99. Ibid, 26.

100. Libicki, *Crisis and Escalation in Cyberspace,* xvii.

101. Futter, "*War Games* Redux?" 6.

102. Austin and Sharikov, "Preemption Is Victory," 1.

103. Ibid.

104. Cimbala and McDermott, "New Cold War?" 105.

105. See Futter, "*War Games* Redux?"

106. Cited by Burns, "Former US Commander."

107. Austin and Sharikov, "Preemption Is Victory," 14.

108. Clarke and Knake, *Cyber War,* 217.

109. Cimbala and McDermott, "New Cold War?" 103.

110. Libicki, *Cyberspace in Peace and War,* 296.

111. Danzig, "Surviving on a Diet of Poisoned Fruit," 6.

PART IV

> Challenges for Our
> Cyber-Nuclear Future

7

> ## Nuclear Weapons Modernization,
> ## Advanced Conventional
> ## Weapons, and the Future
> ## Global Nuclear Environment

THE WORLD is moving inexorably further into a computerized global nuclear order, where many of the things that were taken for granted in the past will probably need to be reassessed in light of an ever more distorted military-technological nuclear context. Although a diverse mix of new cyber threats are undoubtedly a key part of this, the challenges posed by cyber operations are also being exacerbated by other developments in the strategic sphere. Two emerging trends, one domestic and one international, which have both been facilitated by the current information revolution (and may therefore be thought of as cyber enabled), are particularly significant in this regard. First is the fact that *all* nuclear-armed states are currently in the process of modernizing their nuclear weapons and command and control systems; placing more reliance on sophisticated, complex, digitized software in all parts of their nuclear enterprise; and increasingly blending the apparatuses used for nuclear and conventional command and control. Although more powerful, networked, real-time systems may offer greater functionality, options, speed, and processing power, they also increase the chances of errors and unintended consequences, and the potential for attackers to interfere with or compromise these systems. Nuclear modernization is therefore very much a double-edged sword in the computer era.

Second, and at the same time, the global nuclear environment is becoming increasingly distorted by the development of a new suite of advanced conventional weapons (ACW) with nuclear counterforce potential that are intermingling with established nuclear processes in complex, and often unhelpful and unpredictable, ways. These ACW have been driven by advances in computing and processing power, and are increasingly likely to complicate strategic stability and the possibility of nuclear arms control, as well as further muddy the water in future nuclear crises.[1] The combined impact of these technologies on nuclear thinking, utility, strategy, and balances is only likely to increase in the years ahead as systems, platforms, and capabilities mature and proliferate.

To be sure, the extent of the challenges posed by nuclear modernization and developments in ACW will vary depending on the types of system being used and the nature of a particular state's nuclear doctrines and strategic requirements. But taken together—and alongside the challenges posed by cyber operations—these dynamics suggest that all nuclear-armed actors—including established, new, and possible future proliferators—will need to revisit and rethink the processes, mechanisms, and dogma that govern their national nuclear styles and strategies. It also suggests that the nuclear orthodoxy of the past may no longer apply directly to the cyber-nuclear context of today or tomorrow. As Stephen Cimbala suggests, the "coexistence of nuclear weapons with advanced conventional weapons and information-based concepts of warfare will be the most important military con-tradiction of the twenty-first century."[2] Ultimately, restraint in the application of new technologies in both the domestic and international cyber-nuclear realms may be the best way to ensure future nuclear security and stability in an increas-ingly complex global nuclear order. However, given the *technological determin-ism*—the idea that technology drives social and societal change, and that new and more capable technologies are *inevitably* taken up by society—that appears to underpin both nuclear modernization and the development of ACW, whether this is possible remains to be seen.

In order to consider the future impact and implications of an ever more com-plex and computerized domestic and global nuclear environment, this chapter proceeds in three sections. The first considers the adversarial implications of nuclear modernization, and particularly the inherent problems of building pro-gressively more complex, sophisticated, and integrated systems to control nuclear weapons. The second situates cyber threats alongside and within a broader suite of emerging strategic weapons technologies, all of which have implications for nuclear thinking and strategy and, when they are taken together, may well repre-sent a significant transformation in the central dynamics of the global nuclear environment within which all states are acting. The third section goes on to examine what this means for the future of global nuclear stability and order, and particularly the thinking, strategy, and policies of different groups of nuclear-armed states as they progress into what might conceivably be thought of as an incipient computerized "third nuclear age."

The Double-Edged Sword of Nuclear Modernization

It has become conventional wisdom in today's society to assume that more sophis-ticated, powerful, and faster technology is necessarily a good thing and should be adopted as soon as practicable.[3] Indeed, rapid developments in computer, networking, and processing technologies have seemed to acquire a certain *tech-nological determinism*—a belief that technology drives societal developments, rather than the other way around, and a certain *technological imperative*—the idea technologies are inevitable and essential and that they must be developed and accepted for the good of society. This also appears to be the case in the nuclear realm, where nuclear weapons and other strategic munitions have tended to exude a strong "directional force" when it comes to technological determinism.[4] In fact, all nuclear-armed states are currently in the process of modernizing not just their nuclear forces,[5] but also the command and control systems and broader infrastructures that support them (notwithstanding, perhaps, the processes governing nuclear personnel).[6] This is at least in part due to the new possibilities, speed, and functionality offered by the fruits of the latest information revolution. The United States, for example, has been explicit about its desire to move toward more "internet like" systems for nuclear command and control, and others are likely doing the same.[7] Although in some cases this is to be welcomed (parts of the US command and control infrastructure can be traced back to the 1960s[8]), this does not make modernization an automatically good or useful development in the nuclear realm. In fact, it may be quite the opposite; more technological capability does not necessarily mean more security or safety. In this way, nuclear modernization should not automatically mean doing business as usual in an increasingly computerized context.

As each nuclear-armed state goes about modernizing its nuclear forces and associated infrastructure, new and more complex computers and coding are likely to play a progressively more important and influential role in all types of nuclear operations. To be sure, such advances will help functionality, particularly real-time decision making and data processing; provide more options to war planners and operators; and guard against the risks of relying on "static technology" that an adversary might eventually compromise. It is even conceivable that more sophisticated systems—with built-in firewalls and other protective measures—may provide some new types of defense against attackers, particularly against those attacking from cyberspace. But at the same time, this move is equally likely to make these systems less secure and more difficult to protect overall, and therefore theoretically easier to compromise, attack, or at least interfere with.[9] It may even make them a more attractive target for would-be attackers, given that older analogue systems are far harder to "hack" or attack over networks. Thus, several important problems stem from nuclear modernization in the cyber age—particularly the implications of moves toward greater complexity, functionality, and digitization—and need to be understood and balanced against their perceived benefits. These are explained in the following paragraphs.

First, a greater reliance on increasingly complex computer systems for nuclear operations raises the possibility of mistakes, accidents, and unintended outcomes. As has been explained earlier in this book, nuclear weapons systems have always been vulnerable to mishaps and errors, but their increasing complexity—and particularly digitization—is likely to magnify this problem considerably. These more complex systems are likely to provide more software glitches and bugs that could cause systems to fail in unusual ways or be exploited by an attacker. They also make interactions between different systems and different components more complex and multifaceted, and therefore more difficult to understand. The net result is that it will probably become far harder to diagnose and fix any problems that arise, and to do so in a timely manner.[10]

A good example of this situation of complexity being bad for security is the US Rapid Execution and Combat Targeting (REACT) system. This system was installed during the 1990s with the intention of decreasing the time needed to retarget nuclear missiles, and was described at the time by the political commentator William Arkin as "bringing nuclear weapons into the internet age."[11] Although REACT makes different war-fighting options much easier to process, it also relies on far more complex algorithms and processes that could go wrong. The same is true for the more recent US Integrated Strategic Planning and Analysis Network (ISPAN), which will allow rapid planning, targeting, and customized mission solutions for operators. It is particularly important that this will be capable of linking nuclear war plans with other conventional and perhaps cyber operations. According to Lockheed Martin, ISPAN's developer, it "supports the full spectrum of USSTRATCOM's new responsibilities for global strike, missile defense and information operations, in addition to their traditional role of nuclear deterrence."[12] The potential for mistakes stemming from this commingling of nuclear and nonnuclear systems is a major concern.

The same logic also seems to be underpinning future developments in weapons, warheads, and delivery vehicles; as Werner Dahm, the chair of the Air Force Scientific Advisory Board, put it, "These systems are going to be quite different from the ones that they may replace. In particular, they will be much more like all systems today, network connected. They'll be cyber enabled."[13] For example, the new long-range stand-off weapon (nuclear cruise missile) being developed by the US Air Force will for the first time communicate digitally with the aircraft that will deliver it.[14] Although moves toward using more capable computer systems for planning, operations, and inside the weapons themselves, will offer a considerable new range of functions and options for war planners and operators, this shift will also magnify the possibilities of mistakes and the likelihood of creating a vulnerability that an attacker may be able to exploit.

Second, and linked to this, issues of complexity are underpinned and compounded by the fact that those in charge of these systems may "find it difficult to keep pace with problems that arise much less train operators to recognize, diagnose, and fix them—and quickly."[15] The increased complexity of this next generation of nuclear systems means that the coding and processes on which computers and their operators will rely will be almost incomprehensible to all but a handful of programmers, and almost certainly will be beyond the understanding of military operators. This has several important implications, but perhaps most significantly, it will likely become almost impossible to determine whether the system is free from bugs or malicious interference and backdoors that might be exploited in the future. But it will also, therefore, make understanding and diagnosing system problems far more difficult than in the past (especially in a short period of time). To give an example, in the 1990s the US nuclear war plan was thought to have contained millions of lines of complex computer coding, and it is likely that this has grown substantially in the past two decades.[16] For security reasons, it is likely that only a handful of people really know what the coding says and what different parts mean and do. The same is also increasingly true for other parts of the nuclear weapons command and control system. As Gary Brewer and Paul Bracken argued as far back as the 1980s, the worry is that "the performance of millions of lines of untested command software in dozens of different computer systems is ignored. . . . Not knowing how they work, how they might fail or even how they might be realistically tested, one has few ideas about making necessary improvements in them or about picking priorities according to the relative importance of imagined deficiencies in the past."[17]

The result is that it may no longer be as easy to respond in the correct way to system errors, malfunctions, and false alarms (or for that matter actual attacks), such as those experienced at the North American Aerospace Defense Command (known as NORAD) in the 1980s. Although it was relatively straightforward to comprehend the meaning of sparks coming from a mechanical component, or to identify that the wrong cassette tape had been loaded into a machine, it will be far more difficult to recognize and diagnose problems at the level of the microchip and coding consisting of hundreds if not thousands of 0s and 1s. This adds even more strength to the argument that in the nuclear weapons business, the goal is risk management, not risk avoidance at all costs.[18]

Third, there also seems to be a tendency within nuclear modernization programs to increasingly share assets between nuclear and conventional systems. This is perhaps most pronounced in China, where public accounts suggest that the command and control structures for nuclear and conventional weapons (particularly missiles) are both operationally and geographically intertwined.[19] But it is also a trend that is developing in the United States and for other nuclear-armed actors as well.[20] As was explained in the previous chapter, this increases the possibility of misperceptions and mistakes, and presents added complications for the successful management of crises between nuclear actors.[21] The worst-case scenarios here are that a cyber operation or an attack against a conventional target (either a weapons system, its central control nodes, or communications infrastructure) could be misinterpreted as a strike on nuclear systems. As Lawrence Cavaiola and his colleagues explain, "The most severe risk would come in attacking systems that support C4ISR [command, control, communications, computers, intelligence, surveillance, and reconnaissance] of immediate tactical military relevance, and in doing so affecting more strategic C4ISR, such as links between political leadership and military commanders or, worse, control of strategic weapons."[22]

But it is also conceivable that nuclear systems, or the systems essential for nuclear command and control, could be targeted or even compromised by an accident, in turn creating considerable (inadvertent) escalatory pressures. Another possibility is that the ever-closer commingling of nuclear and conventional forces could lead to mistakes or even unintentional nuclear use when it comes to advanced conventional war-fighting operations, particularly when systems and operators are placed under pressure. Each of these challenges is being intensified by the fact that many nuclear-armed states are now diversifying and dispersing nuclear forces to make them harder to target or compromise, and at the same time retaining or even increasing their alert status and reducing the time it takes for weapons to be fired.[23] Taken together, the developments are placing increasing pressures on nuclear command and control systems.[24] Ironically, this is likely to drive the case for more modernization and sophistication rather than less.

A final associated risk is the growing reliance on commercial off-the-shelf technologies for these systems, which in turn creates serious concerns about "future-proofing" nuclear forces. The worry here is that nuclear actors are increasingly utilizing commercial products—particularly hardware, but also software—in parts of the nuclear mission that have been built and purchased from outside that country, and that could be deliberately faulty or, worse, laced with malware. For example, in 2008 the UK Royal Navy began upgrading the computer systems on its nuclear-armed submarines by installing Microsoft Windows XP–based local-area network software and operating systems. This choice came under heavy scrutiny from the international software community, which viewed the decision not to purchase the more expensive Linux software as very dangerous, suggesting that it could lead to losses of security, reliability, and assurance.[25] As a former UK Royal Navy officer, Lewis Page, explains: "Many in the software community have viewed the Royal Navy's wholesale move to Windows-based command systems with concern, feeling that the savings are not such as to justify possible loses in security, reliability, and assurance."[26] The system, known colloquially as "Windows for Submarines," appears to have been chosen primarily because it was the best value for the money.[27]

Interestingly, the US Navy decided to adopt a GNU/Linux-based platform for its nuclear submarines after deciding to drop the Windows operating system. This was primarily due to the increased security provided by the Linux system (principally because it is designed with security as a primary goal rather than trying to add in security as an afterthought as is often the case with Windows). In fact, a significant proportion of cyber operations have targeted Windows-based systems for this reason, perhaps most notably both the Flame and Stuxnet malware used against Iran.[28] The problem, of course, is that it is likely to be almost impossible to check and verify the soundness of all nuclear-weapons-related coding, software, and hardware before a system is deployed, and to do this in both a timely and cost-effective way.[29] Moreover, and perhaps even more worrying, there are rumors that several nuclear-armed states rely on commercial off-the-shelf technologies and other components purchased from abroad for their sensitive nuclear operations.[30] Part of the problem is that some nuclear-armed states simply do not have the internal capacity to manufacture all of the high-technology components and computer chips required in their nuclear weapons and support systems.

As nuclear-armed states go about modernizing their nuclear systems, and especially command and control and support apparatuses, intrinsic tensions and problems are likely to become aggravated and possibly exacerbated, and new potential vulnerabilities are almost certain to emerge. It this way, modernization should be seen as a balance, and not as an a priori good thing to do. In fact, it may be that the less sophisticated nuclear systems are, the less tightly they are coupled (both to warning sensors and other nonnuclear weapons systems), and the less they rely on complex software and high-technology computers for their operations, the safer and more secure they will prove to be. As the former commander of the US Strategic Command, Gen. Robert Kehler, puts it, "The age of the US command and control system might inadvertently offer some protection against the latest hacking techniques."[31] As such, we should not be too quick to discard legacy systems or components, such as the now-much-maligned 8-inch floppy disks and the cabinet-size computers previously used by the US military to send emergency action messages to nuclear forces.[32] Ultimately, as Peggy Morse, the director for intercontinental ballistic missile (ICBM) systems at Boeing, succinctly explains, "While it's old, it's very secure."[33]

Cyber Threats and Advanced Conventional Weapons

Developments in cyber capabilities—and particularly information technology, computing, and processing power—are also having a transformative effect on other weapons systems.[34] In fact, though cyber capabilities and the concurrent threats are often viewed as being the primary product of the latest information age and of the burgeoning computerized global security context, such progress is also facilitating the development of more advanced "smart" weapons with ever greater capabilities and precision. Although these changes are manifesting principally on the battlefield and through networked conceptions of tactical operations and warfare, the most sophisticated of these weapons systems are increasingly showing the potential to make an impact on nuclear thinking and strategy. What we are essentially seeing is that the developments in information technology and engineering that facilitated a new suite of weapons systems at the tactical level more than two decades ago have now begun to permeate upward to the strategic level. In effect, the battlefield Revolution in Military Affairs from the 1980s and 1990s is now beginning to play out at the strategic and nuclear levels,[35] resulting in a new suite of ACW (also known as "strategic conventional weapons"[36]), with considerable implications for nuclear thinking. Essentially, cyber-enabled technologies have facilitated significant qualitative enhancements in accuracy, precision, speed, and networked sensors, which are increasingly improving the capabilities and lethality of conventional weapons and making them usable against a wider range of targets, potentially in a counter–nuclear force capacity. This is particularly the case for targets or missions previously only held vulnerable by—or at least best targeted with—nuclear weapons. That said, technological transformations are also making nuclear weapons more accurate and capable.[37] As Paul Bracken puts it, "Cyber is spilling over into precision strike and nuclear."[38]

In addition to cyberattack capabilities, ACW include (but are not limited to) (1) ballistic missile defenses (BMD) that utilize kinetic hit-to-kill technologies (as opposed to blast fragments or a nuclear explosion), which can be used to intercept nuclear-armed missiles; (2) various antisubmarine warfare capabilities, which might compromise the invulnerability of a submarine-based nuclear force; (3) long-range, precision-strike capabilities and other conventional-armed munitions, which could be used to directly attack nuclear weapons systems and command and control centers; and (4) antisatellite weapons, which can be used to take out the communications, early warning, and navigation capabilities on which nuclear decision makers rely. These weapons systems primarily fall under two separate (albeit increasingly blurred) categories, both of which offer renewed possibilities for deterrence by *denial*: (1) new technologies designed to intercept missiles and warheads after they have been launched and (2) technologies that might be used to stop nuclear weapons systems from working or operating as planned. Individually, each set of systems has the potential to undermine secure second-strike capabilities—long held as the bedrock of nuclear deterrence. But taken together, and when combined with the many new challenges posed by cyber operations, these developments represent a fundamental challenge to the thinking that has underpinned the management of nuclear weapons for more than five decades. In this way, improvements in cyber capabilities (and particularly the ever more pervasive cyber context) are both helping to drive a new range of nonnuclear counterforce weaponry and at the same time are augmenting them as part of a broader shift in the nuclear context at the strategic level. When viewed holistically, these developments raise substantial questions for nuclear security, thinking, and strategy, which are only slowly beginning to be realized by the governments of nuclear-armed states.[39]

The first component of this new challenge, and the most established one, is the rise and spread of ever more capable BMD—though it should also be noted that air defenses (e.g., missiles that could be used against nuclear-armed bombers) have also continued to improve. The pursuit of defense against ballistic missiles can be traced back as far as the 1940s, but only really in the past decade or so has the technology matured to a point whereby it might credibly be deployed against certain types of threats, and the pursuit of such systems has become politically neutralized. In fact, for years BMD was seen as a huge waste of money and as strategically destabilizing, due to the likelihood that such moves would undermine an opponent's second-strike nuclear forces and drive a nuclear arms race. Indeed, in 1972 the United States and the Soviet Union signed the Anti–Ballistic

Missile (ABM) Treaty, placing stringent limits on such systems (the ABM Treaty limited each side to 200 interceptor missiles at two sites; this was later reduced to 100 interceptors at just one site).[40] It was also—perhaps more important for the discussion here—seen as being technologically unworkable. The incredulity that met US president Ronald Reagan's Strategic Defense Initiative (known as Star Wars) in the 1980s was perhaps the most obvious manifestation of this.

However, due in part to the technological improvements facilitated by advancements in information technology (as well as a shifting conception of what was required for deterrence), the United States began to rethink the role of missile defenses as part of a modified deterrence strategy during the 1990s. A few years later, in 2001, US president George W. Bush chose to abrogate the ABM Treaty and begin the pursuit of a limited national missile defense as part of a new conception of strategic deterrence. This then became codified in the 2002 US Nuclear Posture Review and in the unveiling of a "new triad" by the Bush administration.[41] Since that time, the idea of BMD has become normalized in the US political debate,[42] and various systems have been deployed with ever-increasing capability.[43] Early signs suggest that President Donald Trump will also look to push ahead with BMD.[44]

The notion of BMD has also become normalized elsewhere in the world, and several organizations and states are pursuing and even deploying such systems. Russia,[45] whose missile defense plans can be traced back to the late 1940s,[46] already operates a number of defensive systems, while NATO,[47] China,[48] India,[49] Israel,[50] Japan,[51] and others are all engaged on research and development or have begun deploying BMD systems.[52] Although these systems vary considerably in sophistication, intention, and scale, they are clearly part of a broader trend toward reliance on defensive systems in strategic and perhaps nuclear operations, and an overturning of the Cold War–era defensive taboo. They also demonstrate the almost inevitable cascade of missile defense technology to more actors as systems improve.

But the spreading of missile defense capabilities is also creating new concerns for nuclear-armed states—particularly those with a limited nuclear weapons strike capability. The manifestation of advances in BMD are most clearly seen in the United States–Russia nuclear dyad and in Europe, but also increasingly in other nuclear-armed regions, such as Northeast Asia, South Asia, and the Middle East.[53] Although there may well be some logic in deploying defenses against new ostensibly "undeterrable" nuclear threats, the move toward a greater reliance on defenses is creating pressures for nuclear balances around the globe. To put it bluntly, defenses cast doubt on the ability of one state to always hold targets vulnerable in another one—a key component of mutually assured destruction and retaliatory deterrence.

The second component involves a mixture of advanced technologies that might be used for a nonnuclear counterforce role—that is, used against nuclear weapons, delivery vehicles, and associated command and control systems before these weapons can be used. Historically, this was a mission that could only be carried out—or at least was best carried out—using nuclear weapons, such as heavily armed ICBMs designed to penetrate hardened missile silos, command bunkers, or destroy airfields, and nuclear-armed torpedoes or depth charges to attack stealthy submarines, but this is increasingly not the case. Major advances in precision, tracking, and processing power have meant that these tasks can now also potentially be undertaken with nonnuclear weaponry.

The first of these new technologies is the growth of conventional prompt/precision-strike weapons with either regional or global range. Such conventionally armed weapons might be used against nuclear facilities (e.g., a missile waiting to be fired, a command and control center, or a key communications node). This could involve any number of different technologies, but at the moment, it principally involves conventionally armed cruise or ballistic missiles, or new hypersonic and boost-glide systems.[54] The worry is that such weapons could provide a nonnuclear strike capability against an adversary's nuclear systems. In fact, one of the stated desires of the US prompt global strike (PGS) system is to hit targets anywhere in the world—such as a missile being readied to fire—in under 30 minutes.[55] The problem of course is that this also causes concerns for strategic competitors such as Russia and China, which in turn seem likely to develop and deploy high-technology precision weapons themselves.[56] Although many of these systems remain in their infancy, it is perfectly possible to see the beginning of a new arms race in these dual-use technologies, as adversaries race to prevent a conventional-strike gap and the creation of new vulnerabilities. Given the problems of differentiating between nuclear and nonnuclear weapons based on ballistic or cruise missiles, this would also present considerable escalatory pressures.

Significant progress has also been made in other potentially destabilizing counterforce technologies, such as antisubmarine warfare (ASW) and antisatellite/space (ASAT) weaponry. Although ASW capabilities have always been an important component of nuclear strategy, emerging technologies, particularly "underwater drones," raise new questions for the supposed invulnerability of nuclear-armed submarines (literally, submarine submersible ballistic nuclear, known as SSBNs)—and, by implication, for states that rely on SSBNs for nuclear delivery.[57] Unmanned underwater vehicles might be able to silently track an adversary's nuclear-armed submarines while on patrol, sending back location data to a central server (perhaps via buoys or underwater relays) or to a nearby attack submarine, or even be able to carry weapons themselves.[58] These technologies are unlikely to make the vast oceans transparent overnight, and there are undoubtedly problems with operating an underwater fleet of "killer drones," but they will increase the doubt in the minds of planners who assume undersea invulnerability as the norm.

Kinetic ASAT capabilities—that is, the ability to shoot down military assets in space—will create unfamiliar dynamics for crisis management and communications and build on the challenges posed by cyber threats discussed in earlier chapters. Although ASAT weapons are not direct counterforce capabilities in the same way as PGS and ASW, they pose a distinct indirect threat to nuclear relations, particularly given the reliance of leading nuclear powers (especially the United States) on space. This seems likely to be particularly important during a crisis. For example, any adversary of the United States would be likely to target the space assets on which its advanced forces (including BMD and PGS) rely. This in turn could well cause escalatory pressures and complicate crisis stability in unforeseen and unplanned ways. China and Russia may well already be planning attacks on US space assets,[59] and China successfully demonstrated an ASAT capability in a test in 2007.[60] US Air Force general John Hyten, the commander of the US Air Force Space Command, has already warned that "adversaries are developing kinetic, directed energy, and cyber tools to deny, degrade, and destroy our [US] space capabilities."[61] Although there are countermeasures available against each of these subsystems of ACW, the trend seems to be toward both qualitative and quantitative improvements in these capabilities in the future.

For a while, the development of ACW was a distinctly US phenomenon designed principally—or at least ostensibly—for the new deterrence requirements posed by so-called rogue states or nonstate actors (and a broader "second nuclear age"). But these capabilities are increasingly being considered, developed, and deployed by all major nuclear-armed powers.[62] The fear is that advanced monitoring capabilities (including cyber espionage) could be used to locate nuclear assets and find out sensitive information about how they function; new conventional and cyber strike systems would then be used to target weapons (missiles, submarines, etc.) and associated command and control, while ballistic missile (as well as air) defenses would then be used to nullify any subsequent retaliation.

The world therefore stands at a technological and policy crossroads regarding future thinking about the deployment and role of ACW and the possibilities of deterrence by nonnuclear *denial*. In fact, it is possible to foresee a strategic environment where nuclear weapons might be compromised, deterrence might fail, arms racing returns,[63] escalation becomes unmanageable, and the threshold of nuclear use is lowered as a result of developments in ACW and cyber operations.[64] When all these developments are taken together, the net result is that we are arguably standing on the cusp of a new epoch of nuclear affairs. This new context could see advanced conventional weaponry become a significant military factor, if not the key capability, for all nuclear-armed states.[65] As a result, we now face the prospect of a future strategic context in which several states deploy a variety of ACW facilitated by—and including—cyber techniques, and where many of the central tenets of global nuclear order will be challenged if not transformed.

Implications for Nuclear Stability, Strategy, and Posture

The ever-evolving cyber-nuclear context—both domestically and internationally—will have considerable implications for the way that nuclear-armed states think about nuclear posture, strategy, force structure, the need for differentiated weapons systems, and for the types of changes and problems that they will face in the years ahead. Although some components of this challenge hold true across all cases, the different requirements and specifics of nuclear policy create slightly different questions for different actors. These range from challenges associated with reliance on a single nuclear system, to challenges caused by having diverse and alerted forces, and from states with sophisticated weaponry to those that are newly armed or are seeking to acquire a nuclear capability. These dynamics are explained in the following paragraphs.

The first set of challenges is for states that might be termed "maximum deterrent powers," and particularly those that retain nuclear forces on high alert. These new challenges are therefore specifically for the United States and Russia and, to a lesser extent, China. The risk here is twofold; first, developments in cyber operations and ACW create pressures for each of these states to retain highly sophisticated and alerted forces to ensure that their nuclear weapons systems remain credible and cannot be compromised—the so-called threat of *disablement*. This is being driven by a perception that cyber capabilities present new opportunities for preemptive attacks on nuclear systems.[66] Second, unfortunately, this in turn will create more pressures on these systems, increase the chances of mistakes and accidents, and ultimately raise the possibility of *enabling* cyberattacks. In the United States–Russia context, this becomes particularly worrisome, given the large number of forces that are retained at high levels of alert. This is because keeping ICBMs at a high-alert status makes them more vulnerable to cyberattacks, particularly those seeking to cause an unauthorized launch.[67] Approximately 1,800 heavily armed US and Russian ICBMs, often deployed in silos far away from central command and control facilities and tightly coupled with warning networks and sensors, are kept on high alert and primed for launch within minutes—or even just seconds—of receiving the order via a short stream of computer signals.[68] In fact, in 2014, the Russian Glonass system (used for Russian aerospace defense forces) malfunctioned due to a couple of small mathematical mistakes in the software. If this had occurred during a crisis, it could easily have led to inadvertent and unintended outcomes.[69] Unfortunately, as long as the threat of disablement—exacerbated by the threat of cyberattacks and developments in ACW for nuclear systems—predominates in these countries' strategic thinking, it seems unlikely that nuclear forces will be de-alerted, which in turn increases the risks of nuclear use.[70]

The mixture of cyber threats and other types of ACW will also have an impact on the United States–China nuclear relationship, albeit in slightly different ways than for the United States and for Russia. The increasing perception that China could become vulnerable to a US nonnuclear first strike (conventional, cyber, or both) and that the small surviving Chinese nuclear force might be nullified by US ballistic missile defenses will clearly create pressures for the modernization, diversification, and proliferation of Chinese nuclear systems. As M. Taylor Fravel and Evan Medeiros explain, taken together, these capabilities seem to China to provide "the United States with the ability to eliminate China's deterrent in a crisis without crossing the nuclear threshold, reopening the door to coercion of China."[71] The close links between Chinese conventional and nuclear command and control systems, as well as the likelihood that Chinese antisatellite weapons would be targeted by conventional prompt strike capabilities early on in any future conflict, is also worrying.[72] This emerging digital strategic context is therefore also likely to create new pressures to rethink the viability of China's No-First-Use policy. As Joshua Pollack explains, "While nuclear missiles are deterrent weapons, conventional missiles are available for use in the early stages of an armed conflict. In such an event, the United States would have incentives to attack Second Artillery command and control nodes, raising difficult questions about the precise boundaries of China's no-first-use pledge."[73]

A similar set of pressures and dynamics are likely to play out between India and Pakistan. Ever since the overt nuclear tests of 1998, both India and Pakistan have been searching for a workable strategic nuclear balance; but their relations remain unstable, and it is hard to see how the specter of cyberattacks against conventional or nuclear forces, and the broader development of ACW, will help encourage stability and confidence in South Asia.[74] Both India and Pakistan are rumored to be developing cyberattack capabilities that may have a nuclear counterforce role, in addition to programs to develop various other types of ACW.[75] The geographical proximity of these two states also magnifies problems of early warning, and particularly their confidence in the integrity of the information on which decisions are based. As was explained in the previous chapter, this places extra pressure on policymakers and military commanders in any future crisis. Although the nuclear dimension may not currently be as pronounced, the development of cyberattack capabilities alongside other types of ACW in the Middle East is unlikely to help encourage stability in that region either, and may even create pressures for nuclear proliferation among other actors. More broadly, recent and new nuclear proliferators will have little margin for error with their nuclear operations in the emerging cyber context, particularly if they share contiguous borders, given the challenges of building reliable command and control systems and especially early warning networks.[76]

A third set of challenges applies specifically to states that retain a "minimum nuclear deterrent" force, and particularly those that retain a monad—or a single means of nuclear delivery. In the case of the United Kingdom, which relies on just one type of delivery platform—an SSBN (again, a nuclear-armed submarine)—the challenge appears to be particularly acute regarding the possibility of cyber disablement. The threat does not just have to be to the warhead or missile, but given the UK policy of having only one boat on patrol at any one time (a policy known as continuous-at-sea-deterrence), it could be almost anything to do with the operation of the submarine or its crew. It might also involve compromising its stealth capabilities or patrol area through some type of cyber espionage.[77] When cyber threats are augmented by other new technologies, as discussed earlier in this chapter, the possible future threat to the credibility of UK nuclear weapons is in fact quite compelling.[78]

Indeed, the former UK secretary of state for defence, Des Browne, warned in late 2015 that UK nuclear weapons could "be rendered obsolete by hackers" and that without a comprehensive assessment of this risk to the Trident system, a future prime minister might not be certain that the country had a "reliable deterrent" that could be used when needed.[79] This raises questions about relying on a homogeneous nuclear weapons system for deterrence in the emerging global cyber context—and is likely to be another reason why larger nuclear powers will opt to retain or even augment their diverse nuclear force postures.[80] The new techno-military context could, therefore, also provide a further rationale for the continuation of a French nuclear dyad—both submarines and nuclear-armed aircraft.

The final set of challenges is for states that have recently acquired nuclear weapons or that might seek to do so in the future. In the case of North Korea, for example, the challenges posed by a possible *disabling* cyberattack against its nuclear forces, potentially in combination with other types of ACW, is obviously a very serious threat. North Korea is clearly—although not officially—the target of the embryonic US "full spectrum missile defense" plan, which has purportedly included attacks (or at least the planning of attacks) against its missile and perhaps nuclear program.[81] For North Korea and other nuclear aspirants, as Peter Feaver explains, this is likely to mean prioritizing the risk of a decapitating strike (seen as the most urgent problem) rather than the safety and security of nuclear forces.[82] This, in turn, might create pressures to build more nuclear forces, diversify nuclear systems, or, perhaps more worryingly, increase the measures designed to ensure that nuclear weapons can be used (positive control), such as heightened alert status, airborne nuclear alerts, and tighter coupling between warning and use.[83]

These challenges are likely to be aggravated considerably in cases where newly armed nuclear states lack experience with nuclear weapons management and where early warning and other communications systems may be rudimentary or unreliable. It also increases the risks of things simply going wrong. It is unclear what this might mean for a possible future nuclear-armed Iran (or other would-be proliferator), but it would likely increase the pressure to ensure that nuclear forces are usable, and perhaps therefore to compromise safety and security in order to enhance credibility. Taken together, these dynamics raise the risks of mistakes, accidents, third-party interference, and inadvertent nuclear use. Indeed, nuclear arsenals are almost always at their most vulnerable during their early stages of development, and these pressures are likely to be magnified in the evolving global cyber context. That said, it is at least possible that smaller and newer nuclear-armed states might benefit from the limitations and relative simplicity of their forces and command structures when it comes to cyber risks.[84]

Consequently, the emerging and burgeoning cyber-nuclear context means asking new questions and seeking to understand various new pressures across the nuclear weapons enterprise. Although these vary between cases, it is clear that cyber capabilities, in conjunction with the development and deployment of other types of ACW, are creating new pressures for the maintenance of secure second nuclear strike forces (key to stable deterrence and mutually assured destruction) and raising new problems for policymakers as they think about strategy and force structure. Likewise, this new cyber-nuclear context well may necessitate a rethinking of sole-purpose and no-first-use declarations, and lead to increased pressures to deploy more, more diverse, and increasingly differentiated nuclear forces. Ultimately, the new technomilitary context, of which cyber is a key aspect, may well require a comprehensive rethinking—or at least reevaluation—of the orthodoxy that underpins state nuclear strategies and the broader global nuclear order.

Conclusion: Toward a Revolution in Nuclear Affairs?

All nuclear-armed states are updating, upgrading, and/or modernizing their nuclear weapons complexes at a time of great flux in the global nuclear environment, where new technologically driven pressures are playing out in both the domestic and international nuclear contexts. Many of the new cyber-enabled technomilitary developments and programs driving internal modernization—though certainly providing more capability and functionality—are at the same time creating significant new pressures and vulnerabilities that might be exploited through cyber operations, operations involving cyber components, or cyber-enabled weapons systems. The fact that this is also happening at the same time that a broader suite of advanced conventional weaponry is being developed and deployed internationally makes for an increasingly complicated and dangerous global nuclear environment. These concurrent developments are creating new pressures for nuclear thinking, posture, and strategy, and have different implications for different actors—many of which appear antagonistic, and many of which appear to require certain trade-offs when it comes to safety and security. Taken together, this suggests that we stand on the cusp of a more complex and intricate era of global nuclear order, where many of the axioms of the past may need to be reassessed in light of the new cyber context. Moreover, this new context may well be qualitatively and quantitatively different from previous nuclear technological shake-ups of the past, such as those provided by the development of ICBMs, nuclear-armed submarines, and missile defense.[85]

Much has been made of the transition from a first to a second nuclear age with the end of the Cold War, but the evidence suggests that the cyber revolution may well mean that we are on the cusp of a third nuclear age, where the challenges and threats will shift again. This third nuclear age will be characterized by a much more blurred computerized global nuclear order, where advanced and exotic nonnuclear, cyber-enabled technologies play an ever-increasing role in deterrence thinking, strategic balances, crisis management, and proliferation. It remains unclear whether the frameworks, strategies, and thinking that have governed our nuclear world since 1945 will remain fit for purpose in the more complex nuclear future.

Notes

1. This is as I have argued elsewhere with regard to the UK Trident program; see Futter, "Trident Replacement." See also Futter and Zala, "Conventional Prompt Global Strike."

2. Cimbala, *Nuclear Weapons in the Information Age*, 1.

3. This section draws on and expands ideas first published as Futter, "Double-Edged Sword."

4. For an interesting discussion of this, see Roland, "Was the Nuclear Arms Race Deterministic?"

5. See Mecklin, "Disarm and Modernize."

6. Oswald, "Congress Wants Pentagon to Upgrade Nuclear Command and Control."

7. See US Department of Defense, "Nuclear Matters Handbook," 53.

8. See US Government Accountability Office, "Information Technology."

9. Futter, "Double-Edged Sword."

10. Libicki, *Conquest in Cyberspace*, 293–94.

11. Arkin, "Six-Hundred-Million-Dollar Mouse," 68.

12. PR Newswire, "Lockheed Martin Wins $213 Million Strategic Mission Planning Contract." See also Lockheed Martin, "Integrated Strategic Planning and Analysis Network (ISPAN)," www.lockheedmartin.co.uk/us/products/ispan.html.

13. Quoted by Tucker, "Will America's Nuclear Weapons Always Be Safe from Hackers?"

14. Giangreco, "Analysis."

15. Futter, "Double-Edged Sword."

16. Ainslie, *Future of the British Bomb*, 61.

17. Brewer and Bracken, "Some Missing Pieces," 457.

18. Denning, *Information Warfare and Security*, 12.

19. Logan, "Drawing a Line between Conventional and Nuclear Weapons in China."

20. See Futter, "Double-Edged Sword"; and Freedberg, "New Nuclear C2 Should Be Distributed and Multi-Domain."

21. Futter, "Double-Edged Sword."

22. Cavaiola, Gompert, and Libicki, "Cyber House Rules," 87.

23. Blair, "Lowering the Nuclear Threshold."

24. Ibid., 1.

25. See, e.g., Lettice, "OSS Torpedoed."

26. Page, "Royal Navy Completes Windows for Submarines Rollout."

27. It is more formally called the "Submarine Command System Next Generation (SCS NG)"; see www.baesystems.com/en/product/submarine-command-system-next-generation.

28. Tech Khabaren, "US Navy Rejects Windows for Linux."

29. US Department of Defense, Defense Science Board, *Task Force Report: Resilient Military Systems*, 15.

30. This is based on a series of confidential interviews with the author.

31. Quoted by Schlosser, *Command and Control*, 475.

32. Thompson, "Pentagon's Huge Atomic Floppies."

33. Quoted by Reed, "Keeping Nukes Safe."

34. Parts of this section draw on research that I have conducted with Benjamin Zala of the Australian National University.

35. On the Revolution in Military Affairs, see Collins and Futter, *Reassessing the Revolution in Military Affairs*.

36. See Acton, "Russia and Strategic Conventional Weapons."

37. See, e.g., Lieber and Press, "New Era of Counterforce."

38. Bracken, "Cyber Threat to Nuclear Stability," 200.

39. See, e.g., UK Defence Select Committee, "Deterrence in the 21st Century."

40. See "Treaty between the United States of America and the Union of Soviet Socialist Republics on the Limitation of Anti-Ballistic Missile Systems," www.State.Gov/Www/Global/Arms/Treaties/Abm/Abm2.html.

41. On this, see McDonough, *Nuclear Superiority*; and US Department of Defense, "Nuclear Posture Review Report," foreword.

42. See Futter, *Ballistic Missile Defence*.

43. See the US Missile Defense Agency's website: www.mda.mil/system/system.html.

44. See the White House's website: www.whitehouse.gov/making-our-military-strong-again.

45. On this, see Interfax, "Russia Creates New Missile Defense Systems."

46. See Podvig, *Russian Strategic Nuclear Forces*, 399–438.

47. See, e.g., Thranert and Kartchner, "From Offensive to Defense: Extended Deterrence and Missile Defense," in *Future of Extended Deterrence*, ed. von Hlatky and Wenger.

48. See MacDonald and Ferguson, "Chinese Strategic Missile Defense."

49. Nagal, *India and Ballistic Missile Defense.*

50. Levite and Brom, "From Dream to Reality: Israel and Missile Defense," in *Regional Missile Defense*, ed. Kelleher and Dombrowski, 137–59.

51. Pekkanen, "Japan's Ballistic Missile Defense and 'Proactive Pacifism,'" in *Regional Missile Defense*, ed. Kelleher and Dombrowski, 217–37.

52. See also Kelleher and Dombrowski, *Regional Missile Defense.*

53. Khoo and Steff, "'This Program Will Not Be a Threat.'"

54. For a good overview of this, see Acton, *Silver Bullet.*

55. See, e.g., Gormley, "US Advanced Conventional Systems."

56. Gertz, "Pentagon Studies Ways to Counter Hypersonic Missile Threat from China, Russia."

57. See, e.g., Long and Green, "Stalking the Secure Second Strike."

58. See Merchant, "DARPA Is about to Start Testing"; and Hambling, "Underwater Drones."

59. Gertz, "China, Russia Planning Space Attacks."

60. See Forden, "After China's Test."

61. Quoted by Gertz, "China, Russia Planning Space Attacks."

62. See, e.g., Futter and Zala, "Advanced Conventional Weapons."

63. Le Mière, "Spectre of an Asian Arms Race."

64. Podvig, "Blurring the Lines."

65. Futter, Zala, and Moore, "Correspondence," 291.

66. Austin and Sharikov, "Preemption Is Victory," 13.

67. Burns, "Former US Commander: Take Nuclear Missiles Off High Alert."

68. Blair, "Lowering the Nuclear Threshold"; and Global Zero Commission, "De-Alerting and Stabilizing the World's Nuclear Force Postures," 8.

69. Paikowsky and Baram, "Space Wars."

70. For a discussion of this, see Futter, "*War Games* Redux?"

71. Fravel and Medeiros, "China's Search for Assured Retaliation," 83.

72. Pollack, "Emerging Strategic Dilemmas," 59.

73. Ibid., 57.

74. For a discussion of these issues, see Sarkar, "Three Concrete Steps."

75. See, e.g., Jaspal, "Introduction of Ballistic Missile Defense in South Asia," in *Nuclear Learning in South Asia*, ed. Khan, Jacobs, and Burke.

76. Sagan and Waltz, *Spread of Nuclear Weapons*, 79. See also Cunningham and Fravel, "Assuring Assured Retaliation."

77. For a more detailed discussion of this, see Futter, "Is Trident Safe from Cyber-Attack?"

78. Futter, "Trident Replacement," 64.

79. Quoted by BBC News, "Trident Could Be Rendered Obsolete."

80. Bracken, "Cyber Threat to Nuclear Stability," 201.

81. See Sanger and Broad, "Trump Inherits a Secret Cyberwar against North Korean Missiles."

82. Feaver, "Command and Control," 167–68.

83. Sagan and Waltz, *Spread of Nuclear Weapons*, 168.

84. See Seng, "Less Is More," 53.

85. Bracken, "Cyber Threat to Nuclear Stability," 202.

Conclusion: Managing Our Cyber-Nuclear Future

THE NEW DYNAMICS, challenges, and threats associated with both the incipient cyber age and the new tools and capabilities that might be used for cyber operations will not supersede nuclear weapons as the ultimate symbol or guarantor of national security. Neither will they represent a strategic or existential threat on their own any time soon. To believe so would be to misunderstand both the nature and scope of the cyber phenomenon as well as the fundamental differences between the cyber challenge and nuclear weapons. That said, the latest revolution in information technology does unquestionably present an important shift in the context and environment within which we think about nuclear weapons and nuclear security, manage nuclear relationships and strategic stability, and regulate the global nuclear order more broadly. If we take the cyber phenomenon as an all-inclusive concept that includes not just the internet but also the software, hardware, and myriad associated infrastructure, as well as the people who operate and interact with nuclear systems, then the cyber challenge is in fact multifaceted, albeit in some cases subtler and more nuanced, and exacerbates rather than transforms established nuclear tensions, problems, and challenges.

The nuclear weapons enterprise has always been, and will likely remain, a complex, convoluted, and complicated business. But as we progress further into the computer age—and as nuclear-armed states come to rely more acutely on sophisticated information technology and complex systems, and ever-increasing lines of software code to manage every aspect of nuclear operations—the pressures surrounding the possession and role of these weapons will be exacerbated, recast, and transformed. It is particularly important that this process will be shaped not just with new methods of warfare and attack but also with new types of inherent and perceived system vulnerability and strategic risk, as part of a broader cyber-nuclear context. In this way, the cyber challenge primarily builds on a set of existing dynamics that have always been part of nuclear weapons management, especially the antagonistic demands of positive and negative nuclear command and control, the protection of sensitive information, and the need to guard against outside or unauthorized interference. This is also true for the role of humans. Indeed, the human–computer interface remains a key "battle-field" in the cyber-nuclear realm—computers do not think (at least not yet); they do what they are programmed to do. It is people who design systems, write software, and place their faith in computers and machines to carry out tasks as intended—and it is also humans who base their decisions and actions on the information that computerized systems provide to them. The burgeoning digitized environment is therefore presenting new ways into these processes and different opportunities to interfere with how they function, and at the same time creating new challenges for those who build, operate, and rely on them to carry out nuclear operations. Consequently, the emergence of a more complex global nuclear context and the concurrent spread of associated cyber tools, weapons, and capabilities is indisputably changing, recasting, and exacerbating existing tensions right across the nuclear weapons enterprise and providing new dynamics and challenges that must be understood and addressed.

It is important to be clear that the cyber threat to nuclear weapons is not homogeneous and that systems and associated infrastructure are vulnerable in different ways—and that this also varies for different systems and actors. It is not just the threat of remotely hacking directly into a weapons system through interconnected networks and causing a launch or detonation that needs to be guarded against—although this remains a worst-case possibility. Instead, the overwhelming number of attacks on nuclear-related systems are best classified as hacking, nuisances, or espionage—and though these clearly do have implications for the credibility and efficacy of weapons systems, nuclear proliferation, and possible future sabotage—it is important to be clear about the nature of the challenge. Only a handful of cyberattacks have caused major disruption and damage, most notably Stuxnet, although the potential for this to expand in the future is clear. In this way, the most likely implication of the cyber challenge is that weapons will be compromised due to espionage; more worrying is the possibility that systems might be sabotaged or indirectly impaired so they do not work as expected, and the worst-case scenario (though perhaps the least likely one) is that attacks could somehow facilitate a nuclear launch or explosion. The respective roles of deterrence (including nuclear retaliation), security, and defense in responding to cyber threats in the nuclear sphere will therefore be different depending on the specifics of the challenge being faced.

It is equally important to understand that the nature of the cyber threat to nuclear weapons varies between both who is involved—nation-states and non-state actors or terrorists—and between the intentions of these actors—either *enabling* and *disabling* attacks. For example, the main goal of a nation-versus-nation cyberattack, in addition to espionage, is likely to be to disable an opponent's conventional or nuclear forces or command and control networks, or at least erode confidence that these systems will work as expected. However, such actions are riddled with uncertainties, and one would hope that no rational actor is likely to take this risk against a nuclear peer-competitor, unless the situation is already dire (notwithstanding the worrying recent trend to use cyberattacks against the nuclear and missile programs of "rogue states"). Conversely, terrorists or other third-party actors are more likely to seek to use cyber capabilities or operations to precipitate a crisis and/or facilitate miscalculation and possible nuclear use (in addition to stealing sensitive information that might help them build their own nuclear devices). The balance between the threat of enabling versus disabling attacks is therefore a fundamental part of the emerging cyber-nuclear security dilemma, and of the possibility that cyber operations (and the broader instability bequeathed by the cyber context) could escalate a conflict toward nuclear use (either through outside interference or inadvertent miscalculation).

Cyberattacks may also be used alongside actions in other military "domains," especially if the goal is sabotage or major interference, and cyber operations are therefore likely to act as a force multiplier rather than a stand-alone tool at the strategic level. Indeed, major advances in information technology are also allowing for considerable enhancement across other domains and weapons systems. In this way, it is more useful to think of the cyber challenge as constituting an environment or context rather than as simply another domain of military operations. Finally, and in addition to discrete and focused attacks on nuclear weapons systems, widespread cyber operations against society and critical infrastructure also have implications for nuclear weapons, and particularly for the question of whether nuclear weapons can or should play a role in deterring such attacks. This holds true for both national and extended nuclear deterrence guarantees. Although nuclear weapons may not currently represent a particularly attractive, credible, or proportionate response to a cyberattack, the two domains are intrinsically linked, and this link *could* become more significant in the future.

It is also important to think about the broader global strategic environment. Although it may well make sense to treat cyber operations as a separate domain of military activity for administrative or academic purposes, it is highly unlikely that future warfare will be fought solely in cyberspace. Indeed, instead of cyberwarfare, it is arguably much more useful to think of future warfare that will involve cyber operations or weapons and will be conducted in a broader cyber context. This plays out on two different levels. First, cyber capabilities are likely to be used alongside other kinetic military capabilities in any future low-level conflict, which will have an impact on crisis management and could lead to possible unintended escalation. Second, at the strategic level, and once conflict between nuclear-armed states deepens, cyberattacks will almost certainly be used in conjunction with other cyber-enabled advanced conventional weaponry with potentially destabilizing dynamics, such as missile defense, developments in conventional prompt strike weapons, antisubmarine warfare technologies, and antispace capabilities. When these systems are taken together as a whole, they could constitute a serious threat to assured retaliation or even be viewed as facilitating a nonnuclear first-strike capability.

Consequently, as well as creating innumerable new challenges for nuclear command and control systems and associated infrastructure, cyber threats will also have a variety of subsequent implications for the global nuclear order on a much larger scale. The possibility (and even the perception) that nuclear systems might be compromised, attacked, and not work as intended seems unlikely to help the push for global nuclear reductions. It may also be cited as a strong reason for nuclear modernization, and the increased sophistication and diversity of nuclear forces, which both present their own trade-offs vis-à-vis enhanced vulnerabilities, tensions, and cyber security. Perhaps more troubling is the fact that this could also create incentives to retain nuclear forces on high levels of alert, and could serve as a further driver of both horizontal and vertical nuclear proliferation.

Although the implications are of course different for different actors, and much depends on the posture and requirements placed on nuclear forces by individual states, these new dynamics together clearly do represent a challenge to the so-called nuclear orthodoxy and the ideas that have underpinned the international nuclear order since the 1960s. It will also provide an interesting contextual shift in the nuclear proliferation debate. As such, it seems difficult to see how cyber threats will not make an impact on both current bilateral arms control agreements and also on global nuclear regimes—notably, the Nuclear Non-Proliferation Treaty—and provide another barrier to further nuclear cuts and the goal of nuclear disarmament. In fact, the various challenges and threats of cyber-attacks may need to be included as part of future nuclear dialogues and strategic discussions (see below).

Finally, we must think about what the future cyber-nuclear strategic environment might look like, and what types of challenges are likely to emerge. Five key dynamics stand out here. The first is the ever-increasing possibility that attackers could "jump the air gap"—that is, attack systems not connected directly to the outside world through other electromagnetic measures.[1] Although air-gapped systems have always been vulnerable, not least to human insiders,[2] and though total isolation is rarely if ever feasible, it is clear that research is under way on new technologies that can be used to insert programs remotely into a system disconnected from the internet or outside networks in other ways.[3] In fact, a full fifty-page "catalogue" was leaked by Edward Snowden to *Der Spiegel* detailing the numerous different exotic attack plans that had been developed by the US National Security Agency, many of which would involve jumping the gap.[4] Being able to jump the air gap could potentially transform the boundaries of the cyber challenge, and particularly cyber defense.

Second, technologies such as additive manufacturing, or "3D printing," seem set to fundamentally alter the challenge of nuclear nonproliferation, and make the protection of sensitive nuclear secrets and particularly weapon designs even more important. Given the scale of the current cyber-nuclear espionage challenge, this could well become one of the most important nuclear proliferation risks in the next few years. The third dynamic, which is linked to the second one, is cyber proliferation, and the likelihood that cyberattack capabilities and know-how will spread to more actors and become ever more sophisticated. Cyber prolif-eration is likely to be very different from previous weapons systems because when you "fire" or use a cyberweapon, you also send the weapon's blueprints. This means the weapon can be used back against you—albeit perhaps in an updated or altered form. As the journalist Kim Zetter put it, this is "comparable to a scenario where, if in 1945, it wasn't just radioactive fallout that rained down from bombs onto Hiroshima and Nagasaki but all of the scientific equations and schematics for constructing them as well."[5] This also seems likely to undermine the possibilities of cyber arms control and to expand the number of actors that could—if they wished to—carry out strategic cyberattacks, perhaps even on nuclear systems.

The fourth dynamic consists of the considerable issues presented by nuclear modernization, and particularly the current tendency—even fetishization—for ever more sophisticated nuclear weaponry and control systems. This propensity for functionality, flexibility, and speed will unquestionably have implications for the security of these systems and the possibility of future mistakes, accidents, and unintended outcomes. New nuclear proliferators, and those with nascent nuclear command and control infrastructures, will also face a new spate of challenges as they set about securing their positions as members of the elite nuclear club in an international cyber environment. Fifth and finally, though the notion that com-puting power will double every two years—the so-called Moore's Law, developed in the 1960s—is perhaps no longer fully applicable, the dynamics and scope of what can be done to, through, and by computers will undoubtedly increase in the years ahead.[6] In fact, we may still only be at the start of this new epoch and have yet to fully understand the possibilities and dangers of our cyber-shaped world order.[7] Arguably, the next greatest challenge in this regard will be the develop-ment and increased utilization of artificial intelligence for all aspects of daily life, including perhaps the command and control of nuclear weapons.

Although the nuclear weapons enterprise has always been plagued by uncer-tainty, risk, and vulnerability—indeed, to paraphrase the Nobel Prize–winning economist Thomas Schelling, the nuclear game is one that always "leaves some-thing to chance"—the difficulties of nuclear force management are being and will continue to be exacerbated as we move further into the latest information age.[8] In general, it seems that the more reliant we become on information technology and complex systems that very few people understand, the greater the risks of maintaining and operating nuclear weapons will become.[9]

Taken together, these five emerging dynamics suggest a much more complex future battlespace for nuclear weapons thinking and operations, and another strong addition to the "pessimistic" argument about our nuclear future.[10] The threat of accidents, mistakes, and inadvertent use has long been a major con-cern of proliferation pessimists and organization theorists, and this seems likely to be exacerbated in the emerging digital environment. Indeed, the view that proliferation will produce stable deterrence and predictable nuclear relation-ships—so-called proliferation optimism—arguably needs to be reassessed con-sidering the burgeoning global cyber context. Ultimately, it seems that we may be standing on the cusp of a new and far less certain era of global nuclear order because of the latest information technology revolution that we are living through. In the words of Gen. Michael Hayden, former director of both the US National Security Agency and Central Intelligence Agency: "Something has shifted in the nature and calculation of warfare, just as it had after the United States dropped atomic bombs on Hiroshima and Nagasaki at the end of World War II. I don't want to pretend it's the same effect, . . . but in one sense at least, it's August 1945."[11] In fact, we may even be on the cusp of a cyber-enabled third nuclear age.[12]

Recommendations and a Way Forward

There are no easy fixes or obvious panaceas to mitigate this new and diverse suite of cyber challenges in the nuclear realm, but there are some options that could be considered and pursued to help minimize the impact and risks of the cyber age for nuclear weapons. A fecund and potentially propitious starting point is the need to properly understand the nature of the challenge, to come to some type of agreement on what the term "cyber" means and to be clear how it is being used, and to share thoughts on how new cyber dynamics might play out in the nuclear context. It is too easy to misunderstand or misconstrue the cyber challenge, either by focusing too narrowly or too broadly, which often leads participants in the debate to talk past each other or create hyperbole, and this does not help in for-mulating methods and mechanisms of protection or a productive way forward. Core concepts need to be properly defined and agreed on, and only then can we begin to ask the right questions and perhaps develop new frameworks and tem-plates to better understand and manage these challenges. This might also include cyber-nuclear "rules of the road," building on the excellent work pioneered by the NATO Cyber Defence Centre of Excellence in Tallinn and the Budapest Con-vention on Cyber Crime.[13] It might even involve some type of glossary on key cyber-nuclear concepts (perhaps akin to the glossary for nuclear weapons being developed as part of the "P5 Process").[14] Cyber threats vary markedly, and it is important to be clear about exactly what is at stake and what the implications of these threats are and could be for nuclear thinking and strategy, especially as states seek to modernize their nuclear infrastructures and we progress further into the latest information age.

Equally, it is essential that the cyber and nuclear communities speak with each other both in the academic and think tank world as well as inside national secu-rity bureaucracies. This should certainly be done internally, and where possible, internationally as well. The fact that nuclear and cyber expertise so often seem to inhabit different worlds is a big problem, particularly when nuclear weapons management either involves people who "cut their nuclear teeth" in a very different generation and/or who may not have much understanding or familiarity with cyber operations.[15] Moreover, a lack of familiarity with the cyber challenge is not just a generational thing, and improved cyber education (particularly making sure that both senior leaders and new recruits understand the full nature of the challenges[16]), alongside better cyber hygiene more broadly, is also clearly a key part of the way forward.

Establishing global cyber-nuclear norms would also seem a particularly prudent thing to do to. This might mean foreswearing possible cyberattack capabilities, limiting cyber operations to military and not civilian networks and targets, and using restraint as a model for others.[17] This could even be the basis of a cyber "taboo" or "norm of nonuse," such as has appeared to develop in the nuclear realm,[18] although in the cyber case perhaps it would be placed on targets rather than weapons.[19] For example, though the United States may be ahead in the cyber realm for now (at least that seems to be the consensus), almost inevitably, others will catch up—making everyone less secure in the long run. Moreover, the dominance of US conventional forces and the US military's already extensive and growing use of information technology make cyberattacks an increasingly attractive and effective weapon to use against the United States.[20] US decisions about setting precedents and norms in the cyber-nuclear realm are therefore key to how the future cyber-nuclear context will play out.[21] Striking agreements and working together to reduce cyber risks will not be easy, but all nuclear-armed states stand to benefit from doing so in the medium and long terms. The alternative is a less secure cyber-nuclear future for all.

A second set of recommendations would be for all nuclear-armed states to work to harden and protect their nuclear systems against direct cyberattacks, and perhaps above all to build more time into the nuclear decision-making processes. Better protection might be achieved through enhanced network defenses, security architectures, and firewalls, and by embracing measures that minimize the implications of indirect cyber interference—such as upgraded and highly redundant early warning and communications systems (although these should be kept as simple as possible because greater redundancy can create its own problems by increasing complexity and the chances for things to go wrong); better training and screening of operators; and possibly also much more robust (and in-house) supply chain management, personnel reliability programs, and full control of coding and manufacturing processes for sensitive systems.[22] In 2016, it was announced that the US Air Force's Scientific Advisory Board would be conducting a study into nuclear security for emerging systems and modernization, and the same should be true for other nuclear states.[23] Nevertheless, there is still an overwhelming propensity to focus more on attacks or offensive cyber capabilities than on defense and security—and it often seems that those in charge of the two aspects of the cyber challenge do not necessarily communicate. The result could be a bizarre situation where one branch of government is creating a cyber weapon of which another branch of the same government is not aware and thus cannot protect against if it is ever used against them.

Efforts to reduce cyber risks could also involve measures designed to reduce the alert levels of forces, and the time it takes for weapons to be fired (from a matter of minutes to 12 hours, 24 hours, or perhaps even longer). This would not necessarily have to be through a universal treaty, but could simply be part of broader collaborative security efforts. In turn, this could prevent hackers from being able to cause or somehow precipitate a nuclear launch, and ultimately prevent them from causing a nuclear war, which would clearly be of interest to all parties involved.[24] As the Global Zero Commission explains, "It would offer protection from computer error, cyber seizure of nuclear command and control, accidental detonations, unauthorized 'insider' launch, false warning of enemy missile attack, and rushed nuclear decision making."[25]

High-level and regular "red teaming" against nuclear systems by groups of insiders, or even by carefully chosen outside experts, would undoubtedly help with this.[26] This might include the use of internal people to test employees with, for example, spoofed email—and perhaps this might become part of normal nuclear practice if it is not already.[27] Groups of "antihackers" specifically assigned directly to nuclear forces in order to reduce vulnerabilities and protect these systems from attack could be deployed, as Russia is rumored to be doing.[28] In a similar move, the US Air Force has also announced a project to pay "white hat hackers" a "bug bounty" for any weak points and vulnerabilities they can discover in sensitive systems—albeit, for the moment, only public-facing business systems rather than those used for weapons and command and control.[29] Each of these measures might be bolstered by "war gaming," which could in turn be used to aid the design of new protocols, procedures, and "work-arounds."[30] Security and defense might also be enhanced by the creation of multinational forensic assistance and incident response teams.[31] Finally, it might be a good idea to ensure that a sufficient number of "cyber first responders," or at least people with enough understanding of sensitive computer systems and particularly their coding, are on hand at all times to diagnose and if possible fix computer problems or deal with attacks on nuclear systems.

Some of these measures could possibly be done cooperatively, certainly between allies, and possibly also between erstwhile adversaries and competitors. There have been suggestions of cooperative talks or dialogues between the United States, Russia, and China about the issue of strategic command and control network security.[32] These could potentially be broadened to include all nuclear-armed states and focus on issues such as best practices, security systems for storage sites, weapons system safety design improvements, and personnel reliability programs.[33] Such discussions might also form the basis of a set of moratoriums or agreements between states not to target each other's nuclear command and control systems with cyber operations.[34] Plans have already been mooted about explicitly prohibiting cyberattacks on nuclear power plants, and this could potentially be extended to include other nuclear facilities, and also perhaps even nuclear weapons.[35] That said, such measures would of course do little against an attack by a third party.

Another potential avenue is for some type of global early warning system, as has been mooted by Peter Hayes.[36] Although this would not rule out attacks by third parties or all of the risks posed by accidents or mistakes, it could present an opportunity for trust and cooperation building, and help with crisis management in the cyber-nuclear context.[37] Although this might be limited to start with, it could potentially begin with exchanging nonclassified information, and build up to sharing data on mutual threats (e.g., third-party, nonstate actors).[38] More broadly, this might also include regular meetings of experts to share best practices,[39] dialogues between policy professionals, and possibly even the creation of international consultative frameworks and regimes.[40] The establishment of a cyber security hotline between the United States and Russia in 2013 is a positive move in this direction,[41] as was the use of the hotline connecting the Nuclear Risk Reduction Centers in 2016 that both parties have subsequently agreed can be used for cyber incidents.[42] At the same time, it might be possible to utilize (again, potentially cooperatively) cyber techniques as a method of counterproliferation against both states and nonstate actors suspected of seeking nuclear weapons and contravening international norms.[43]

Finally, cyber operations need to be at least included alongside other emerging strategic dynamics in nuclear-related discussions, dialogues, and, ultimately perhaps, even arms control agreements. Specific arms control efforts could potentially be split between prevention and regulation models, and build on those that have gone before.[44] Although broader, all-inclusive cyber arms control efforts might remain some way off or even be impossible, more targeted agreements might be easier to negotiate and codify. These might include moratoriums on not targeting each other's nuclear command and control systems (as mentioned above), although these would be difficult to verify, and of course would not include nonstate actors determined to cause trouble. They might also include serious thinking about how cyber capabilities might be used to aid verification and monitoring, or enhance and also undergird other arms control and nonproliferation objectives. The project named Geo4nonpro, run by the James Martin Center at Middlebury College, is a good example of this.[45] Although the cyber threat to nuclear facilities (both weapons and civilian) has permeated the informal world of pressure groups and global civil society—notably, the Humanitarian Impacts Initiative—it might also be something that needs to be included in formal global nuclear forums, such as at the Nuclear Non-Proliferation Treaty review process and/or the Geneva Conference on Disarmament. Although this will certainly not be easy, reducing the pressures on nuclear systems and their operators will help minimize the chances of something going wrong because of cyber operations. The arms control efforts coordinated by China and Russia in 2011 at the United Nations are a useful start in this regard.[46] The proposal sought a code of conduct whereby states were "not to use information and communications technologies, including networks, to carry out hostile activities or acts of aggression, pose threats to international peace and security, or proliferate information weapons or related technologies."[47] It might be time now to revisit this.

Ultimately, the best way to prepare for our cyber-nuclear future may be to adhere to three basic principles when it comes to nuclear weapons management: Systems must be *simple*—not overcomplicated or unnecessarily complex; they must be *secure*—both from traditional forms of attack and increasingly from those conducting digital operations in cyberspace; and they must be *separate*—that is, kept distinct from other weapons systems, planning processes, and sensors as much as possible. All three of these measures would potentially give planners and operators more time, an essential commodity in the cyber-nuclear context, and also help reduce the perception that cyber-enabled nuclear modernization programs are not secretly designed to facilitate nuclear superiority or make nuclear weapons more usable. Adhering to these three basic principles would represent a good start for managing the ultimate weapon in an increasingly uncertain future cyber-nuclear environment.

Notes

1. See, e.g., Fryer-Biggs, "DoD Looking to 'Jump the Gap'"; and Goodin, "Meet 'Bad BIOS.'"
2. Kello, "Meaning of the Cyber Revolution," 17.
3. See Sanger and Mazzetti, "US Had Cyberattack Plan."
4. See Appelbaum, Horchert, and Stocker, "Shopping for Spy Gear."
5. Zetter, *Countdown to Zero Day*, 376.
6. See, e.g., Schaller, "Moore's Law."
7. Lewis, "Cyber Attacks."
8. See Schelling, *Strategy of Conflict*, chap. 8.
9. Drell, Shultz, and Andreasen, introduction to *Nuclear Enterprise*, ed. Shultz and Drell, 6.
10. On this, see Sagan and Waltz, *Spread of Nuclear Weapons*.
11. Quoted by Kaplan, *Dark Territory*, 215.
12. See Futter, "Emerging Technologies."
13. On the NATO Cyber Defence Centre of Excellence, see Schmitt, *Tallinn Manual*. On the Budapest Convention on Cyber Crime, see "Convention on Cybercrime," November 23, 2001, www.gov.uk/government/uploads/system/uploads/attachment_data/file/238194/8309.pdf.
14. See Berger, *P5 Process*.
15. I am grateful to Michael Sulmeyer, former director for plans and operations for cyber policy at the US Department of Defense, for raising this point.
16. Gartzke and Lindsay, "Thermonuclear Cyberwar," 10.
17. This is an idea raised by Cavaiola, Gompert, and Libicki, "Cyber House Rules," 99.

18. On this, see Tannenwald, *Nuclear Taboo.*
19. Nye, "Deterrence and Dissuasion," 61.
20. Adams, "Virtual Defense," 99.
21. See Danzig, "Surviving on a Diet of Poisoned Fruit," 6.
22. The United Kingdom now operates a broader "cyber essentials" scheme to protect the military supply chain; see "MoD Cyber Essentials Requirements Contractors and Sub Contractors," www.qgstandards.co.uk/cyber-essentials-mod/. However, it is not clear how this applies to nuclear weapons systems and associated components.
23. See Osborn, "Air Force to 'Cyber-Secure' Nuclear Arsenal."
24. Burns, "Former US Commander: Take Nuclear Missiles Off High Alert."
25. Global Zero Commission on Nuclear Risk Reduction, "De-Alerting and Stabilizing the World's Nuclear Force Postures," 15.
26. This was an idea discussed by the Nuclear Threat Initiative's Nuclear Weapons and Cyber Threats Task Force meeting in Washington in September 2016. Such red-teaming might draw on ideas utilized by the US National Security Agency as part of Operation Eligible Receiver in 1997.
27. I would like to thank Aliya Sternstein for this idea.
28. Russia Today, "Cyber Security Units."
29. Freedberg, "Hack Us, Please."
30. Wirtz, "Cyber Pearl Harbor," 8–9.
31. Nye, "Deterrence and Dissuasion," 62.
32. See, e.g., Union of Concerned Scientists and American Association for the Advancement of Science, "Workshop on US Nuclear Weapons Safety," 20.
33. Sagan and Waltz, *Spread of Nuclear Weapons*, 88.
34. See Danzig, "Surviving on a Diet of Poisoned Fruit," 26–27.
35. Sprenger, "Q&A."
36. Private conversation with the author. See also Hayes, "Nuclear Command and Control," 11.
37. Gady and Austin, "Russia, the United States and Cyber Diplomacy."
38. Ibid.
39. See, e.g., Yarynich, C3, 269.
40. Mazanec, *Evolution of Cyber War*, 214.
41. Rashid, "Russia and US Set Up Cybersecurity Hotline"; and Sanger, "White House Confirms Pre-Election Warning to Russia over Hacking."
42. Sanger, "White House Confirms Pre-Election Warning to Russia over Hacking."
43. For a discussion of this, see Roscini, "Cyber Operations as Nuclear Counterproliferation Measures."
44. Meyer, "Cyber-Security through Arms Control," 25.
45. See "Project on Crowdsourced Imagery Analysis: About," www.geo4nonpro.org/about.
46. "Developments in the Field of Information and Telecommunications in the Context of International Security," letter dated September 12, 2011, from the permanent representatives of China, the Russian Federation, Tajikistan, and Uzbekistan to the United Nations, addressed to the UN secretary-general.
47. Ibid.

⠕ BIBLIOGRAPHY

Abbany, Zulfikar. "Has Germany's Patriot Missile System Been Hacked?" *DW.com*, July 8, 2015. www.dw.com/en/has-germanys-patriot-missile-system-been-hacked/a-18571292?utm_source=Sailthruandutm_medium=emailandutm_term=%2ASituation%20Reportandutm_campaign=SitRep0709.

Acton, James. "Russia and Strategic Conventional Weapons: Concerns and Response." *Nonproliferation Review* 22, no. 2 (2015): 141–54.

————. *Silver Bullet: Asking the Right Questions about Conventional Prompt Global Strike.* Washington, DC: Carnegie Endowment for International Peace, 2013.

Adams, James. "Virtual Defense." *Foreign Affairs* 80, no. 3 (2001): 98–112.

Ainslie, John. *The Future of the British Bomb.* London: WMD Awareness Programme, 2006. www.swordofdamocles.org/pdf/future.pdf.

Albright, David, Paul Brannan, and Christina Walrond. "Did Stuxnet Take Out 1,000 Centrifuges at the Natanz Enrichment Plant?" Institute for Science and International Security, December 22, 2010. http://isis-online.org/uploads/isis-reports/documents/stuxnet_FEP_22Dec2010.pdf.

Allison, Graham. *Nuclear Terrorism: The Ultimate Preventable Catastrophe.* New York: Times Books, 2004.

Anderson, James, P. *Computer Security Technology Planning Study, ESD-TR-73–51, Vol. II.* Bedford, MA: US Air Force, Deputy for Command and Management Systems, HQ Electronic Systems Division, L. G. Hanscom Field, 1972. http://csrc.nist.gov/publications/history/ande72.pdf.

Anderson, Ross. *Security Engineering: A Guide to Building Dependable Distributed Systems.* Indianapolis: Wiley, 2008.

Andreasen, Steve, and Richard Clarke, "Cyberwar's Threat Does Not Justify a New Policy of Nuclear Deterrence." *Washington Post*, June 14, 2013.

Andres, Jason, and Steve Winterfeld. *Cyber Warfare: Techniques, Tactics and Tools for Security Practitioners.* Waltham, MA: Syngress, 2011.

Appelbaum, Jacob, Judith Horchert, and Christian Stocker. "Shopping for Spy Gear: Catalogue Advertises NSA Toolbox." *Der Spiegel*, December 29, 2013. www.spiegel.de/international/world/catalog-reveals-nsa-has-back-doors-for-numerous-devices-a-940994.html.

Arkin, William. "The Six-Hundred-Million-Dollar Mouse." *Bulletin of the Atomic Scientists* 52, no. 6 (1996): 68.

Arquilla, John. "Deterrence after Stuxnet." *Communications of the* ACM, August 4, 2015. https://cacm.acm.org/blogs/blog-cacm/190371-deterrence-after-stuxnet/fulltext.

Arquilla, John, and David Ronfeldt. "Cyberwar Is Coming!" *Comparative Strategy* 12, no. 2 (1993): 141–65.

―――, eds. *In Athena's Camp: Preparing for Conflict in the Information Age.* Santa Monica, CA: RAND Corporation, 1997.

Ashford, Warwick. "NATO to Adopt New Cyber Defence Policy." *ComputerWeekly.com,* September 3, 2014. www.computerweekly.com/news/2240228071/Nato-to-adopt-new-cyber-defence-policy.

Austin, Greg. "The Costs of American Cyber Superiority." *ChinaUSFocus.com,* August 6, 2013. www.chinausfocus.com/peace-security/costs-of-american-cyber-superiority/.

Austin, Greg, and Pavel Sharikov. "Preemption Is Victory: Aggravated Nuclear Instability in the Information Age." Unpublished working paper.

Axe, David. "New Navy Jammer Could Invade Networks, Nukes Sites." *Wired,* January 2011. www.wired.com/2011/01/jammer-could-invade-nets/.

Barzashka, Ivanka. "Are Cyber-Weapons Effective? Assessing Stuxnet's Impact on the Iranian Enrichment Programme." *RUSI Journal* 158, no. 2 (2013): 48–56.

BBC News. "Trident Could Be Rendered Obsolete by Hackers." November 24, 2015. www.bbc.co.uk/news/uk-politics-34903327.

Bendel, Thomas R., and William S. Murray. "The Bounds of the Possible: Nuclear Command and Control in the Information Age." *Comparative Strategy* 18, no. 4 (1999): 313–28.

Bender, Jeremy. "Russia May Still Have an Automated Nuclear Launch System Aimed across the Northern Hemisphere." *Business Insider,* September 4, 2014. www.businessinsider.com/russias-dead-hand-system-may-still-be-active-2014-9?IR=T.

Benedict, Kennette. "Stuxnet and the Bomb." *Bulletin of the Atomic Scientists,* June 15, 2012. http://thebulletin.org/stuxnet-and-bomb.

Berger, Andrea. *The P5 Process Five Years On.* RUSI Occasional Paper. London: Royal United Services Institute, 2014. https://rusi.org/sites/default/files/201407_op_the_p5_nuclear_dialogue.pdf.

Berkowitz, Bruce, and Robert W. Hahn. "Cybersecurity: Who's Watching the Store?" *Issues in Science and Technology* 19, no. 3 (Spring 2003): 55–62.

Berlinger, Joshua. "Could the US Take Out North Korea's Missiles before Launch?" *CNN.com,* April 18, 2017. http://edition.cnn.com/2017/04/18/asia/cyber-missile-defense-north-korea/index.html.

Bitzinger, Richard. "Why China Should Fear the US Military's Third Offset Strategy." *National Interest,* August 28, 2016. http://nationalinterest.org/blog/the-buzz/why-china-should-fear-the-us-militarys-third-offset-strategy-17505.

Blagden, David. "Anonymity, Preference Revelation, and the Deterrence of Cyber Coercion." Unpublished working paper shared by the author.

Blair, Bruce. "Could Terrorists Launch America's Nuclear Missiles?" *Time,* November 11, 2010.

―――. *The Logic of Accidental Nuclear War.* Washington, DC: Brookings Institution Press, 1993.

———. "Lowering the Nuclear Threshold: The Dangerous Evolution of World Nuclear Arsenals toward Far-Flung Dispersal, Hair-Trigger Launch Readiness, and First Use Doctrines." Remarks given at the Vienna conference on the Humanitarian Impact of Nuclear Weapons, Vienna, December 8–9, 2014. www.thesimonsfoundation.ca/sites /all/files/Presentation%20by%20Bruce%20Blair%20at%20the%20Vienna%20Con ference%20on%20the%20Humanitarian%20Impact%20of%20Nuclear%20Weap ons,%20Dec%208,%202014.pdf.

———. "Russia's Doomsday Machine." Op-ed, *New York Times*, October 8, 1993. www .globalzero.org/files/bb_russias_doomsday_machine_10.08.1998.pdf.

———. *Strategic Command and Control: Redefining the Nuclear Threat.* Washington, DC: Brookings Institution Press, 1985.

———. "Why Our Nuclear Weapons Can Be Hacked." *New York Times*, March 14, 2017.

Blank, Stephen. "Can Information Warfare Be Deterred?" *Defense Analysis* 17, no. 2 (2001): 121–38.

Blechman, Barry, ed. *Technology and the Limitation of International Conflict.* Washington, DC: Foreign Policy Institute of Johns Hopkins University, 1989.

Blitz, James. "UK Becomes First State to Admit to Offensive Cyber Attack Capability." *Financial Times*, September 29, 2013.

Born, Hans, Bates Gill, and Heiner Hänggi. *Governing the Bomb: Civilian Control and Democratic Accountability of Nuclear Weapons.* New York: Oxford University Press for Stockholm International Peace Research Institute, 2010.

Borning, Alan. "Computer System Reliability and Nuclear War." *Communications of the ACM* 30, no. 2 (1987). www.ee.stanford.edu/~hellman/Breakthrough/book/chapters /borning.html.

Borrie, John, Tim Caughley, and Wilfred Wan, eds. *Understanding Nuclear Weapon Risks.* New York: United Nations Institute for Disarmament Research, 2017. www.unidir.org /files/publications/pdfs/understanding-nuclear-weapon-risks-en-676.pdf.

Boulanin, Vincent, and Tanya Ogilvie-White. *Cyber Threats and Nuclear Dangers.* Policy Brief 17. Seoul: Asia-Pacific Leadership Network for Nuclear Non-Proliferation and Disarmament and Centre for Nuclear Non-Proliferation and Disarmament, 2014. https://cnnd.crawford.anu.edu.au/sites/default/files/publication/cnnd_crawford_anu _edu_au/2014-11/policy_brief_no_17_-_cyber_threats_and_nuclear_dangers.pdf.

Bowen, Clayton P., and Daniel Wolven. "Command and Control Challenges in South Asia." *Nonproliferation Review*, Spring–Summer 1999, 25–35. www.nonproliferation .org/wp-content/uploads/npr/bowen63.pdf.

Bracken, Paul. *The Command and Control of Nuclear Forces.* New Haven, CT: Yale University Press, 1983.

———. "The Cyber Threat to Nuclear Stability." *Orbis* 60, no. 2 (2016): 188–203.

———. *The Second Nuclear Age: Strategy, Danger and the New Power Politics.* New York: St. Martin's Press, 2012.

Breene, Keith. "Who Are the Cyberwar Superpowers?" *World Economic Forum*, May 4, 2016. www.weforum.org/agenda/2016/05/who-are-the-cyberwar-superpowers/.

Brewer, Gary, and Paul Bracken. "Some Missing Pieces of the C3I Puzzle." *Journal of Conflict Resolution* 28, no. 3 (1994): 451–69.

Brewin, Bob. "DOD Reveals Viral Infection." *FCW.com*, August 31, 2004. http://fcw.com /articles/2004/08/31/dod-reveals-viral-infection.aspx.

————. "Kosovo Ushered in Cyberwar." *FCW.com*, September 27, 1999. https://fcw.com/articles/1999/09/27/kosovo-ushered-in-cyberwar.aspx.

Broad, William. "Computer Security Worries Military Experts." *New York Times*, September 25, 1983.

————. "Computers and the US Military Don't Mix." *Science* 207, no. 14 (1980): 1183–87.

Brock, Gerald. *The Second Information Revolution*. Cambridge: Cambridge University Press, 2003.

Bronk, Christopher, and Eneken Tikk-Ringas. "The Cyber Attack on Saudi Aramco." *Survival* 55, no. 2 (2013): 81–96.

Brown, Davis. "A Proposal for an International Convention to Regulate the Use of Information Systems in Armed Conflict." *Harvard International Law Journal* 47, no. 1 (2006): 179–221.

Buchanan, Ben. *The Cybersecurity Dilemma: Hacking, Trust and Fear between Nations*. London: Hurst, 2017.

————. "The Life Cycles of Cyber Threats." *Survival* 58, no. 1 (2016): 38–58.

Burkeman, Oliver. "Forty Years of the Internet: How the World Changed Forever." *Guardian*, October 23, 2009. www.theguardian.com/technology/2009/oct/23/internet-40-history-arpanet.

Burns, Robert. "Former US Commander: Take Nuclear Missiles Off High Alert." Associated Press, April 29, 2015. http://hosted2.ap.org/APDEFAULT/89ae8247abe8493fae244055 46e9a1aa/Article_2015-04-29-US-Nuclear-Weapons-Cyber/id-83b7c14d6f504aa2ad2f8 8b00f7ad5b6.

Campbell, Matthew. "Logic Bomb Arms Race Panics Russia." *Sunday Times*, November 30, 1998. https://cryptome.org/jya/ru-panic.htm.

Carr, Jeffrey. *Inside Cyberwarfare: Mapping the Cyber Underworld*. Sebastopol, CA: O'Reilly Media, 2010.

Carter, Ashton, John Steinbruner, and Charles Zraket, eds. *Managing Nuclear Operations*. Washington, DC: Brookings Institution Press, 1987.

Cartwright, James. "Joint Terminology for Cyberspace Operations." Memorandum from the Vice Chairman of the Joint Chiefs of Staff, United States Department of Defense, Washington DC, 20318-9999, www.nsciva.org/CyberReferenceLib/2010-11joint%20 Terminology%20for%20Cyberspace%20Operations.pdf.

————. "Whither the Forward-Basing of US Troops?" Presentation at the Center for International and Strategic Studies, Washington, June 4, 2009. www.google.co.uk /url?sa=tandrct=jandq=andesrc=sandsource=webandcd=1andved=0ahUKEwiViZm M8LLTAhXPI1AKHbGcDQcQFgglMAAandurl=https%3A%2F%2Fwww.defense .gov%2FPortals%2F1%2Ffeatures%2FdefenseReviews%2FQDR%2Ftranscript_Cart wright_20090604.docxandusg=AFQjCNHym34EXGWPn75la6e4eLHt2MHAr Qandsig2=9xaHJTY9TE7BN58X445ujg.

Cavaiola, Lawrence, David Gompert, and Martin Libicki. "Cyber House Rules: On War, Retaliation and Escalation." *Survival* 57, no. 1 (2015): 81–104.

Caylor, Matt. "The Cyber Threat to Nuclear Deterrence." *War on the Rocks*, February 1, 2016. http://warontherocks.com/2016/02/the-cyber-threat-to-nuclear-deterrence/.

Charles, Deborah. "US Homeland Chief: Cyber 9–11 Could Happen 'Imminently.'" Reuters, January 24, 2013. www.reuters.com/article/2013/01/24/us-usa-cyber-threat -idUSBRE90N1A320130124.

Cho, Meeyoung, and Jack Kim. "South Korea Nuclear Plant Operator Says Hacked, Raising Alarm." Reuters, December 22, 2014. http://uk.reuters.com/article/2014/12/22/uk-south korea-nuclear-idUKKBN0K008G20141222.

Cimbala, Stephen. "Cyber War and Deterrence Stability: Post-START Nuclear Arms Control." *Comparative Strategy* 33, no. 3 (2014): 276–86.

———. *The New Nuclear Disorder.* Farnham, UK: Ashgate, 2015.

———. "Nuclear Deterrence in Cyber-ia." *Air and Space Power Journal,* Fall 2016, 54–63.

———. *Nuclear Weapons in the Information Age.* London: Continuum International, 2012.

Cimbala, Stephen, and Roger McDermott. "A New Cold War? Missile Defenses, Nuclear Arms Reductions, and Cyber War." *Comparative Strategy* 34, no. 1 (2015): 95–111.

Cirenza, Patrick. "Cyberweapons Aren't like Nuclear Weapons." *Slate,* March 15, 2016. www.slate.com/articles/technology/future_tense/2016/03/cyberweapons_are_not _like_nuclear_weapons.html.

———. "An Evaluation of the Analogy between Nuclear and Cyber Deterrence." Thesis, Center for International Security and Cooperation, Freeman Spogli Institute for International Studies, Stanford University, June 2015. https://fsi.stanford.edu/sites/default /files/cirenza_final_thesis_2015.pdf.

Claburn, Thomas. "CIA Admits Cyberattacks Blacked Out Cities." *Information Week,* January 18, 2008. www.informationweek.com/cia-admits-cyberattacks-blacked-out -cities/d/d-id/1063513.

Clark, Colin. "As GAO Finds DoD Wobbly on Cyber Policies, Carter Launches HackerOne." *Breaking Defense,* April 7, 2016. http://breakingdefense.com/2016/04/ as-gao-finds-dod-wobbly-on-cyber-policies-carter-launches-hackerone/.

Clarke, Richard, and Steven Andreasen. "Cyberwar's Threat Does Not Justify a New Policy of Nuclear Deterrence." *Washington Post,* June 14, 2014.

Clarke, Richard, and Robert Knake. *Cyber War: The Next Threat to National Security and What to Do about It.* New York: HarperCollins, 2010.

Colby, Elbridge. "Cyberwar and the Nuclear Option." *National Interest,* June 24, 2013. http://nationalinterest.org/commentary/cyberwar-the-nuclear-option-8638.

Collins, Catherine, and Douglas Frantz. "Down the Nuclear Rabbit Hole." *Los Angeles Times,* January 3, 2011. http://articles.latimes.com/2011/jan/03/opinion/la-oe-frantz -khan-20110103.

Collins, Jeffrey, and Andrew Futter. *Reassessing the Revolution in Military Affairs: Transformation, Evolution and Lessons Learnt.* Basingstoke, UK: Palgrave Macmillan, 2015.

Computerworld. "Moth in the Machine: Debugging the Origins of 'Bug.'" September 4, 2011. www.computerworld.com/article/2515435/app-development/moth-in-the-machine —debugging-the-origins-of—bug-.html.

Constantin, Lucian. "Satellite Communications Systems Are Rife with Security Flaws, Vulnerable to Hackers." *Computerworld,* April 18, 2014. www.computerworld.com /article/2488396/malware-vulnerabilities/satellite-communication-systems-are-rife -with-security-flaws—vulnerable-to-.html.

Cordesman, Anthony, and Justin Cordesman. *Cyber-Threats, Information Warfare, and Critical Infrastructure Protection.* Westport, CT: Praeger, 2002.

Corera, Gordon. *Intercept: The Secret History of Computers and Spies.* London: Weidenfeld & Nicolson, 2015.

———. *Shopping for Bombs: Nuclear Proliferation, Global Insecurity and the Rise and Fall of the A. Q. Khan Network.* London: Hurst, 2006.

Cornish, Paul, David Livingstone, Dave Clemente, and Claire Yorke. *On Cyber Warfare*. London: Chatham House, 2010. www.chathamhouse.org/sites/files/chathamhouse/public/Research/International%20Security/r1110_cyberwarfare.pdf.

Cornwall, Hugo. *Hackers' Handbook*. Garfield, MN: Arthur Brown, 1986.

Cosby, Neale. *Simnet: An Insider's Perspective*. Report for US Defense Advanced Research Projects Agency. Alexandria, VA: Institute for Defense Analyses, 1995. www.dtic.mil/dtic/tr/fulltext/u2/a294786.pdf.

Craigen, Dan, Nadia Diakun-Thibault, and Randy Purse. "Defining Cybersecurity." *Technology Innovation Management Review* 4, no. 10 (2014): 13–21.

Crawford, David. "UN Probes Iran Hacking of Inspectors." *Wall Street Journal*, May 19, 2011. www.wsj.com/news/articles/SB10001424052748704281504576331450055868830?mod=_newsreel_1.

Cromer Logan, David. "Drawing a Line between Conventional and Nuclear Weapons in China." *Bulletin of the Atomic Scientists*, May 6, 2015. http://thebulletin.org/drawing-line-between-conventional-and-nuclear-weapons-china8304.

Cross, Tim. "After Moore's Law." *Economist*, March 12, 2016. www.economist.com/technology-quarterly/2016-03-12/after-moores-law.

Cunningham, Fiona S., and M. Taylor Fravel. "Assuring Assured Retaliation: China's Nuclear Posture and US–China Strategic Stability." *International Security* 40, no. 2 (2015): 7–50.

Curtis, Sophie. "Cambridge Researchers Uncover Backdoor in Military Chip." *Techworld*, May 29, 2012. www.techworld.com/news/security/cambridge-researchersuncover-backdoor-in-military-chip-3360617/.

Danzig, Richard. "Surviving on a Diet of Poisoned Fruit: Reducing the National Security Risks of America's Cyber Dependencies." Center for a New American Century, July 2014. www.cnas.org/sites/default/files/publications-pdf/CNAS_PoisonedFruit_Danzig_0.pdf.

Davis, Joshua. "Hackers Take Down the Most Wired Country in Europe." *Wired*, October 2007. http://archive.wired.com/politics/security/magazine/15-09/ff_estonia?currentPage=all.

Degaut, Marcos. "Spies and Policymakers: Intelligence in the Information Age." *Intelligence and National Security* 31, no. 4 (2016): 509–31.

Demchak, Chris, and Peter Dombrowski. "Cyber Westphalia: Asserting State Prerogatives in Cyberspace." *Georgetown Journal of International Affairs*, 2013, 29–38.

———. "The Rise of a Cybered Westphalian Age." *Strategic Studies Quarterly*, Spring 2011, 32–61.

Denning, Dorothy. *Information Warfare and Security*. Reading, MA: Addison-Wesley, 1999.

———. "Rethinking the Cyber Domain and Deterrence." *Joint Forces Quarterly* 77, no. 2 (April 2015): 8–15.

Devries, Jennifer Valentino, and Danny Yadron. "Cataloguing the World's Cyberforces." *Wall Street Journal*, October 11, 2015. www.wsj.com/articles/cataloging-the-worlds-cyberforces-1444610710.

Dharapak, Charles. "Pentagon Gets Cyberwar Guidelines." *USA Today*, June 22, 2011. http://usatoday30.usatoday.com/news/military/2011-06-22-pentagon-cyber-war_n.htm.

Dunn, William. "UK Government under Targeted Cyber Attack." *CIO News*, February 7, 2011. www.cio.co.uk/news/3259725/uk-government-under-targeted-cyberattack/.

EastWest Institute. "A Measure of Restraint in Cyberspace: Reducing Risk to Civilian Nuclear Assets." January 2014. www.ewi.info/sites/default/files/A%20Measure%20of %20Restraint%20in%20Cyberspace.pdf.

Edwards, Rob. "Trident Whistleblower William McNeilly 'Discharged' from Royal Navy." *Guardian*, June 17, 2015. www.theguardian.com/uk-news/2015/jun/17/trident-whistle blower-william-mcneilly-discharged-from-royal-navy.

Elwell, Andrew. "Cyber War! What Is It Good For? Absolutely Not . . . Stealing Commercial Secrets." *DefenceIQ.com*, November 21, 2011. www.defenceiq.com/defence -technology/articles/cyber-war-what-is-it-good-for-absolutely-not-steal/.

————."MI5 Boss Reveals 'Astonishing' Number of Cyber Attack Secrets." *DefenceIQ. com*, June 25, 2012. https://www.defenceiq.com/defence-technology/articles/mi5-boss -reveals-astonishing-cyber-attack-secrets.

Ewing, Philip. "The Pentagon's New Cyber Attack Plan: 'Blunt Force Trauma.'" *Politico*, April 18, 2015. www.politico.com/story/2015/04/dod-hopes-cyber-can-create-blunt -force-trauma-117095.html.

Falliere, Nicholas, Liam O. Murchu, and Eric Chien. "W32.Stuxnet Dossier Version 1.4." Symantec, February 2011. www.symantec.com/content/en/us/enterprise/media/security _response/whitepapers/w32_stuxnet_dossier.pdf.

Farmer, Ben. "Trident Upgraded to Protect against Cyber Attack." *Telegraph*, March 30, 2016. www.telegraph.co.uk/news/uknews/defence/12206756/Trident-upgraded-to -protect-against-cyber-attack.html.

Farnsworth, Timothy. "Is There a Place for Nuclear Deterrence in Cyberspace?" *Arms Control Now*, May 30, 2013. http://armscontrolnow.org/2013/05/30/is-there-a-place -for-nuclear-deterrence-in-cyberspace/.

————. "Study Sees Cyber Risk for US Arsenal." *Arms Control Today* 43, no. 3 (April 2013): 22–23.

Farwell, James, and Rafal Rohozinski. "The New Reality of Cyber War." *Survival* 54, no. 4 (2012): 107–20.

Feaver, Peter. "Command and Control in Emerging Nuclear Nations." *International Security* 17, no. 3 (1992): 160–87.

————. *Guarding the Guardians: Civilian Control of Nuclear Weapons in the United States*. Ithaca, NY: Cornell University Press, 1992.

Feng, Brian. "The Hacking Group That Leaked NSA Secrets Claims It Has Stolen Data on Foreign Nuclear Programs." *Washington Post*, May 16, 2017.

Fidler, David. "The Relationship between the Biological Weapons Convention and Cybersecurity." *Council on Foreign Relations Net Politics Blog*, March 26, 2015. http:// blogs.cfr.org/cyber/2015/03/26/the-relationship-between-the-biological-weapons -convention-and-cybersecurity/.

Fischer, Benjamin. "Canopy Wing: The US War Plan That Gave the East Germans Goosebumps." *International Journal of Intelligence and Counter Intelligence* 27 (2014): 431–64.

Follarth, Eric, and Holger Stark. "The Story of Operation Orchard: How Israel Destroyed Syria's Al Kibar Nuclear Reactor." *Spiegel Online*, November 2, 2009. www.spiegel.de /international/world/the-story-of-operation-orchard-how-israel-destroyed-syria-s-al -kibar-nuclear-reactor-a-658663.html.

Forden, Geoffrey. "After China's Test: Time for a Limited Ban on Anti-Satellite Weapons." *Arms Control Today* 37 (April 2007). www.armscontrol.org/act/2007_04/Forden.

Forsythe, Michael. "Chinese General with Dempsey Compares Cyber-Attack to Nukes." *Bloomberg News*, April 23, 2013. www.bloomberg.com/news/articles/2013-04-22/china -seeks-to-forge-new-type-of-military-relationship-with-u-s-.

Fravel, Taylor, and Evan Medeiros. "China's Search for Assured Retaliation: The Evolution of Chinese Nuclear Strategy and Force Structure." *International Security* 35, no. 2 (2010): 48–87.

Freedberg, Sydney. "Hack Us, Please: Air Force Pays $130K in 'Bug Bounties' under Obama Program." *Breading Defense*, August 10, 2017. http://breakingdefense.com/2017/08 /hack-us-please-air-force-pays-130k-in-bug-bounties-under-obama-program/.

———. "NATO Hews to Strategic Ambiguity on Cyber Deterrence." *Breaking Defense*, November 7, 2014. http://breakingdefense.com/2014/11/natos-hews-to-strategic -ambiguity-on-cyber-deterrence/.

———. "New Nuclear C2 Should Be Distributed and Multi-Domain: STRATCOM Deputy." *Breaking Defense*, April 5, 2017. http://breakingdefense.com/2017/04/new-nuclear -c2-should-be-...7u4Jk0coiZRjNE05xXiHfvzGudXZUdZY4oF66WPguhp-wand _hsmi=49960271.

Fritz, Jason. "Hacking Nuclear Command and Control." International Commission on Nuclear Non-Proliferation and Disarmament, 2009. www.icnnd.org/Documents/Jason _Fritz_Hacking_NC2.doc.

Fryer-Biggs, Zachary. "DoD Looking to 'Jump the Gap' into Adversaries' Closed Networks." *Defense News*, January 15, 2013. http://archive.defensenews.com/article/2013 0115/C4ISR01/301150010/DoD-Looking-8216-Jump-Gap-8217-Into-Adversaries -8217-Closed-Networks.

Fulghum, David. "Why Syria's Air Defenses Failed to Detect Israel's." *Aviation Week and Space Technology*, November 12, 2013. www.imra.org.il/story.php3?id=36291.

Futter, Andrew. *Ballistic Missile Defence and US National Security Policy: Normalisation and Acceptance after the Cold War*. New York: Routledge, 2013.

———. *Cyber Threats and Nuclear Weapons: New Questions for Command and Control, Security and Strategy*. RUSI Occasional Paper. London: Royal United Services Institute, 2016. https://rusi.org/publication/occasional-papers/cyber-threats-and-nuclear-weapons -new-questions-command-and-control.

———. "Cyber Threats and the Challenge of De-Alerting US and Russian Nuclear Forces." NAPSNet Policy Forum, June 15, 2015. http://nautilus.org/napsnet/napsnet-policy -forum/cyber-threats-and-the-challenge-of-de-alerting-us-and-russian-nuclear-forces/.

———. "The Danger of Using Cyber Attacks to Counter Nuclear Threats." *Arms Control Today* 46 (July–August 2016). www.armscontrol.org/ACT/2016_07/Features/The -Dangers-of-Using-Cyberattacks-to-Counter-Nuclear-Threats.

———. "The Double-Edged Sword: US Nuclear Command and Control Modernization." *Bulletin of the Atomic Scientists*, June 29, 2016. http://thebulletin.org/double-edged -sword-us-nuclear-command-and-control-modernization9593.

———. "Emerging Technologies and Global Nuclear Order." Paper presented at Nobel Peace Symposium, Oslo, May 23, 2017.

———. "Hacking Missile Defence: The Cyber Challenge to BMD." *Missile Defense Review*, March 2015. http://missiledefensereview.org/2015/03/01/hacking-missile-defence-the -cyber-challenge-to-bmd/.

———. *Is Trident Safe from Cyber Attack?* Policy Brief. London: European Leadership Network, 2016. www.europeanleadershipnetwork.org/is-trident-safe-from-cyber-attack_3506.html.

———. "Trident Replacement and UK Nuclear Deterrence: Requirements in an Uncertain Future." *RUSI Journal* 160, no. 5 (2015): 60–66.

———. "*War Games* Redux? Cyber Threats, US–Russian Strategic Stability and New Challenges for Nuclear Security and Arms Control." *European Security* 24, no. 2 (2016): 163–80.

Futter, Andrew, and Benjamin Zala. "Advanced Conventional Weapons and Nuclear Disarmament: Why the Obama Plan Won't Work." *Nonproliferation Review* 20, no. 1 (2013): 107–22.

———. "Conventional Prompt Global Strike: Arms Racing and Strategic Stability in a Post-Unipolar World." *Nonproliferation Review* 22, no. 3 (2015): 291–99.

Futter, A., B. Zala, and G. Moore. "Correspondence: Conventional Prompt Global Strike—Arms Racing and Strategic Stability in a Post-Unipolar World." *Nonproliferation Review* 22 (2015): 291–99.

Gady, Franz-Stefan. "Could Cyber Attacks Lead to Nuclear War?" *The Diplomat*, May 4, 2015. http://thediplomat.com/2015/05/could-cyber-attacks-lead-to-nuclear-war/.

Gady, Franz-Stefan, and Greg Austin. "Russia, the United States and Cyber Diplomacy: Opening the Doors." New York: EastWest Institute, 2010. www.eastwest.ngo/sites/default/files/ideas-files/USRussiaCyber_WEB.pdf.

Gartzke, Erik. "The Myth of Cyberwar: Bringing War in Cyberspace Down to Earth." *International Security* 38, no. 2 (2013): 41–73.

Gartzke, Erik, and Jon R. Lindsay. "Thermonuclear Cyberwar." *Journal of Cybersecurity* 3, no. 1 (2017): 37–48.

———. "Weaving Tangled Webs: Offense, Defense, and Deception in Cyberspace." *Security Studies* 24, no. 2 (2015): 316–48.

Geers, Kenneth, ed. *Cyber War in Perspective: Russian Aggression against Ukraine*. Tallinn: NATO Cooperative Cyber Defence Centre of Excellence, 2015.

Gertz, Bill. "China, Russia Planning Space Attacks on US Satellites." *Washington Free Beacon*, March 16, 2016. http://freebeacon.com/national-security/china-russia-planning-space-attacks-on-u-s-satellites/.

———. "Pentagon Studies Ways to Counter Hypersonic Missile Threat from China, Russia." *Washington Times*, February 22, 2017. www.washingtontimes.com/news/2017/feb/22/china-russia-hypersonic-missile-threat-under-review/.

Ghoshal, Debalina. "China Hacking Iron Dome, Arrow Missile Defense Systems." Gatestone Institute, August 5, 2014. www.gatestoneinstitute.org/4578/china-hacking-missile-defense.

Giangreco, Leigh. "Analysis: The Future of Nuclear Weapons Will Be Networked." *Flight Global*, February 8, 2017. https://www.flightglobal.com/news/articles/analysis-the-future-of-nuclear-weapons-will-be-netw-433472/.

Gibbs, Samuel. "Eugene Kaspersky: Major Cyberterrorist Attack Is Only a Matter of Time." *Guardian*, May 1, 2014. www.theguardian.com/technology/2014/may/01/eugene-kaspersky-major-cyberterrorist-attack-uk.

Gibson, William. *Neuromancer*. New York: Ace, 1984.

Gilbert, David. "US Charges Cyber-Spies with Stealing Nuclear Power Plant Plans." *International Business Times*, May 19, 2014. www.ibtimes.co.uk/us-charges-chinese-cyber-spies-stealing-nuclear-power-plant-plans-1449175.

Gjelten, Tom. "Is All the Talk about Cyberwarfare Just Hype?" NPR, March 15, 2015. www.npr.org/2013/03/15/174352914/is-all-the-talk-about-cyberwarfare-just-hype.

Glaser, Charles. "Deterrence of Cyber Attacks and US National Security." George Washington University Cyber Security Policy and Research Institute, June 1, 2011. http://static1.squarespace.com/static/53b2efd7e4b0018990a073c4/t/54b94136e4b0ad6fb5e16716/1421426998290/2011-5_cyber_deterrence_and_security_glaser.pdf.

Global Security Newswire. "Chinese Hacking Targets US Missile Defense Designs." May 28, 2013. www.nti.org/gsn/article/chinese-hacking-targets-us-missile-defense-designs/.

———. "Hacked Israeli Military Twitter Account Declared Nuclear Leak." July 7, 2014. www.nti.org/gsn/article/hack-israeli-military-account-erroneous-postannounces-nuclear-leak/.

———. "Indian Naval Computers Targeted in Chinese Cyber Attack." July 2, 2012. www.nti.org/gsn/article/indian-naval-computers-victim-chinese-cyber-attack-report/.

Global Zero Commission on Nuclear Risk Reduction. "De-Alerting and Stabilizing the World's Nuclear Force Postures." April 2015. www.globalzero.org/files/global_zero_commission_on_nuclear_risk_reduction_report_0.pdf.

Gompert, David, and Martin Libicki. "Cyber Warfare and Sino-American Crisis Instability." *Survival* 56, no. 4 (2014): 7–22.

Goodin, Dan. "Meet 'Bad BIOS,' the Mysterious Mac and PC Malware That Jumps Airgaps." *Arstechnica*, October 31, 2013. http://arstechnica.com/security/2013/10/meet-badbios-the-mysterious-mac-and-pc-malware-that-jumps-airgaps/.

Gorman, Siobhan, and Julian Barnes. "Cyber Combat: Act of War." *Wall Street Journal*, May 31, 2011. www.wsj.com/articles/SB10001424052702304563104576355562313578 2718.

Gormley, Dennis. "US Advanced Conventional Systems and Conventional Prompt Global Strike Ambitions: Assessing the Risks, Benefits, and Arms Control Implications." *Nonproliferation Review* 22, no. 2 (2015): 123–39.

Gray, Colin. *Making Strategic Sense of Cyber Power: Why the Sky Is Not Falling In*. Carlisle, PA: Strategic Studies Institute, US Army War College, 2013.

Green, Joshua. "The Myth of Cyberterrorism: There Are Many Ways Terrorists Can Kill You—Computers Aren't One of Them." *Washington Monthly*, November 2002. www.washingtonmonthly.com/features/2001/0211.green.html.

Greenberg, Andy. "'Crash Override': The Malware That Took Down a Power Grid." *Wired*, June 12, 2017. https://www.wired.com/story/crash-override-malware/.

———. "Shopping List for Zero-Days: A Price List for Hackers' Secret Software Exploits." *Forbes*, March 23, 2013. www.forbes.com/sites/andygreenberg/2012/03/23/shopping-for-zero-days-an-price-list-for-hackers-secret-software-exploits/.

Gregory, Shaun. *The Hidden Cost of Nuclear Deterrence: Nuclear Weapons Accidents*. London: Brassey's, 1990.

Gromyko, Anatoly, and Martin Hellman, eds. *Breakthrough: Emerging New Thinking—Soviet and Western Scholars Issue a Challenge to Build a World beyond War*. New York: Walker, 1988.

Hagestad, William. *21st-Century Chinese Cyberwarfare*. Ely, UK: IT Governance Publishing, 2012.

Haggard, Stephen, and Jon Lindsay. "North Korea and the Sony Hack: Exporting Instability through Cyberspace." *Asia Pacific Issues* (EastWest Center) 117 (May 2015). www .eastwestcenter.org/system/tdf/private/api117.pdf?file=1andtype=nodeandid=35164.

Halpin, Edward, Philippa Trevorrow, David Webb, and Steve Wright, eds. *Cyberwar, Netwar and the Revolution in Military Affairs*. Basingstoke, UK: Palgrave Macmillan, 2006.

Hambling, David. "Underwater Drones May Make Hiding a Nuclear Missile Sub Harder." *New Scientist*, February 24, 2016. www.newscientist.com/article/2078466-underwater drones-may-make-hiding-a-nuclear-missile-sub-harder/.

Hamilton, Keegan. "The Plan to Make America's Nukes Great Again Could Go Horribly Wrong," *Vice News*, April 20, 2017. news.vice.com/story/the-plan-to-make-americas -nukes-great-again-could-go-horribly-wrong.

Harding, Luke. *The Snowden Files: The Inside Story of the World's Most Wanted Man*. London: Guardian Faber, 2014.

Hayes, Peter. "Nuclear Command and Control in the Millennials' Era." NAPSNet Special Report, February 17, 2015. http://nautilus.org/napsnet/napsnet-special-reports/nuclear -command-and-control-in-the-millenials-era/.

Healey, Jason, ed. *A Fierce Domain: Conflict in Cyberspace 1986 to 2012*. Arlington, VA: Cyber Conflict Studies Association, 2013.

Hennign, W. J., and Brian Bennett. "Pentagon Seeks Cyberweapons Strong Enough to Deter Attacks." *Los Angeles Times*, July 31, 2016. www.latimes.com/nation/la-na-cyber -deterrent-20150731-story.html.

Hirschfeld Davis, Julie. "Hacking of Government Computers Exposed 21.5 Million People." *New York Times*, July 9, 2015. www.nytimes.com/2015/07/10/us/office-of -personnel-management-hackers-got-data-of-millions.html.

Hjortdal, Magnus. "China's Use of Cyber Warfare: Espionage Meets Strategic Deterrence." *Journal of Strategic Security* 4, no. 2 (Summer 2011): 1–24.

Hoffman, David. *Dead Hand: The Untold Story of the Cold War Arms Race and Its Dangerous Legacy*. New York: Anchor Books, 2009.

Holloway, David. *Stalin and the Bomb: The Soviet Union and Atomic Energy, 1939–1956*. New Haven, CT: Yale University Press, 1996.

Ingersoll, Geoffrey. "US Navy: Hackers 'Jumping the Air Gap' Would 'Disrupt the World Balance of Power.'" *Business Insider*, November 19, 2013. www.businessinsider.com /navy-acoustic-hackers-could-halt-fleets-2013-11?IR=T.

Interfax. "Russia Creates New Missile Defense Systems." *Russia beyond the Headlines*, December 8, 2014. http://asia.rbth.com/news/2014/12/08/russia_creates_new_missile _defense_systems_42050.html.

Ivanov, Igor. "The Missile-Defense Mistake: Undermining Strategic Stability and the ABM Treaty." *Foreign Affairs* 59, no. 5 (2000): 15–20.

Jacobsen, Annie. *The Pentagon's Brain: An Uncensored History of DARPA, America's Top Secret Military Research Agency*. Boston: Little, Brown: 2015.

Jervis, Robert. *Perception and Misperception in International Politics*. Princeton, NJ: Princeton University Press, 1976.

Jones, Sam. "NATO Holds Largest Cyber War Games." *Financial Times*, November 20, 2014. www.ft.com/cms/s/0/9c46a600-70c5-11e4811300144feabdc0.html#axzz3NIsB8FG2.

Kan, Shirley. *China: Suspected Acquisition of US Nuclear Weapon Secrets*. Report RL30143. Washington, DC: US Congressional Research Service, 2006. http://fas.org/sgp/crs/nuke /RL30143.pdf.

Kaplan, Fred. *Dark Territory: The Secret History of Cyber War*. London: Simon & Schuster, 2016.

———. "'War Games' and Cybersecurity's Debt to a Hollywood Hack." *New York Times*, February 19, 2016. www.nytimes.com/2016/02/21/movies/wargames-and-cybersecuritys -debt-to-a-hollywood-hack.html.

Keck, Zachary. "S. Korea Seeks Cyber Weapons to Target North Korea's Nukes." *Diplomat*, February 21, 2014. http://thediplomat.com/2014/02/s-korea-seeks-cyber-weapons-to -target-north-koreas-nukes/.

Kelleher, Catherine McArdle, and Peter Dombrowski, eds. *Regional Missile Defense from a Global Perspective*. Stanford, CA: Stanford University Press, 2015.

Keller, Jon. "Navy Plans Cyber Security Upgrades for Fleet of Submarine-Launched Nuclear Missiles." *Military and Aerospace Electronics*, July 25, 2016. www.militaryaero space.com/articles/2016/07/cyber-security-nuclear-missiles.html.

Kelley, Michael. "Anonymous Hacks Top Nuclear Watchdog Again to Force Investigation of Israel." *Business Insider*, December 3, 2012. /www.businessinsider.com/anonymous -hack-iaea-nuclear-weapons-israel-2012-12?IR=T.

Kello, Lucas. "The Meaning of the Cyber Revolution: Perils to Theory and Statecraft." *International Security* 38, no. 2 (2013): 7–40.

Khan, Feroz Hassan, Ryan Jacobs, and Emily Burke, eds. *Nuclear Learning in South Asia: The Next Decade*. Monterey, CA: US Naval Postgraduate School, 2014.

Khoo, Nicholas, and Reuben Steff. "'This Program Will Not Be a Threat to Them': Missile Defense and US Relations with Russia and China." *Defense and Security Analysis* 30, no. 1 (2014): 17–28.

Koblentz, Gergory D. *Strategic Stability in the Second Nuclear Age*. Special Report 71. New York: Council on Foreign Relations, 2014.

Koebler, Jason. "US Nukes Face up to 10 Million Cyber Attacks Daily." *US News & World Report*, March 20, 2012. www.usnews.com/news/articles/2012/03/20/us-nukes-face-up -to-10-million-cyber-attacks-daily/.

Kostin, Sergei, and Eric Raynaud. *Farewell: The Greatest Spy Story of the Twentieth Century*. Las Vegas: AmazonCrossing, 2011.

Kramer, Franklin, Robert Butler, and Catherine Lotrionte. "Cyber, Extended Deterrence, and NATO." Atlantic Council, May 26, 2016. www.atlanticcouncil.org/blogs/nato source/cyber-extended-deterrence-and-nato.

Kramer, Franklin, Stuart Starr, and Larry Wentz, eds. *Cyberpower and National Security*. Dulles, VA: Potomac Books, 2009.

Krepinevich, Andrew. *Cyber Warfare: A Nuclear Option?* Washington, DC: Center for Strategic and Budgetary Assessments, 2012.

Kroenig, Matthew, and Tristan Volpe. "3-D Printing the Bomb? The Nuclear Nonproliferation Challenge." *Washington Quarterly* 38, no. 3 (2015): 7–19.

Kulikova, Alexandra. "Is a Cyber Arms Race between the US and Russia Possible?" *Russia Direct*, January 28, 2015. www.russia-direct.org/analysis/cyber-arms-race-between-us -and-russia-possible.

Lake, Eli. "Operation Sabotage." *New Republic*, July 14, 2010. www.newrepublic.com /article/world/75952/operation-sabotage.

Langner, Ralph. "To Kill a Centrifuge: A Technical Analysis of What Stuxnet's Creators Tried to Achieve." Langner Group, Arlington, VA, November 2013. www.langner .com/en/wp-content/uploads/2013/11/To-kill-a-centrifuge.pdf.

Lanoszka, Alexander. "Russian Hybrid Warfare and Extended Deterrence in Eastern Europe." *International Affairs* 92, no. 1 (2016): 175–95. www.alexlanoszka.com/Lanosz kaIAHybrid.pdf.

Lebow, Richard Ned. *Nuclear Crisis Management: A Dangerous Illusion.* Ithaca, NY: Cornell University Press, 1987.

Lee, Bernice, and Felix Preston, with Gemma Green. *Preparing for High-Impact, Low-Probability Events.* London: Chatham House, 2012. www.chathamhouse.org/sites/files /chathamhouse/public/Research/Energy,%20Environment%20and%20Development /r0112_highimpact.pdf.

Lee, Robert M., and Thomas Rid. "OMG Cyber: Thirteen Reasons Why Hype Makes for Bad Policy." *RUSI Journal* 159, no. 5 (2014): 4–12.

Le Mière, Christian. "The Spectre of an Asian Arms Race." *Survival* 56 (2004): 139–56.

Lettice, John. "OSS Torpedoed: Royal Navy Will Run on Windows for Warships." *Register*, September 6, 2004. www.theregister.co.uk/2004/09/06/ams_goes_windows_for _warships/.

Lewis, James. "Cross-Domain Deterrence and Credible Threats." Center for Strategic and International Studies, Washington, July 2010. http://csis.org/files/publication/100701 _Cross_Domain_Deterrence.pdf.

———. "Cyber Attacks, Real or Imagined, and Cyber War." Center for Strategic and International Studies, Washington, July 2011. www.csis.org/analysis/cyber-attacks -real-or-imagined-and-cyber-war.

Lewis, Patricia, Heather Williams, Benoît Pelopidas, and Sasan Aghlani. *Too Close for Comfort: Cases of Near Nuclear Use and Options for Policy.* London: Chatham House, 2014. /www.chathamhouse.org/sites/files/chathamhouse/field/field_document/20140428 TooCloseforComfortNuclearUseLewisWilliamsPelopidasAghlani.pdf.

Leyden, John. "Israel Suspected of 'Hacking' Syrian Air Defences: Did Algorithms Clear Path for Air Raid?" *Register*, October 4, 2007. www.theregister.co.uk/Print/2007/10/04 /radar_hack_raid/.

Liang, Qiao, and Wang Ziangsui. *Unrestricted Warfare: China's Master Plan to Destroy America.* Dehradun, India: Natraj, 2007.

Libicki, Martin. *Conquest in Cyberspace: National Security and Information Warfare.* New York: Cambridge University Press, 2007.

———. *Crisis and Escalation in Cyberspace.* Santa Monica, CA: RAND Corporation, 2012.

———. *Cyberdeterrence and Cyberwar.* Santa Monica, CA: RAND Corporation, 2009.

———. *Cyberspace in Peace and War.* Annapolis, MD: Naval Institute Press, 2016.

———. "Cyber War Will Not and Should Not Have Its Grand Strategist." *Strategic Studies Quarterly*, Spring 2014, 23–39.

———. *What Is Information Warfare?* Washington, DC: National Defense University, 1995.

Liebelson, Dana. "Are US Nuke Secrets Vulnerable to Cyber Attack?" *Mother Jones*, December 2012. www.motherjones.com/politics/2012/12/us-nukes-may-be-risk-cyber-attack.

Lieber, Kier, and Daryl Press. "The New Era of Counterforce: Technological Change and the Future of Nuclear Deterrence." *International Security* 41, no. 4 (Spring 2017): 9–49.

Liff, Adam P. "Cyberwar: A New 'Absolute Weapons?' The Proliferation of Cyber Warfare Capability and Interstate War." *Journal of Strategic Studies* 35, no. 4 (2012): 401–28.

Lindsay, Jon. "Stuxnet and the Limits of Cyber Warfare." *Security Studies* 22, no. 3 (2013): 365–404.

Loeb, Vernon, and Walter Pincus. "Los Alamos Security Breach Confirmed." *Washington Post*, April 29, 1999. www.washingtonpost.com/wp-srv/national/daily/april99/spying 29.htm.

Logan, David Cromer. "Drawing a Line between Conventional and Nuclear Weapons in China." *Bulletin of the Atomic Scientists*, May 6, 2015. http://thebulletin.org/drawing -line-between-conventional-and-nuclear-weapons-china8304.

Long, Austin, and Brendan Rittenhouse Green. "Stalking the Secure Second Strike: Intelligence, Counterforce, and Nuclear Strategy." *Journal of Strategic Studies* 38, nos. 1–2 (2015): 38–73.

Lonsdale, David. *The Nature of War in the Information Age: Clausewitzian Future*. London: Frank Cass, 2004.

Lynn, William. "Defending a New Domain: The Pentagon's Cyber Strategy." *Foreign Affairs* 89, no. 5 (2010): 97–108.

MacDonald, Bruce W., and Charles D. Ferguson. "Chinese Strategic Missile Defense: Will It Happen, and What Could It Mean?" *Arms Control Today*, November 2015. www. armscontrol.org/ACT/2015_11/Features/Chinese-Strategic-Missile-Defense-Will-It -Happen-and-What-Would-It-Mean.

Madory, Doug. "UK Traffic Diverted through Ukraine." Dyn Research, March 13, 2015. http://research.dyn.com/2015/03/uk-traffic-diverted-ukraine/.

Mahnaimi, Uzi. "Fake Rock Spying Device Blows Up Near Iranian Nuclear Site." *Sunday Times* (London), September 23, 2012. www.thesundaytimes.co.uk/sto/news/world _news/Middle_East/article1131847.ece.

Makovsky, David. "The Silent Strike: How Israel Bombed a Syrian Nuclear Reactor and Kept It Secret." *New Yorker*, September 17, 2012. www.newyorker.com/magazine /2012/09/17/the-silent-strike.

Mangan, Dan. "US Military Uses 8-Inch Floppy Disks to Coordinate Nuclear Force Oper- ations." CNBC, May 25, 2016. www.cnbc.com/2016/05/25/us-military-uses-8-inch -floppy-disks-to-coordinate-nuclear-force-operations.html.

Manson, George Patterson. "Cyberwar: The United States and China Prepare for the Next Generation of Conflict." *Comparative Strategy* 30, no. 2 (2011): 121–33.

Markoff, John, David Sanger, and Thom Shanker. "In Digital Combat, US Finds No Easy Deterrent." *New York Times*, January 25, 2010. www.nytimes.com/2010/01/26/world /26cyber.html?pagewanted=alland_r=0.

Markoff, John, and Thom Shanker. "Halted '03 Iraq Plan Illustrates US Fear of Cyberwar Risk." *New York Times*, August 1, 2009. www.nytimes.com/2009/08/02/us/politics/02 cyber.html.

Masood, Rahat. "Assessment of Cyber Security Challenges in Nuclear Power Plants: Security Incidents, Threats, and Initiatives." Cyber Security and Privacy Research Institute, George Washington University, August 15, 2016. https://static1.squarespace. com/static/53b2efd7e4b0018990a073c4/t/57af79d6e58c62414bda0daf/147111 7785529/GW-CSPRI-2016-03+MASOOD+Rahat+Nuclear+Power+Plant+Cyber security.pdf.

Matthews, Owen. "Russia's Greatest Weapon May Be Its Hackers." *Newsweek*, May 7, 2015. http://europe.newsweek.com/russias-greatest-weapon-may-be-its-hackers-326974 ?rm=eu.

Maybaym, M., A.-M. Osulaand, and L. Lindstrom, eds. *Architectures in Cyberspace: 7th International Conference on Cyber Conflict*. Tallinn: NATO, 2015.

Mazanec, Brian. *The Evolution of Cyber War: International Norms for Emerging Technology Weapon*. Dulles, VA: Potomac Books, 2015.

McConnell, Mike. "Cyberwar Is the New Atomic Age." *New Perspectives Quarterly* 26, no. 3 (2009): 72–77.

McDonough, David S. *Nuclear Superiority: The "New Triad" and the Evolution of American Nuclear Strategy*. Adelphi Paper 33. London: Routledge for International Institute for Strategic Studies, 2006.

McGoogan, Cara. "Ministry of Defence Switches to the Cloud as Microsoft Opens First UK Data Centres." *Telegraph*, September 7, 2016. www.telegraph.co.uk/technology /2016/09/07/ministry-of-defence-switches-to-the-cloud-as-microsoft-opens-fir/.

McGraw, Gary. "Cyber War Is Inevitable (Unless We Build Security In)." *Journal of Strategic Studies* 36, no. 1 (2013): 109–19.

McKeon, Brian P. "Statement before the Senate Armed Services Subcommittee on Strategic Forces," April 13, 2016. www.armed-services.senate.gov/imo/media/doc/mckeon _04-13-16.pdf.

Mecklin, John. "Disarm and Modernize." *Foreign Policy* 211 (2015): 52–59.

Medetsky, Anatoly. "KGB Veteran Denies CIA Caused '82 Blast." *Moscow Times*, March 18, 2004. www.themoscowtimes.com/news/article/kgb-veteran-denies-cia-caused-82-blast /232261.html.

Melman, Yossi. "Exclusive: Israel's Rash Behavior Blew Operation to Sabotage Iran's Computers, US Officials Say." *Jerusalem Post*, February 16, 2016. www.jpost.com /Middle-East/Iran/Israels-rash-behavior-blew-operation-to-sabotage-Irans-computers -US-officials-say-444970.

Merchant, Brian. "DARPA Is about to Start Testing an Autonomous, Submarine Hunting Ocean Drone." *Motherboard*, November 10, 2015. http://motherboard.vice.com /read/darpa-isbuilding-an-autonomous-submarine-hunting-drone-boat.

Meserve, Jeanne. "Mouse Click Could Plunge City into Darkness, Experts Say." CNN, September 27, 2007. http://edition.cnn.com/2007/US/09/27/power.at.risk/index .html.

Meyer, Paul. "Cyber-Security through Arms Control: An Approach to International Cooperation." *RUSI Journal* 156, no. 2 (2011): 22–27.

Michaels, Jim. "US Could Use Cyberattack on Syrian Air Defenses." *USA Today*, May 16, 2013. www.usatoday.com/story/news/world/2013/05/16/syria-attack-pentagon-air-force -military/2166439/.

Mitchell, Paul. *Network-Centric Warfare: Coalition Operations in the Age of US Primacy*. Adelphi Paper 385. Abingdon, UK: Routledge for International Institute for Strategic Studies, 2006.

Mitra, Subhasish, H.-S. Philip Wong, and Simon Wong. "Stopping Hardware Trojans in Their Tracks." *IEEE Spectrum*, January 20, 2015. http://spectrum.ieee.org/semiconduc tors/design/stopping-hardware-trojans-in-their-tracks.

Moore, Daniel, and Thomas Rid. "Cryptopolitik and the Darknet." *Survival* 58, no. 1 (2016): 7–38.

Muncaster, Phil. "Researchers Jump the Security Air Gap with a Feature Phone." *Infosecurity Magazine*, July 29, 2015. www.infosecurity-magazine.com/news/researchers-jump -security-air-gap/.

Munger, Frank. "Lab Halts Web Access after Cyber Attack." *Knoxville News Sentinel*, April 19, 2011. www.knoxnews.com/news/local-news/lab-halts-web-access-after-cyber-attack.

Murchu, Liam O. "Stuxnet Using Three Additional Zero-Day Vulnerabilities." Symantec Official Blog, September 14, 2010. www.symantec.com/connect/blogs/stuxnet-using -three-additional-zero-day-vulnerabilities.

Murdock, Jason. "North Korea Hackers Accessed 'War Plans' Detailing US Military Response to Conflict." *International Business Times*, April 5, 2015. www.ibtimes.co.uk /north-korean-hackers-accessed-war-plans-detailing-us-military-response -conflict-1615494.

Nagal, Balraj. *India and Ballistic Missile Defense: Furthering a Defensive Deterrent.* Regional Insight. Washington, DC: Carnegie Endowment for International Peace, 2016. http:// carnegieendowment.org/2016/06/30/india-and-ballistic-missile-defense-furthering -defensive-deterrent-pub-63966.

Nakashima, Ellen. "Confidential Report Lists US Weapons System Designs Compromised by Chinese Cyberspies." *Washington Post*, May 27, 2013. www.washingtonpost.com /world/national-security/confidential-report-lists-us-weapons-system-designs -compromised-by-chinese-cyberspies/2013/05/27/a42c3e1c-c2dd-11e2-8c3b-0b5e9 247e8ca_story.html.

———. "Cyber-Intruder Sparks Massive Federal Response—and Debate over Dealing with Threats." *Washington Post*, December 8, 2011. www.washingtonpost.com/national /national-security/cyber-intruder-sparks-response-debate/2011/12/06/gIQAxLuFgO _story.html.

———. "List of Cyber-Weapons Developed by Pentagon to Streamline Computer War-fare." *Washington Post*, May 31, 2011. www.washingtonpost.com/national/list-of-cyber -weapons-developed-by-pentagon-to-streamline-computer-warfare/2011/05/31 /AGSublFH_story.html.

Nakashima, Ellen, Greg Miller, and Julie Tate. "US, Israel Developed Flame Computer Virus to Slow Iranian Nuclear Efforts, Officials Say." *Washington Post*, January 8, 2012. www.washingtonpost.com/world/national-security/us-israel-developed-computer -virus-to-slow-iranian-nuclear-efforts-officials-say/2012/06/19/gJQA6xBPoV_story .html.

Nakashima, Ellen, and Matt Zapotosky. "US Charges Iran-Linked Hackers with Targeting Banks, NY Dam." *Washington Post*, March 24, 2016. www.washingtonpost.com/world /national-security/justice-department-to-unseal-indictment-against-hackers-linked -to-iranian-goverment/2016/03/24/9b3797d2-f17b-11e5-a61f-e9c95c06edca_story .html?utm_term=.4ea7d0c17b99.

National Research Council of the National Academies. *Proceeding of a Workshop on Deterring Cyber Attacks: Informing Strategies and Developing Options for US Policy.* Wash-ington, DC: National Academies Press, 2010.

National Security Archive. "First Documented Evidence That US Presidents Predelegated Nuclear Weapons Release Authority to the Military." http://nsarchive.gwu.edu/news /19980319.htm.

Neumann, Peter. *Computer-Related Risks.* New York: Addison-Wesley, 1995.

Newman, Lily Hay. "The Ransomware Meltdown Experts Warned about Is Here." *Wired*, May 2017. www.wired.com/2017/05/ransomware-meltdown-experts-warned/.

Newsweek. "We're in the Middle of a Cyberwar." September 19, 1999. www.newsweek .com/were-middle-cyerwar-166196.

New York Times. "Deterring Cyber Attacks from North Korea." December 29, 2014. www .nytimes.com/2014/12/30/opinion/deterring-cyberattacks-from-north-korea.html ?_r=0.

————. "Iran Says Nuclear Equipment Was Sabotaged." September 22, 2012. www.nytimes .com/2012/09/23/world/middleeast/iran-says-siemens-tried-to-sabotage-its-nuclear -program.html?_r=1and.

Norton-Taylor, Richard. "Chinese Cyber-Spies Penetrate Foreign Office Computers." *Guardian*, February 4, 2011. www.theguardian.com/world/2011/feb/04/chinese-super -spies-foreign-office-computers.

Nye, Joseph. "Deterrence and Dissuasion in Cyberspace." *International Security* 41, no. 3 (2016–17): 44–71.

————. "From Bombs to Bytes: Can Our Nuclear History Inform Our Cyber Future?" *Bulletin of the Atomic Scientists* 69, no. 5 (2013): 8–14.

————. "Nuclear Lessons for Cyber Security?" *Strategic Studies Quarterly*, Winter 2011, 18–38.

Office of the President of the United States. "International Strategy for Cyberspace." May 2011. www.whitehouse.gov/sites/default/files/rss_viewer/international_strategy _for_cyberspace.pdf.

Opall-Rome, Barbara. "Israeli Cyber Game Drags US, Russia to Brink of Mideast War." *Defense News*, November 14, 2013. www.defensenews.com/article/20131115/C4ISR NET07/311150020/Israeli-Cyber-Game-Drags-US-Russia-Brink-Mideast-War.

Osborn, Kris. "Air Force to 'Cyber-Secure' Nuclear Arsenal." *Scout.com*, November 8, 2016. www.scout.com/military/warrior/story/1725859-air-force-fights-nuclear-weapons-hackers.

————. "Russia's Satellite Nuclear Warning System down until November." *Defensetech*, June 30, 2015. www.defensetech.org/2015/06/30/russias-satellite-nuclear-warning-system -down-until-november/.

Oswald, Rachel. "Congress Wants Pentagon to Upgrade Nuclear Command and Control." *DefenseOne.com*, December 18, 2018. www.defenseone.com/management/2013/12 /congress-wants-pentagon-upgrade-nuclear-command-and-control/75645/.

Owens, William, Kenneth Dam, and Herbert Lin, eds. *Technology, Policy, Law, and Ethics Regarding US Acquisition and Use of Cyberattack Capabilities*. Washington, DC: National Academies Press, 2009. www3.nd.edu/~cpence/eewt/Owens2009.pdf.

Page, Lewis. "Royal Navy Completes Windows for Submarines Rollout." *Register*, December 16, 2012. www.theregister.co.uk/2008/12/16/windows_for_submarines_rollout/.

Paikowsky, Deganit, and Gil Baram. "Space Wars: Why Our Space Systems Need an Upgrade." *Foreign Affairs*, January 7, 2015. www.foreignaffairs.com/articles/142690 /deganit-paikowsky-and-gil-baram/space-wars.

Palmer, Danny. "Yes, Trident Really Could Be Vulnerable to a Cyber Attack, Warn Experts." *Computing*, November 24, 2015. www.computing.co.uk/ctg/news/2436369 /yes-trident-really-could-be-vulnerable-to-a-cyber-attack-warn-experts#.

Panetta, Leon. "Remarks by Secretary Panetta on Cybersecurity to the Business Executives for National Security, New York City," October 11, 2012. www.defense.gov /transcripts/transcript.aspx?transcriptid=5136.

Penenberg, Adam. "Hacking Bhabha." *Forbes*, November 16, 1998. www.forbes.com /1998/11/16/feat.html.

Perlroth, Nicole. "In Cyberattack on Saudi Firm, US Sees Iran Firing Back." *New York Times*, October 23, 2012. www.nytimes.com/2012/10/24/business/global/cyberattack -on-saudi-oil-firm-disquiets-us.html.

Perlroth, Nicole, and David Sanger. "North Korea Loses Its Link to the Internet." *New York Times*, December 22, 2014. www.nytimes.com/2014/12/23/world/asia/attack-is -suspected-as-north-korean-internet-collapses.html.

Perrow, Charles. *Normal Accidents: Living with High-Risk Technologies.* Princeton, NJ: Princeton University Press, 1999.

Peterson, Dale. "Offensive Cyber Weapons: Construction, Development and Employment." *Journal of Strategic Studies* 36, no. 1 (2013): 120–24.

Podvig, Pavel. "Blurring the Lines between Nuclear and Conventional Weapons." *Bulletin of the Atomic Scientists* 72, no. 3 (2016): 145–49.

———, ed. *Russian Strategic Nuclear Forces.* Cambridge, MA: MIT Press, 2004.

Pollack, Joshua. "Emerging Strategic Dilemmas in US–Chinese Relations." *Bulletin of the Atomic Scientists* 65, no. 4 (July–August 2009): 53–63.

Posen, Barry R. *Inadvertent Escalation: Conventional War and Nuclear Risks.* Ithaca, NY: Cornell University Press, 1991.

Potins, K., J. Stinissen, and M. Maybaum, eds. *Proceedings of the 5th International Conference on Cyber Conflict.* Tallinn: NATO, 2013.

Poulsen, Kevin. "Slammer Worm Crashed Ohio Nuke Plant Network." *Security Focus,* August 18, 2003. www.securityfocus.com/news/6767.

PR Newswire. "Lockheed Martin Wins $213 Million Strategic Mission Planning Contract." August 26, 2004. www.prnewswire.com/news-releases/lockheed-martin-wins -213-million-strategic-mission-planning-contract-71757852.html.

President's Foreign Intelligence Advisory Board, Special Investigative Panel. "Science at Its Best, Security at Its Worst." June 1999. http://energy.gov/sites/prod/files/cioprod /documents/pfiab-doe.pdf.

Price, Alfred. *War in the Fourth Dimension: US Electronic Warfare, from the Vietnam War to the Present.* London: Greenhill Books, 2001.

Rashid, Fahmida Y. "Russia and US Set Up Cybersecurity Hotline to Prevent Accidental Cyberwar." *Security Week,* June 18, 2013. www.securityweek.com/russia-and-us-setup -cybersecurity-hotline-prevent-accidental-cyberwar.

Rattray, George. *Strategic Warfare in Cyberspace.* Cambridge, MA: MIT Press, 2001.

Reagan, Ronald. "National Policy on Telecommunications and Automated Information Systems Security." National Security Decision Directive 145, White House, Washington, September 17, 1984. https://fas.org/irp/offdocs/nsdd/nsdd-145.pdf.

Redmond, Kent, and Thomas M. Smith. *From Whirlwind to MITRE: The R&D Story of the SAGE Air Defense Computer.* Cambridge, MA: MIT Press, 2000.

Reed, John. "Keeping Nukes Safe from Cyber Attack." *Foreign Policy,* September 25, 2012. http://foreignpolicy.com/2012/09/25/keeping-nukes-safe-from-cyber-attack/.

Reed, Thomas. *At the Abyss: An Insider's History of the Cold War.* New York: Ballantine, 2004.

Reed, Thomas, and Danny Stillman. *The Nuclear Express: A Political History of the Bomb and Its Proliferation.* Minneapolis: Zenith Press, 2009.

Richards, Julian. *Cyber-War: The Anatomy of the Global Security Threat.* Basingstoke, UK: Palgrave Macmillan, 2014.

Richelson, Jeffrey. *Spying on the Bomb: American Nuclear Intelligence from Nazi Germany to North Korea.* New York: W. W. Norton, 2007.

Rid, Thomas. *Cyberwar Will Not Take Place.* London: C. Hurst, 2013.

———. *Rise of the Machines: The Lost History of Cybernetics.* London: Scribe, 2016.

Rid, Thomas, and Ben Buchanan. "Attributing Cyber Attacks." *Journal of Strategic Studies* 38, nos. 1–2 (2015): 4–37.

Rid, Thomas, and Peter McBurney. "Cyber-Weapons." *RUSI Journal* 157, no. 1 (2012): 6–13.

Riley, Michael, and Ashlee Vance. "Cyber Weapons: The New Arms Race." *BusinessWeek*, July 20, 2011. www.businessweek.com/magazine/cyber-weapons-the-new-arms-race -07212011.html.

Risen, James. "Energy Department Halts Computer Work at Three Nuclear Weapons Labs." *New York Times*, April 7, 1999. www.nytimes.com/library/tech/99/04/biztech /articles/07nuke.html.

Risen, James, and Jeff Gerth. "Breach at Los Alamos: A Special Report; China Stole Nuclear Secrets for Bombs, US Aides Say." *New York Times*, March 6, 1999. www .nytimes.com/1999/03/06/world/breach-los-alamos-special-report-china-stole-nuclear -secrets-for-bombs-us-aides.html.

Rodriguez, Salvador. "US Tried, Failed to Sabotage North Korea Nuclear Weapons Programme." *International Business Times*, May 29, 2015. www.ibtimes.com/us-tried-failed -sabotage-north-korea-nuclear-weapons-program-stuxnet-style-cyber-1945012.

Roland, Alex. "Was the Nuclear Arms Race Deterministic?" *Technology and Culture* 51, no. 2 (2010): 444–61.

Roscini, Marco. "Cyber Operations as Nuclear Counterproliferation Measures." *Journal of Conflict and Security Law* 19, no. 1 (2014): 133–57.

Rosen, Armin. "A Spherical Bunker in Russia Was the Most Secure Place in the Entire Cold War." *Business Insider*, March 9, 2015. http://uk.businessinsider.com/a -spherical-bunker-in-russia-was-the-most-secure-place-in-the-entire-cold-war-2015-3 ?r=USandIR=T.

Rossiter, Mike. *The Spy Who Changed the World: Klaus Fuchs and the Secrets of the Nuclear Bomb*. London: Headline Publishing Group, 2014.

Rothkopf, David. "Where Fukushima Meets Stuxnet: The Growing Threat of Cyber War." *Foreign Policy*, March 17, 2011. http://foreignpolicy.com/2011/03/17/where-fukushima -meets-stuxnet-the-growing-threat-of-cyber-war/.

Russia Today. "American Atomic Secrets at Risk—Probe." December 21, 2012. http://rt .com/usa/doe-cyber-attack-atomic-risk-526/.

———. "Cyber Security Units to Protect Russia's Nuclear Weapons Stockpiles." October 17, 2014. http://rt.com/news/196720-russia-missile-forces-cybersecurity/.

———. "'Innocent Mistake': UK's Nuclear Weapons Web Data Routed through Ukraine." March 14, 2016. www.rt.com/news/240781-uk-nuclear-data-ukraine/.

———. "US Nuclear Weapons Researchers Targeted with Internet Explorer Virus." May 7, 2013. http://rt.com/usa/attack-department-nuclear-internet-955/.

Ryall, Julian, Nicola Smith, and David Millward. "North Korea's Unsuccessful Missile Launch 'May Have Been Thwarted by US Cyber Attack.'" *Telegraph*, April 16, 2017. www.telegraph.co.uk/news/2017/04/16/north-korea-makes-unsuccessful-missile -launch-day-massive-show/.

Sagan, Scott D. *The Limits of Safety: Organizations, Accidents and Nuclear Weapons*. Princeton, NJ: Princeton University Press, 1993.

Sagan, Scott D., and Kenneth N. Waltz. *The Spread of Nuclear Weapons: A Debate Renewed*. New York: W. W. Norton, 2003.

Sanger, David. *Confront and Conceal: Obama's Secret Wars and Surprising Use of American Power*. New York: Broadway Paperbacks, 2013.

———. "Explosion at Key Military Base in Iran Raises Questions about Sabotage." *New York Times*, October 9, 2014. www.nytimes.com/2014/10/10/world/explosion-at-key-military-base-in-iran-raises-questions-about-sabotage.html.

———. "White House Confirms Pre-Election Warning to Russia over Hacking." *New York Times*, November 16, 2016. www.nytimes.com/2016/11/17/us/politics/white-house-confirms-pre-election-warning-to-russia-over-hacking.html.

Sanger, David, and William J. Broad. "Trump Inherits a Secret Cyberwar against North Korean Missiles." *New York Times*, March 4, 2017. www.nytimes.com/2017/03/04/world/asia/north-korea-missile-program-sabotage.html.

Sanger, David, and Martin Fackler. "NSA Breached North Korean Networks before Sony Attack, Officials Say." *New York Times*, January 18, 2015. www.nytimes.com/2015/01/19/world/asia/nsa-tapped-into-north-korean-networks-before-sony-attack-officials-say.html.

Sanger, David, and Mark Mazzetti. "US Had Cyberattack Plan If Iran Nuclear Dispute Led to Conflict." *New York Times*, February 16, 2016. www.nytimes.com/2016/02/17/world/middleeast/us-had-cyberattack-planned-if-iran-nuclear-negotiations-failed.html?utm_source=Sailthruandutm_medium=emailandutm_campaign=New%20Campaignandutm_term=%2ASituation%20Reportand_r=0.

Sanger, David, and Thom Shanker. "NSA Devises Radio Pathway into Computers." *New York Times*, January 14, 2014. www.nytimes.com/2014/01/15/us/nsa-effort-pries-open-computers-not-connected-to-internet.html.

Sarkar, Jayita. "Three Concrete Steps toward South Asian Nuclear Stability." *Bulletin of the Atomic Scientists*, September 13, 2016. http://thebulletin.org/how-reduce-south-asias-nuclear-dangers.

SC Magazine. "Russia Overtaking US in Cyber-Warfare Capabilities." October 30, 2015. www.scmagazine.com/russia-overtaking-us-in-cyber-warfare-capabilities/printarticle/450518/.

Schaller, R. R. "Moore's Law: Past, Present and Future." *Spectrum IEEE* 34, no. 6 (1997): 52–59.

Schell, Roger R. "Computer Security: The Achilles Heel of the Electronic Air Force?" *Air University Review* 30, no. 2 (January–February 1979): 16–33.

Schelling, Thomas. *The Strategy of Conflict*. Cambridge, MA: Harvard University Press, 1980.

Schiller, Markus, and Peter Hayes. "Could Cyber Attacks Defeat North Korean Missile Tests?" Nautilus Institute, March 6, 2017. http://nautilus.org/napsnet/napsnet-policy-forum/could-cyber-attacks-defeat-north-korean-missile-tests/.

Schlosser, Eric. *Command and Control: Nuclear Weapons, the Damascus Accident, and the Illusion of Safety*. London: Allen Lane, 2013.

———. "Neglecting Our Nukes." *Politico*, September 16, 2013. www.politico.com/story/2013/09/neglecting-our-nukes-96854.html.

Schmidt, Eric, and Jared Cohen. *The New Digital Age: Reshaping the Future of People, Nations and Business*. London: John Murray: 2013.

Schmitt, Eric, and Thom Shanker. "US Debated Cyberwarfare in Attack Plan on Libya." *New York Times*, October 17, 2011. www.nytimes.com/2011/10/18/world/africa/cyber-warfare-against-libya-was-debated-by-us.html?_r=0.

Schmitt, Michael, ed. *Tallinn Manual on the International Law Applicable to Cyber Warfare*. Cambridge: Cambridge University Press, 2013.

Schwartau, Winn. *Information Warfare: Cyberterrorism—Protecting Your Personal Security in the Electronic Age*. 2nd ed. New York: Thunder's Mouth Press, 1996.

Segal, Adam. "Cyberspace: The New Strategic Realm in US–China Relations." *Strategic Analysis* 38, no. 4 (2014): 577–81.

———. *The Hacked World Order: How Nations Fight, Trade, Maneuver, and Manipulate in the Digital Age*. New York: PublicAffairs, 2016.

Seng, Jordan. "Less Is More: Command and Control Advantages of Minor Nuclear States." *Security Studies* 6, no. 4 (1997): 50–92.

Shinkman, Paul D. "American Is Losing the Cyber War." *US News & World Report*, September 29, 2016. www.usnews.com/news/articles/2016-09-29/cyber-wars-how-the-us-stacks-up-against-its-digital-adversaries.

Shultz, George, and Sidney Drell, eds. *The Nuclear Enterprise: High Consequence Accidents—How to Enhance Safety and Minimize Risks in Nuclear Weapons and Reactors*. Stanford, CA: Hoover Institution Press, 2012.

Singer, Peter W., and August Cole. *Ghost Fleet: A Novel of the Next World War*. Boston: Houghton Mifflin Harcourt, 2015.

Singer, Peter W., and Allan Friedman. *Cybersecurity and Cyberwar: What Everyone Needs to Know*. Oxford: Oxford University Press, 2014.

Slayton, Rebecca. *Physics, Computing and Missile Defense*. Cambridge, MA: MIT Press, 2013.

Sokolski, Henry, and Bruno Tertrais, eds. *Nuclear Weapons Security Crises: What Does History Teach?* Carlisle, PA: Strategic Studies Institute, US Army War College, 2013.

Sprenger, Sebastian. "Q&A: Expert Wants Nuclear Plants 'Taken off the Table' in Cyber-Warfare." *Global Security Newswire*, May 30, 2015. www.nti.org/gsn/article/q-expert-wants-nuclear-plants-taken-table-cyber-warfare/.

Stahl, Leslie. "Who's Minding the Nukes?" CBS News, April 27, 2014. www.cbsnews.com/news/whos-minding-the-nuclear-weapons/.

Steinnon, Richard. *Surviving Cyberwar*. Plymouth, UK: Government Institutes, 2010.

Sterling, Bruce. "War Is Virtual Hell." *Wired*, January 1993. www.wired.com/1993/01/virthell/.

Sterner, Eric. "Retaliatory Deterrence in Cyberspace." *Strategic Studies Quarterly*, Spring 2011, 62–80.

Sternstein, Aliya. "Attack on Energy Lab Computers Was Isolated, Officials Say." *Global Security Newswire*, April 26, 2011. www.nti.org/gsn/article/attack-on-energy-lab-computers-was-isolated-and-limited-officials-say/.

———. "Exclusive: Nuke Regulator Hacked by Suspected Foreign Powers." *Nextgov.com*, August 19, 2014. www.nextgov.com/cybersecurity/2014/08/exclusive-nuke-regulator-hacked-suspected-foreign-powers/91643/.

———. "Officials Worry about Vulnerability of Global Nuclear Stockpile to Cyber Attack." *Global Security Newswire*, March 14, 2013. www.nti.rsvp1.com/gsn/article/officials-worry-about-vulnerability-global-nuclear-stockpile-cyber-attack/?mgh=http%3A%2F%2Fwww.nti.organdamp;mgf=1.

———. "Why Cybersecurity Dollars Do Not Add Up at the Pentagon." *DefenseOne.com*, March 31, 2015. www.defenseone.com/technology/2015/03/why-pentagons-cyber security-dollars-dont-add/108895/.

Stober, Dan, and Ian Hoffman. *A Convenient Spy: Wen Ho Lee and the Politics of Nuclear Espionage*. New York: Doubleday, 1989.

Stoll, Clifford. *The Cuckoo's Egg: Tracking a Spy through the Maze of Computer Espionage*. New York: Doubleday, 1989.

Sulick, Michael. *American Spies: Espionage against the United States from the Cold War to the Present*. Washington, DC: Georgetown University Press, 2013.

Syring, James D. (director, Missile Defense Agency). "Unclassified Statement of Testimony before the House Armed Services Committee Subcommittee on Strategic Forces," March 25, 2014. www.mda.mil/global/documents/pdf/ps_syring_032514_HA SC.PDF.

Szoldra, Paul. "North Korea Suspected in Hack of South Korea's Cyber Command." *Business Insider*, December 6, 2016. http://uk.businessinsider.com/north-korea-hacked -south-korea-2016-12?r=USandIR=T.

Tabansky, Lior. "Basic Concepts in Cyber Warfare." *Military and Strategic Studies* 3, no. 1 (2011): 75–92.

Tannenwald, Nina. *The Nuclear Taboo: The United States and the Non-Use of Nuclear Weapons since 1945*. New York: Cambridge University Press, 2007.

Tech Khabaren. "US Navy Rejects Windows for Linux." June 24, 2012. http://techkhaba ren.wordpress.com/2012/06/24/us-navy-rejects-windows-for-linux/.

Thomas, Timothy. *Cyber Silhouettes: Shadows over Information Operations*. Fort Leavenworth, KS: Foreign Military Studies Office, 2005.

———. "Deterring Information Warfare: A New Strategic Challenge." *Parameters* 26, no. 4 (Winter 1996–67): 81–91.

Thompson, Lauren. "Watchdog Agency Warns of 'Weaknesses' in Nuclear War Command Links." *Forbes*, June 22, 2015. www.forbes.com/sites/lorenthompson/2015/06/22 /watchdog-agency-warns-of-weaknesses-in-nuclear-war-command-links/.

Thompson, Mark. "Iranian Cyber Attack on New York Dam Shows Future of War." *Time*, March 24, 2016. http://time.com/4270728/iran-cyber-attack-dam-fbi/.

———. "The Pentagon's Huge Atomic Floppies." *Time*, May 25, 2016. http://time.com /4348494/pentagon-nuclear-floppy-disks/.

Thompson, Nicolas. "Inside the Apocalyptic Soviet Doomsday Machine." *Wired*, September 2009. www.wired.com/2009/09/mf-deadhand/.

Tomlinson, Simon. "Ministry of Defence Top Secret Systems Hacked, Head of Cyber Security Reveals." *Daily Mail*, May 4, 2012. www.dailymail.co.uk/news/article-2139373 /Ministry-Defence-secret-systems-hacked-head-cyber-security-reveals.html.

Trulock, Notra. *Code Name Kindred Spirit: Inside the Chinese Nuclear Espionage Scandal*. San Francisco: Encounter Books, 2002.

Tucker, Patrick. "Why Ukraine Has Already Lost the Cyberwar, Too." *DefenseOne.com*, April 28, 2014. www.defenseone.com/technology/2014/04/why-ukraine-has-already -lost-cyberwar-too/83350/.

———. "Will America's Nuclear Weapons Always Be Safe from Hackers?" *The Atlantic*, December 30, 2016. www.theatlantic.com/technology/archive/2016/12/hacking-into -future-nuclear-weapons-the-us-militarys-next-worry/511904/.

UK Defence Select Committee. "Deterrence in the 21st Century." March 11, 2014. www .publications.parliament.uk/pa/cm201314/cmselect/cmdfence/1066/1066.pdf.

UK Nuclear Decommissioning Authority. "New Cyber Security Requirements." November 6, 2014. http://webarchive.nationalarchives.gov.uk/20150817115932/http://www .nda.gov.uk/2.014/11/new-mandatory-requirements-for-government-supply-chain/.

Union of Concerned Scientists and American Association for the Advancement of Science. "Workshop on US Nuclear Weapons Safety and Security: Summary Report." September 2013. www.ucsusa.org/sites/default/files/legacy/assets/documents/nwgs/nuclear-safety -security-workshop.pdf.

United Nations General Assembly. "Developments in the Field of Information and Telecommunications in the Context of International Security." Letter dated September 12, 2011, from the permanent representatives of China, the Russian Federation, Tajikistan, and Uzbekistan to the United Nations, addressed to the UN secretary-general. Document A/66/359. https://ccdcoe.org/sites/default/files/documents/UN-110912-Code OfConduct_0.pdf.

US Department of Defense. "The Department of Defense Cyber Strategy." April 2015. www.defense.gov/home/features/2015/0415_cyberstrategy/Final_2015_DoD_CYBER _STRATEGY_for_web.pdf.

———. "Final Report of the Federal Advisory Committee on Nuclear Failsafe and Risk Reduction." https://archive.org/details/FinalReportoftheFederalAdvisoryCommittee onNuclearFailsafeandRiskReductionFARR.

———. "Nuclear Matters Handbook." 2016. www.acq.osd.mil/ncbdp/nm/NMHB/index .htm.

———. "Nuclear Posture Review Report." 2002. http://archive.defense.gov/news/Jan 2002/d20020109npr.pdf.

———. "Report of the Defense Science Board Task Force on Mission Impact of Foreign Influence on DOD Software." Office of the Undersecretary of Defense for Acquisition, Technology, and Logistics, September 2007. www.acq.osd.mil/dsb/reports/ADA486949 .pdf.

US Department of Defense, Defense Science Board. "Task Force on Mission Impact of Foreign Influence on DOD Software." May 2008. www.dtic.mil/docs/citations/ADA 486949.

———. *Task Force Report: Resilient Military Systems and the Advanced Cyber Threat.* Washington, DC: US Department of Defense, 2013. www.acq.osd.mil/dsb/reports/Resilient MilitarySystems.CyberThreat.pdf.

US Department of Energy, Office of Inspector General. "Audit Report, Follow-Up Audit of the Department's Cyber Security Incident Management Program, DOE/IG-0878." December 2012. http://energy.gov/sites/prod/files/IG-0878.pdf.

US Government Accountability Office. "Information Security: Agencies Need to Improve Cyber Incident Response Practices." April 2014. www.gao.gov/assets/670/ 662901.pdf.

———. "Information Technology: Federal Agencies Need to Address Aging Legacy Systems." May 25, 2016. www.gao.gov/products/GAO-16-468.

———. "NORAD's Missile Warning System: What Went Wrong?" May 15, 1981. www .gao.gov/assets/140/133240.pdf.

———. "Nuclear Security: Los Alamos National Laboratory Faces Challenges in Sustaining Physical and Cyber Security Improvements." September 25, 2008. www.gao.gov /assets/130/121367.pdf.

US House of Representatives. "The Report of the Select Committee on US National Security and Military/Commercial Concerns with the People's Republic of China (The Cox Report)." 1999. www.house.gov/coxreport/cont/gncont.html.

US National Security Agency. "Learning from the Enemy: The Gunman Project." www
.nsa.gov/public_info/_files/cryptologic_histories/learning_from_the_enemy.pdf.

Valeriano, Brandon, and Ryan C. Maness. "The Dynamics of Cyber Conflict between
Rival Antagonists, 2001–11." *Journal of Peace Research* 51, no. 3 (2014): 347–60.

Van der Meer, Sico. "Cyber Warfare and Nuclear Weapons: Game Changing Consequences?" Netherlands Institute of International Relations, December 2016. www
.clingendael.nl/sites/default/files/SWP_Paper_Chapter_Sico_van_der_Meer.pdf.

Vincent, James. "Schematics from Israel's Iron Dome Missile Shield 'Hacked' by Chinese,
Says Report." *Independent*, July 29, 2014. www.independent.co.uk/life-style/gadgets
-and-tech/israels-iron-dome-missile-shield-hacked-by-chinese-military-hackers-says
-report-9635619.html#.

Von Hlatky, Stefanie, and Andreas Wenger, eds. *The Future of Extended Deterrence: The
United States, NATO, and Beyond.* Washington, DC: Georgetown University Press,
2015.

Warner, Michael. "Cybersecurity: A Pre-History." *Intelligence and National Security* 27, no.
5 (2012): 781–99.

Watt, Nicholas. "Trident Could Be Vulnerable to Cyber-Attack, Former Defence Secretary Says." *Guardian*, November 24, 2015.

Weimann, Gabriel. "Cyberterrorism: The Sum of All Fears?" *Studies in Conflict and Terrorism* 28, no. 2 (2005): 129–49.

Weiner, Norbert. *Cybernetics or Control and Communication in the Animal and the Machine.*
Cambridge, MA: MIT Press, 1948.

Weiss, Gus. "Duping the Soviets: The Farewell Dossier." *Studies in Intelligence* 39, no. 5
(1996): 121–26.

Williams, Dan. "Analysis: Wary of Naked Force, Israeli's Eye Cyberwar on Iran." Reuters,
July 8, 2009. http://in.reuters.com/article/2009/07/08/idINIndia-40888520090708.

Williams, Heather. "Britain's Trident, and the Need to Support Nuclear Personnel." *Bulletin of the Atomic Scientists*, June 1, 2015. http://thebulletin.org/britain's-trident-and
-need-support-nuclear-personnel8363.

Wilson, Clay. *Botnets, Cybercrime, and Cyberterrorism: Vulnerabilities and Policy Issues for
Congress.* Report RL32114. Washington, DC: US Congressional Research Service,
2008. www.fas.org/sgp/crs/terror/RL32114.pdf.

———. *Information Operations, Electronic Warfare, and Cyberwar: Capabilities and Related
Policy Questions.* Report RL31787. Washington, DC: US Congressional Research Service, 2007. www.au.af.mil/au/awc/awcgate/crs/rl31787.pdf.

Wirtz, James. "The Cyber Pearl Harbor." *Intelligence and National Security*, 2017.

Wise, David. *Tiger Trap: America's Secret Spy War with China.* Boston: Houghton Mifflin
Harcourt, 2011.

Wolf, Markus, with Anne McElvoy. *Man without a Face: The Autobiography of Commu-
nism's Greatest Spymaster.* New York: PublicAffairs, 1997.

Wolff, Josephine. "Cyber Is Not a Noun." *Slate*, September 9, 2016. www.slate.com/articles
/technology/future_tense/2016/09/cyber_is_not_a_noun.html.

Yadron, Danny, and Jennifer Valentino-Devries. "This Article Was Written with the Help
of a 'Cyber' Machine: Overuse of Prefix Sparks Backlash, but Alternatives Are Few;
'Computery.'" *Wall Street Journal*, March 4, 2015. www.wsj.com/articles/is-the-prefix
-cyber-overused-1425427767.

Yarynich, Valery E. C3: *Nuclear Command, Control and Cooperation*. Washington, DC: Center for Defense Information, 2003.

Yost, Jeffrey. "Interview Conducted with Roger Schell." Computer History Project, Charles Babbage Institute, University of Minnesota, May 2012. http://conservancy.umn.edu/bitstream/handle/11299/133439/oh405rrs.pdf?sequence=1andisAllowed=y.

Younger, Stephen M. "Written Statement before the Senate Judiciary Subcommittee on Administrative Oversight and the Courts, 'A Continuation of Oversight of the Wen Ho Lee Case.'" October 3, 2000. http://fas.org/sgp/congress/2000/younger.html.

Zenko, Micah. "The Existential Angst of America's Top Generals." *Foreign Policy*, August 4, 2015. http://foreignpolicy.com/2015/08/04/the-existential-angst-of-americas-top-generals-threat-inflation-islamic-state/?wp_login_redirect=0.

Zetter, Kim. "Could Stuxnet Mess with North Korea's New Uranium Plant?" *Wired*, November 2010. www.wired.com/2010/11/could-stuxnet-mess-with-north-koreas-new-uranium-plant/.

———. *Countdown to Zero Day: Stuxnet and the Launch of the World's First Digital Weapon*. New York: Crown, 2014.

———. "A Cyberatttack Has Caused Confirmed Damage for the Second Time Ever." *Wired*, January 2015. www.wired.com/2015/01/german-steel-mill-hack-destruction/.

———. "The Evidence That North Korea Hacked Sony Is Flimsy." *Wired*, December 2014. www.wired.com/2014/12/evidence-of-north-korea-hack-is-thin/.

———. "Inside the Cunning, Unprecedented Hack of Ukraine's Power Grid." *Wired*, March 2016. www.wired.com/2016/03/inside-cunning-unprecedented-hack-ukraines-power-grid/.

———. "Researchers Hack Air-Gapped Computer with Simple Cell Phone." *Wired*, July 2015. www.wired.com/2015/07/researchers-hack-air-gapped-computer-simple-cell-phone/.

⠿ INDEX

Tables are indicated by t following the page number.

⫶ ABOUT THE AUTHOR

Andrew Futter is an associate professor in the School of History, Politics and International Relations at the University of Leicester in the United Kingdom. He is the author of *The Politics of Nuclear Weapons* and *Ballistic Missile Defence and US National Security Policy*, the editor of *The United Kingdom and the Future of Nuclear Weapons*, and the coeditor of *Reassessing the Revolution in Military Affairs*.